CALLED
TO BE
SAINTS

An Invitation to Christian Maturity

GORDON T. SMITH

IVP Academic

An imprint of InterVarsity Press
Downers Grove, Illinois

InterVarsity Press
P.O. Box 1400, Downers Grove, IL 60515-1426
World Wide Web: www.ivpress.com
Email: email@ivpress.com

InterVarsity Press® is the book-publishing division of InterVarsity Christian Fellowship/USA®, a movement of students and faculty active on campus at hundreds of universities, colleges and schools of nursing in the United States of America, and a member movement of the International Fellowship of Evangelical Students. For information about local and regional activities, write Public Relations Dept., InterVarsity Christian Fellowship/USA, 6400 Schroeder Rd., P.O. Box 7895, Madison, WI 53707-7895, or visit the IVCF website at www.intervarsity.org.

Scripture quotations, unless otherwise noted, are from the New Revised Standard Version of the Bible, copyright 1989 by the Division of Christian Education of the National Council of the Churches of Christ in the USA. Used by permission. All rights reserved.

While all stories in this book are true, some names and identifying information in this book have been changed to protect the privacy of the individuals involved.

Cover design: David Fassett
Interior design: Beth Hagenberg
Images: church tiles: © Cole Vineyard/iStockphoto

ISBN 978-0-8308-4030-4 (print)
ISBN 978-0-8308-6489-8 (digital)

Printed in the United States of America ∞

Library of Congress Cataloging-in-Publication Data
A catalog record for this book is available from the Library of Congress.

P	21	20	19	18	17	16	15	14	13	12	11	10	9	8	7	6	5	4	3	2	1
Y	32	31	30	29	28	27	26	25	24	23	22	21	20	19	18	17	16	15	14			

for joella

CONTENTS

INTRODUCTION

THIS IS AN INVITATION TO THINK THEOLOGICALLY about the Christian life and to ask, what does it mean to be a Christian? More specifically, what does it mean to be a *mature* Christian? In order for us to have a complete theology of the Christian life—to address matters of the Christian life and Christian spirituality effectively—we need to find substantive answers to three questions.

First, what is the *beginning* of the Christian life? What do we mean by conversion and initiation into Christian faith? What does it look like and feel like to come to faith in Christ? Second, what is the character of Christian *maturity*? If conversion is a beginning, comparable to infancy, what does it look like to be mature, to grow up in one's faith? Here one would consider the goal or objective—the *telos* of the journey in Christ. And third, what is the approach and means of *formation* so that we grow up in our salvation? How does a person newborn in Christ grow and mature in faith? A comprehensive theology of the Christian life—of religious experience from a biblical perspective—would address all three questions: the beginning, the end or goal, and the means by which one moves toward maturity.

There is a growing number of publications on conversion and initiation into Christian faith. Indeed, I have contributed a few publications myself to this question.[1] And the third question on spiritual formation and practice has also received a great deal of attention. But it seems to

---

[1]Gordon T. Smith, *Beginning Well: Christian Conversion & Authentic Transformation* (Downers Grove, IL: InterVarsity Press, 2001); *Transforming Conversion: Rethinking the Language and Contours of Christian Initiation* (Grand Rapids, MI: Baker, 2010); "Conversion and Redemption," *The Oxford Handbook of Evangelical Theology*, ed. Gerald R. McDermott (New York: Oxford University Press, 2010).

me there is still a gap when it comes to the second question: What does it mean to be mature in our faith? And so this book focuses specifically on that question, contributing to the discussion of the goal or vision of the Christian life.

A focus on this question has implications for our understanding of conversion and our approach to evangelism. If conversion is a good beginning to the Christian life, that naturally raises a question—what, then, *is* the Christian life? The second question also has implications for spiritual discipline and practice. Indeed, we should only speak about practice in light of the grace for which we hope.

So, then, the following chapters focus on what it means to be mature as a Christian. If the Christian life is a journey, a pilgrimage, what is the goal or objective toward which we walk? To what end are we converted? And to what end are our spiritual practices and disciplines?

The opening chapter makes a case for why such a theology of the Christian life is needed. Chapter 2 is the defining chapter of the book, with an insistence that the Christian vision for maturity is maturity "in Christ." Chapters 3 through 6 in turn identify four distinctive features of a mature Christian. Each of these chapters in its distinct way is about the good life, the human vocation—what it means to fulfill the purpose or identity for which we were created. This life is a gift that is offered to us in Christ. But it is also a calling, and this book is a guide to living a life worthy of the calling we have received (Eph 4:1).

This book is offered to the entire Christian community—young, middle-aged and seniors. It seeks to challenge young people to establish early on the kind of life they will live: What goals are worth pursuing and what achievements are worth their due diligence? What patterns of life, work, relationship and worship will foster the life they want to have? This book also offers to guide those in midlife as they make midcourse adjustments to their priorities and thus to their lives, with close attention to what matters most. And finally, it proposes to encourage those moving into their senior years about the choices they make at this crucial juncture. For many people these years are the most rewarding and significant, the time when they ask themselves what kind of legacy they want to leave. For each group it is about stewardship: What does it mean to be a good steward of our early years, our mid-adult years and our senior years?

This book is also offered to church congregations that are eager to take seriously the call to foster maturity and bring about spiritual transformation in disciples of Jesus. What does this look like? What is the character of this maturity? And how is it expressed in congregational priorities and commitments?

Specifically, this book is both a call and invitation to live life "in Christ"—more precisely, to live a life that is the fruit of dynamic participation in the life of Christ. This life will have at least four distinctive marks or features. Each of these is offered as an invitation:

- To be a wise person and to pursue wisdom with passion and persistence.

- To do good work in response to the call of Christ—vocational holiness.

- To love others as one learns to live in love.

- To know the joy of God—the joy that is the deep wellspring of the blessed life.

Each of these—wisdom, good work, love and joy—is offered to us in Christ. And so we can speak of them only as gifts we know in light of what it means to live in union with Christ, to participate in his life. Thus I reference chapter 2 as the central and defining chapter.

Finally, the book includes two appendices. The first is an invitation to pastors to consider what all of this means for the character of congregational life. What would it look like, in other words, if we approached congregational life with a vision of maturity in Christ? And second, I have included an invitation to the leadership and faculty of institutions of higher education—notably Christian universities and seminaries—with this question in mind: Can the university and the theological seminary design its life and curriculum around a vision of transformation in Christ?

1

CALLED TO BE SAINTS

*The Need for a Compelling
Theology of Holiness*

*Happy are those
who do not follow the advice of the wicked,
or take the path that sinners tread,
or sit in the seat of scoffers;
but their delight is in the law of the LORD,
and on his law they meditate day and night.
They are like trees
planted by streams of water,
which yield their fruit in its season,
and their leaves do not wither.
In all that they do, they prosper.*

PSALM 1:1-3

JESUS ASSURES HIS FOLLOWERS that in him they will find life abundant, surely echoing this wonderful line from Psalm 1 that they will be like trees planted by streams of water. What are the contours and what is the character of this abundant life? What is the good life for which we were created and to which we are called? What are the indicators of a life well lived? To what end were we created? And thus, to what end have we been saved?

The whole of the New Testament assumes that a Christian is someone who grows toward spiritual maturity. But what precisely does it look and feel like to be mature in Christ? The confluence of various developments reminds us that more attention needs to be given to this question.

THE SANCTIFICATION GAP

First, I think back to the remarkable insight in Richard Lovelace's book *Dynamics of Spiritual Life*, in which he observed in the late 1970s that evangelical theology and spirituality were marked by a "sanctification gap."[1] He insisted that this was not due to lack of belief in the importance of holiness or spiritual maturity. Rather he demonstrated that evangelicalism's revivalistic heritage had unwittingly undercut this dynamic church doctrine. In the intervening years, good and helpful contributions have been made to this theme, but in many respects evangelical theology and congregational practice are still marked by the same gap. The theology of sanctification or holiness is typically a second-order theme, with little sense that it may well be the goal of theology and the church.

Textbooks in systematic theology that are used in evangelical seminaries give this topic only cursory attention. An example on my bookshelves highlights this. It is a standard textbook in many evangelical seminaries—a massive 1,200-page systematic theology—but it allocates barely ten pages to the question of the character and contours of the Christian life. Admittedly, those within the Wesleyan and Methodist traditions tend to devote more time and space to sanctification. But is this only a Wesleyan concern? Those who are heirs to John Calvin surely appreciate that the nature of the Christian life is a major theme of Calvin's *Institutes*. Could it be that we have neglected this theme even if the fathers of our theological and spiritual traditions recognized its centrality?

Even when sanctification or holiness is addressed in current studies, the focus is typically on the means—the *how* sanctification happens—

---

[1]Richard F. Lovelace, *Dynamics of Spiritual Life: An Evangelical Theology of Renewal* (Downers Grove, IL: InterVarsity Press, 1979), pp. 229-38.

rather than on what it looks like *when* it happens. A book published a few years ago on "five views of sanctification" hardly discusses sanctification itself but instead focuses on the process of sanctification, with diverse views presented on the Spirit's work in bringing it about. But the book leaves unanswered a key question: To what end is the Spirit's work?

An even more profound problem is that most evangelical Christians have an understanding of conversion that presumes they are "good to go." They have prayed a prayer that "assures" them of a future life, and in the meantime they hear preaching on Sunday that, quite simply, does not either call for or rely on a theology of spiritual maturity. The dominant motif is that salvation can be experienced by believing certain things to be true, praying a simple prayer and then carrying on as best one can till Jesus "returns."

This has left the church vulnerable to what has aptly been called "therapeutic deism," and one wonders if this is indeed the religion of the land rather than trinitarian Christian faith.[2] The goal of the church is to get people "saved" so they can be happy and live productive and civil lives, all with the assurance that in the next life they will be in "heaven." Most words spoken in Sunday preaching in evangelical churches do not assume that spiritual maturity is integral to the gospel.

The Barna Group came to a remarkable conclusion based on research conducted in 2009:

> Our studies this year among pastors showed that almost nine out of ten senior pastors of Protestant churches asserted that spiritual immaturity is one of the most serious problems facing the Church. Yet relatively few of those pastors believe that such immaturity is reflected in their church. Few pastors have gone so far as to give their congregants a specific, written statement of how they define spiritual maturity, how it might be measured, the strategy for facilitating such maturity, or what scriptural passages are most helpful in describing and fostering maturity. Those pastors who made any attempt to measure maturity were more likely to gauge depth on the basis of participation in programs than to evaluate people's spiritual understanding or any type of transformational fruit in their lives.

---

[2]See, for example, Christian Smith, *Souls in Transition: The Religious and Spiritual Lives of Emerging Adults* (New York: Oxford University Press, 2009).

Not surprisingly, our research found that a majority of churchgoing adults are uncertain as to what their church would define as a "healthy, spiritually mature follower of Christ" and they were no more likely to have personally developed a clear notion of such a life.[3]

This research suggests there is a place, indeed an urgent need, for something that would help pastors and congregations define spiritual maturity more clearly.

But if we respond to this gap, it is imperative that our response be *theological*. And for evangelical Christians this is a challenge. Are we prepared to think critically about the Christian life, to ask what it would look like to have a congregation defined by such a vision? Evangelical Christians seem particularly vulnerable to perspectives that do not call for critical theological reflection. Mark Noll speaks of this proclivity when he writes, "To put it most simply, the evangelical ethos is activistic, populist, pragmatic, and utilitarian . . . dominated by the urgencies of the moment."[4] And yet what is needed is a theological vision of the human vocation—something with nuance and substance, an articulation of the Christian life that is congruent with the New Testament call to faith in Christ.

I fully acknowledge that there has been an explosion of interest in spiritual formation and spiritual practice or discipline. Evangelical publishers are putting out several books a year on the importance of spiritual discipline and practice, all of which can be linked in some way to the seminal book by Richard Foster, *Celebration of Discipline*.[5] And yet a common observation could be made about these publications: What is the meaning and goal of the Christian life? What is the theological vision that guides us as we engage these practices?

Spiritual disciplines or practices have meaning only as a means to an end. And they have little meaning if we lack clarity about the end. For every spiritual practice we engage in, we should be able to speak of the

---

[3]"Barna Studies the Research, Offers a Year-in-Review Perspective," Barna Group, 2009, www.barna.org/barna-update/article/12-faith-spirituality/325-barna-studies-the-research-offers-a-year-in-review-perspective.
[4]Mark A. Noll, *The Scandal of the Evangelical Mind* (Grand Rapids, MI: Eerdmans, 1994), p. 12.
[5]Richard Foster, *Celebration of Discipline: The Path to Spiritual Growth* (San Francisco: Harper & Row, 1978).

"grace" we seek through this discipline. And if we speak of a specific grace, we need to be clear what it is we hope—speaking theologically—for God to do in us. Spiritual discipline makes sense only if we have a clear and substantive doctrine of sanctification—if we are clear on the goal, or *telos,* of the Christian life.

Finally, in consideration of this sanctification gap, there are two extensive discussions currently taking place within the evangelical church. First, there are those who speak of the need for character development and moral formation. And from what seems to be a very different group, there is focused conversation on the life of prayer and contemplation. Some speak of being transformed into the image of Christ and that character development is about being like Christ (Christ as model of the Christian life). Others focus on the interior life of prayer and meditation. Both speak of maturity in the disciple's life, but each approaches that maturity from a different perspective. Perhaps with a clear definition of what it means to be a mature Christian, we can effectively bring these two streams together.

THE CALL FOR TRANSFORMATION

Before we get any further, we likely need to make a basic case that God's people are called to spiritual maturity in Christ—that there is, indeed, a goal or vision of the Christian life wherein the church and individual Christians are called to sainthood.

While every theological tradition affirms the need for maturity in Christ, or sanctification, we still need to make the case biblically and theologically that it is integral to the gospel and the call of Christ. Indeed, an articulation of the call to spiritual maturity can and ideally should be inherent in each dimension of the church's life and ministry—all preaching, for example, should include an implicit if not explicit call to the fulfillment of the human vocation. Each time the Scriptures are opened, read and preached, some vision of what it means to be human should be expressed.

The Old Testament is essentially the account of a God who forms for himself a people who are specifically called to be holy. When God brings the people of Israel out of Egypt, they are the people of God; that is their identity. This identity as the people of God is the basis on which they are called to reflect—in their life, work and relationships—the holy character of God. And the journey is not merely a geographic journey to the promised land but a journey of a maturing faith in God. God seeks not merely their release from Egypt but to make them into a people who can reflect the purposes of God. God is out to make for himself a people who reflect his holiness, who are marked by righteousness, and who live in justice and the shalom of God.

When we come to the New Testament, we see again and again the expectation that in and through the work of Christ, the church will be a holy community, transformed by Christ through the power of Word and Spirit. When Jesus announces the in-breaking of the kingdom of God, he declares that a new order of life is being launched through his life and work. This new and transformed mode of life will affect every dimension of existence. Jesus does not merely preach a gospel of personal salvation for those who hope for an afterlife in "heaven." Rather, he teaches his disciples to pray, "Your will be done on earth as it is in heaven." He urges them to seek the kingdom and righteousness, which is modeled by the radical actions of the disciples who left everything to follow him. His offer to them was a transformed life—an "abundant life" (Jn 10:10).

Jesus uses language that makes some readers uncomfortable; he speaks of perfection. In the Sermon on the Mount he urges his disciples to "be perfect, therefore, as your heavenly Father is perfect" (Mt 5:48). And in response to the rich young ruler, he is explicit: "If you wish to be perfect," he says—clearly in response to the desire and intent of this young man—then one must leave all and follow Jesus (Mt 19:21).

Often this has been read as advocating a kind of flawless morality, and those who recognize the depth and power of sin in the human race are not inclined to accept that such perfection is possible. Some within the Wesleyan tradition have been inclined to stress that this is a perfection of love, a perfection of intent rather than flawless behavior.

But there is another way to think about perfection—notably, from the perspective of creation, an approach that may be closer to the intent of the New Testament. When we view the human vocation and sanctification from the vantage point of creation, we see the human vocation as fulfillment of creation. To be complete in Christ, to be "perfect," is quite simply to be what one has been created to be. To say "simply," though, is to miss the force and beauty of perfection. When an engine runs exquisitely, when a pen writes effortlessly, when a bridge spans a river with a flawless combination of beauty and structural integrity, or when a coat fits us comfortably in a style and color that suit us and is just right for the day's weather, we rightly use the word *perfect*. Something works; something fits; something is true to its intent.

We can apply the same concept to the human person. When we meet a saint, we encounter beauty, integrity and congruence. The call to perfection is the invitation to be that for which we were created.

This is also the message of the apostle Paul. His benediction to the Thessalonian believers is straightforward and comprehensive: May God sanctify you entirely, he writes (1 Thess 5:23). In Romans 12:1 he urges his readers to be transformed by the renewing of their minds. And the letter to the Colossians from beginning to end is a call to spiritual maturity in Christ, captured eloquently in the affirmation that they have come to faith in Christ—they have received Christ as Lord (Col 2:6), but now that they have come to faith, he urges them to grow up in their faith, rooted and anchored in Christ. Indeed, in the preceding verses Paul describes his own ministry as preaching, struggling and suffering to this end: that they would be complete, perfect and mature in Christ (Col 1:28).

The language of perfection as it is used here is not elitist; rather, it speaks of something we all long for and something we are all called to. The New Testament uses two compelling images or metaphors to profile this call to transformation: sickness-healing and infancy-maturity.

The image of sickness and health—transformation as healing—arises from the profound ways in which Jesus is a healer. Ultimately he is not merely the healer of physical ailments but the healer of our souls, indeed of our whole beings. The promise of healing is anticipated with the coming of the Messiah (Is 58:8); Jesus is then revealed in the Gospels as the divine healer. And the book of Revelation celebrates the one who brings healing to the nations (Rev 22:2).

The second image—infancy-maturity—also emerges as a regular motif, especially in the New Testament Epistles. In 1 Peter, for example, the writer speaks to the readers of their new faith, stressing that their new birth is the fruit of the Word that has been preached to them. He goes on to urge them as babes in Christ to crave the pure spiritual milk by which they will grow up in their salvation (see 1 Peter 1:22–2:2). Ephesians 4 speaks of a fully functioning congregation of believers where each one contributes to the equipping of God's people, so that Christians are not tossed about like a boat at sea by every wind of teaching but rather grow up into Christ as the congregation is built up in the faith. Similarly the book of Hebrews encourages readers to move beyond elementary teachings toward maturity (Heb 6:1).

This image of spiritual growth toward maturity suggests the idea of progress in the faith; spiritual maturity does not come quickly but occurs over time as a person responds to the means of grace and thus "grows." Surely this is precisely what the author of 2 Peter wants his readers to understand. He speaks of faith, goodness, knowledge, self-control and more, concluding with love, and he speaks of possessing these qualities in increasing measure (2 Pet 1:8).

In 2 Peter we are also reminded that new birth is not an end but a beginning; our election or calling in Christ and to Christ is for a particular purpose—maturity in Christ. To put it more bluntly, our conversion has meaning only if it leads to the goal of conversion: namely, this very spiritual maturity (2 Pet 1:10-11).

There are other metaphors in the New Testament. For example, Paul uses the idea of changing clothes when he speaks of putting off the old self—as one might a suit of clothing—and putting on the new self (Eph 4:22-24). In Christ one has a new identity, a new way of being, a radical reorientation. Still, the dominant images used in reference to spiritual maturity are those of sickness-health and infancy-maturity. I will draw on these images often in the chapters that follow.

But before we go further, we need to speak about heresy.

SPEAKING ABOUT HERESY

All theological reflection requires that one think about heresy, asking where there is a teaching or theology that is a partial truth and thus not the whole truth. A partial or half-truth is actually false—and in many ways more dangerous that something that is blatantly false.

There are two heresies connected with a theology of sanctification or spiritual maturity that need to be identified early on. First, we need to consider the dangers of *perfectionism*. The animating and empowering call to transformation in Christ is a call to mature in faith, hope and love—to be "perfect" in Christ. And yet many recoil from such talk largely because they have seen the downside of perfectionism. The fear of perfectionism has even led some New Testament translators to avoid the use of the word *perfect* to translate *telos* (see, for example, the New International Version and New Revised Standard Version translations of Colossians 1:28).

This avoidance is perhaps an overreaction, but we still need to be clear about what we mean and do not mean by use of the word *perfect*. Perfectionism is deadly, whereas the call to full maturity in Christ is animating (that is, it enlivens us). The difference is a matter of location and association.

Perfectionism treats the law of God, and thus the very holiness of God, as a standard in its own right. Perfectionism calls Christians to live according to this law. But though the law is a guide to character and virtue, its effects are deadly when it is disconnected from its source. The Scriptures and the sixteenth-century Reformers speak of how legalism is a curse and a weight rather than a freedom in Christ. The law is good, and Paul clearly expects that it will be fulfilled in the covenant people of God (Rom 13:8-10). But when not linked intimately with faith in Christ, the law is an impossible weight, a crushing burden, an impossible taskmaster.

A sister heresy to perfectionism is moralism. Much Sunday preaching is really little more than urging people to get their lives in order: good advice on how to be a good, morally upright person—whether it is a sermon on how to be a good father (on Father's Day, of course) or whether it is a call to get one's finances in order. Either way it is just good advice—and for many a crushing burden. It is the weight of the law without the gospel. People hear the call and the ideal as nothing but a reminder of their failure.

Thus one of the abiding themes of this book is an insistence that we cannot equate moral formation with spiritual formation. I will explain more what I mean by this statement in the chapters that follow. But for now, I must at least plant the seed and note that spiritual formation is not synonymous with virtue or character development. While it includes these, they are not the heart of the matter. If moral development is not derivative of our union with Christ, it is an impossible burden.

Second, we must speak of *pelagianism*, an ancient heresy that Augustine combated in late fourth and early fifth century. The basic argument is simple: that the human person has an inherent capacity to become mature or holy through consistent practice, diligent effort and strength of will. The label *pelagian* is sometimes used to describe all spiritualities that emphasize the responsibility and capacity of the human person to grow toward spiritual maturity. But that would be a misnomer and false characterization. The problem is more subtle. The Scriptures clearly speak of personal responsibility and effort—witness Paul's affirmation of his struggle for the believers in Colossae (Col 1:29) and for his own soul (Phil 3:12-14).

The biblical vision of holiness is one in which spiritual maturity is the fruit ultimately not of human effort toward an objective standard (a holy law, perhaps), but rather human response to the call and enabling of God. Our theology of the Christian life must, of course, include a reflection on agency—on the significance of both divine and human actions. Often the casual line offered is that we must do our part while God does God's part. But this is not in the end a helpful way to frame this matter, because quite simply it confuses the issue and the very different ways in which we act and God acts. The difference, while subtle, is radical.

When it comes to the life we have in God, God is the actor. It is all of God. It is all gift. But this does not mean the human person is passive or a nonactor. We can and should take human agency seriously. However, the genius of human action is that it is an act of *response* to and *participation* in the actions of God.

The images of sickness-healing and infancy-growth are helpful here. A doctor knows that she is not a healer; she is merely participating in and fostering the healing process that is part of the work of God in creation. Doctors don't heal, but they are active participants in the healing process.

Similarly, farmers know that they do not grow anything. They don't grow corn or vegetables or wheat. Rather, they plant, they water, they weed and they prune their fruit trees. Though their effort and participation is important, the fruit at the end of the apple tree is hardly their "work." Despite all their effort, this fruit—or, for the doctor, this healing— is sheer gift.

Perfectionism, pelagianism, moralism, legalism and all the other "isms" that might undercut true Christian spirituality are indeed a threat, but they cannot keep us from this call to maturity in Christ. John Calvin offers a helpful perspective here. He insists that we not speak of our calling to perfection in any way that fails to acknowledge that we are all sinners, sinners on the road to mature faith in Christ. Though none have become perfect, the standard and the call remain; they are that for which we long and that which we seek. Calvin insists that the dangers of perfectionism do not mean we do not speak of our objective. Rather, he suggests that we speak of it as precisely that—the goal toward which we run.[6] He echoes the language of Paul in Philippians: "I press on toward the goal for the prize of the heavenly call of God in Christ Jesus" (Phil 3:14). Though the objective is not reached, it is nevertheless pursued.

From this vantage point, we can speak of our goal not as something oppressive but rather as that which motivates and inspires us. We may never be in perfect health, but that does not mean we tolerate sickness. A doctor likely knows that his patient will never be "perfectly" healthy, but it would a travesty to then tolerate and accept disease. We may never be as wise, mature and holy as we would like to be. But that does not mean we despair and forsake our calling to Christian maturity.

We can use the language of perfection and completeness and see it as a call to excellence. Having identified the scourge of perfectionism that has often plagued this discussion, we must not let a fear of perfectionism keep from us from articulating a vibrant and compelling vision for Christian holiness.

---

[6]John Calvin, *The Institutes of the Christian Religion*, 3.6.5.

A vital dimension of a church's teaching and preaching is the regular reminder that spiritual maturity is indeed our calling: it is our destiny, our human vocation in Christ. Pastoral ministry must constantly make the case for why spiritual growth is essential, possible and accessible; it is a vital dimension of congregational life.

Congregations that do not pursue with passion and vigor a dynamic maturity in Christ are surely as fraudulent as a hospital that is not passionate and vigorous in its pursuit of healing and wholeness. What follows is an attempt to provide such a vision that I trust is an accessible, compelling and worthy goal for the Christian believer.

SOME DEFINING CRITERIA

How then do we embrace the call to spiritual maturity, indeed to perfection, but avoid these deadly heresies? How can we speak of the call to maturity in Christ in a way that fosters a pastoral vision for God's people—one comparable to the vision a doctor has for his patient's healing or a farmer has for the fruit of the orchard? At the very least we need to approach our theological vision from five distinctive perspectives. These are the criteria by which we will define our theology of spiritual maturity:

- Trinitarian and christocentric
- Salvation as the fulfillment of God's creation
- The interplay of sin and faith
- Individual and communal holiness
- The ordinary and the mundane—particularly the reality of suffering.

Trinitarian and christocentric. First, it is essential that we anchor our vision for the human vocation in the triune character of God—Father, Son and Spirit.

With reference to the Father, it is appropriate to use the language of election and speak of the one who made us and thus longs for us to come into the very identity for which we were created. When we speak of human destiny or purpose, we are referring to the goal to which we are called by our Father in heaven.

Second, a trinitarian vision for Christian maturity or holiness will consistently speak of that maturity as participation in the life and work of Christ Jesus. I will belabor this point: Christian spirituality is demarcated by being "in Christ." In fact, we can speak of holiness only from the perspective of Christ's divine initiative revealed in the mercy of the cross. Everything is formed in us on the basis of the gospel of the Lord Jesus Christ. It is this gospel that compels and transforms us, but more, it is through the gospel that we are drawn into the very life of Christ.

And third, this trinitarian vision profiles the fundamental gospel truth that spiritual maturity is effected in our lives through the gracious ministry of the Holy Spirit. I am reminded of a line from Richard Lovelace: "True spirituality is not a superhuman religiosity; it is simply true humanity released from bondage to sin and renewed by the Holy Spirit."[7]

Christian spirituality is a life of radical dependence on the Spirit. We do not live self-created or self-constructed lives, but rather lives of active response to the grace of God. Many books on the Christian life seem like nothing more than a christianized version of Stephen Covey's *Seven Habits of Highly Effective People*, a classic of American civil religion with its implicit and explicit assumption that if we are successful it is because we have managed to get our lives together. If not, it is because we are lazy or lack resolve. The biblical vision is a life lived in radical dependence on God and in deep mutual interdependence with others; for Covey, the individual controls his or her destiny by commitment to certain habits.

Much preaching on Sunday is about getting these habits right: You too can be a good father, husband, employee—whatever—if you just get the practices right and keep them up. But the answer to the fatalistic quietism of nominal Christianity is not a religious self-help program.

Rather, we must be thoroughly trinitarian and speak of the gift of holiness that comes through the grace of the Spirit. The call to holiness comes from the Father as an invitation to participate in the life of Christ Jesus and to do so in radical dependence on the grace of the Spirit. All three dimensions of this trinitarian vision speak to the fact that our holiness is a miracle of divine initiative—an initiative in grace and mercy.

---

[7]Lovelace, *Dynamics*, p. 19.

Thus our holiness brings glory to God. And our theology of spiritual maturity will then ask, what does true humanity look like when released from the oppressive power of sin and infused with the life of the Holy Spirit who, in the language of the Nicene Creed, is "the Lord and giver of life"?

Baptism, then, is a rite of initiation into a life that is demarcated by the triune God. The Lord's Supper is the rite of the faith community where we respond to the Creator who in Christ has loved us and given his very God-self for us and who invites us in the Spirit to live the life to which we are called. Both baptism and the Lord's Supper are rites of gracious empowerment, equipping and feeding us to live in response to God's call.

As already indicated, this emphasis on the work of the Spirit does not diminish or discount the significance of human agency; it is merely that our actions come in response to the Spirit's work and are sustained through the grace given by the Spirit.

Salvation as the fulfillment of God's creation. A second crucial criterion is the affirmation that our salvation is the fulfillment of the purposes of God in creation. We can ask the holiness question only if we also attend to an intimately related question: To what end were we created? If we affirm with the creed that "I believe in God the Father almighty, maker of heaven and earth," what does this mean for our understanding of God's redemptive purposes? It means that we speak of maturity, or perfection, as the fulfillment of creation.

In technical language, it means we see a profound continuity between the order of creation and the order of redemption. It means we speak of "perfection" as nothing other that the end for which we were made or designed, for, as Thomas Aquinas noted, "A thing is said to be perfect in so far as it attains its proper end, which is the final perfection of the thing."[8] It is to the glory of God that we be fully and completely who we were created to be.

We can rightly ask, then, what it means to be created in the image of God and what it looks like for this image to be renewed, restored and

---

[8]Thomas Aquinas, *Summa Theologiae: A Concise Translation*, ed. Timothy McDermott (Westminster, MD: Christian Classics, 1989), p. 456.

brought to full completion or maturity. What I hope to demonstrate is that a saint is one who lives to the glory and praise of the Father and Creator. Thus there is a profound beauty to holiness—not merely the holiness of God, but the holiness, indeed the glory, of the human person who is the image, icon or reflection of God. This means that for each dimension of holiness we must consider the interplay between creation and redemption. We must consider how the grace of God infuses the whole of creation: healing, restoring and transforming all that God has made.[9]

It is important that we keep the two distinct—the order of creation and the order of redemption. They are not identical; this is so because of the presence and power of sin. We only experience a created order that is wracked with the power of evil. But the continuity between creation and redemption means that we can never speak of God's salvation except in the light of the wonder and beauty of the creation. And one notable implication is that we do not think in terms of two distinct zones to our lives—a secular and a sacred zone. Rather the grace of God infuses all that we are and all that we are called to be.

One implication is that holiness is not equated with religious activities or church participation. The Christian life and church life are not identical. Yes, we are called to be full participants in the life of the church. But we do not reduce Christian living to church activities and involvements. There is much more to our lives than that which is prescribed or contained within it.

Most of all, it means that we long and hope for the renewal of God's creation. The whole creation, we read in Romans 8, groans in anticipation of the revelation of the children of God (Rom 8:18-20). Our hope, our longing, is not for an otherworldly existence. We affirm life in the created order; we affirm and delight in life as God created it to be. Thus when we speak of the reign of Christ—of the in-breaking of the kingdom of God—by praying, "Your will be done on earth as it is in heaven," we

---

[9]In this regard, I particularly appreciate the work of Karl Rahner. See for example his *The Christian Commitment: Essays in Pastoral Theology*, trans. Cecily Hastings (New York: Sheed and Ward, 1963), p. 39, where he writes that God's grace "actually penetrates the created order itself, healing and sanctifying it; that it incorporates the world, in all its abiding naturality, into the 'mysterium Christi'; and that this process of taking the world by grace into the life of God" is meant to inform the human calling or vocation.

are praying for and participating in the renewal of all things under the benevolent authority of Christ.

The interplay of sin and faith. We cannot speak of transformation and Christian maturity unless we have a clear understanding of the biblical doctrine of sin. It is the necessary point of reference in any discussion of what it means to be a saint. And it is not sufficient to speak of sin as deliberate transgression—bad people doing bad things. Rather, we need to speak of sin as a sickness that has infected the whole of God's creation; we need to speak of it as an incipient, oppressive power, an addictive and deadly force.

An awareness of sin's power reminds us of our need for both compassion and patience as we attend to and respond to the grace of God in our lives. Yes, we must speak of Christ's victory over sin, and yes we must speak of the possibilities of grace in our lives. And yet our vision of what it means to be mature or complete in Christ must without apology take full account of the insidious power of sin in our lives, in our communities, in the church and in the world.

When we are naive to the power of sin or speak as though it no longer has real control in our lives, we unwittingly become more susceptible to its devastating hold. In the timing and purposes of God, sin is not yet eliminated from the equation; we still live with its effects even though we are confident of its ultimate defeat. And so our discussion of what it means to be mature in Christ must recognize that we will live out our entire lives struggling with sin's debilitating effects: the wrongs of others, the strains on mental health, the flaws great and small that afflict us all.

This does not mean we tolerate sin—any more than a doctor tolerates sickness. It merely means we acknowledge the power of sin and recognize that God's transforming work can seem slow and incremental. It also means we must respond to ourselves and to others with compassion, generosity and patience, learning to bear with one another in love (Col 3:13).

Quite apart from the power of sin in our lives, we must speak of the priority of faith. Our calling is one of radical dependence on God as creatures who grow into maturity and learn to trust in him. And the sin factor in our lives and in our world is what more than anything else calls us back to a deep recognition of our need for Christ, of what it means to live under the mercy and in radical dependence on his grace.

In faith we can sing, "Just as I am, without one plea, but that thy blood was shed for me." This is our disposition of heart and mind each day, each hour; we always fall short of the glory to which we are called and thus always turn again to Christ in dependence on God's gracious work in him. There is nothing quite like our sin, failure and weakness to force us, indeed compel us, to turn from the foolishness of our self-constructed lives to live instead in faith and quiet, childlike trust. Thus we speak of this life in Christ as a gift—a gift that is received with humility.

Individual and communal holiness. Our vision of Christian maturity must include a doctrine of holiness that accounts for the interplay between the individual person, called to maturity in Christ, and the church, which is also called to grow up in Christ. Both the individual and the communal (or ecclesial) body need to be understood in light of the other. Personal maturity in Christ will always be found in dynamic communion with the faith community. And it is not merely a matter of being in community; it must be the church with whom we are in community (thus our definition of the church matters). Our understanding and experience of the faith is anchored in a rich theological and spiritual tradition; we are part of a faith community that has an apostolic foundation.

To be complete in Christ is to know the holiness of God who calls us into fellowship with himself as a triune being. Indeed, the holiness of God cannot be construed apart from the love and fellowship found within his triunity. In similar fashion, the holiness of the Christian can find expression only within the love and fellowship of the church. Our individual sanctification is part of God's overall plan for the church. So in the end we cannot speak of the call to holiness apart from the calling of God's people to be, together, the one holy catholic and apostolic church.

And so in the discussion that follows we will address the formative power of liturgy and worship. We will speak of the central practices of the faith community and affirm how we grow in grace together as God's people. We will speak of worship, the proclamation of the Scriptures, the practice of the Lord's Supper and the common work of witnessing in word and deed to the reign of Christ. The church is not merely an instrument of the kingdom; it is also an embodiment and foretaste of the kingdom. And so the church is the fruit of the in-breaking of the kingdom in the world.

Yet the individual does have a personal identity, and we speak of corporate holiness without denying the significance and power of the individual. The individual is not lost within the corporate identity of the church but rather flourishes in this community as one who gives and receives the love of God. Still, what must be stressed is that individual spiritual maturity cannot be contemplated apart from the shared practices of the faith community. Furthermore, it is important to affirm that we are on this journey together not merely as companions on the road but as mutually dependent sisters and brothers growing up into Christ as each one contributes (Eph 4:13-16).

All of this means, at the very least, two things. First, the call of the church to be the holy people of God must form the backdrop for any discussion of the human vocation. And second, our vision of spiritual maturity in Christ needs to be one that can be translated into practice within congregations. This way congregations can clearly see how they are on this journey together, and individuals can see and feel this very dynamic of interdependence on one another even as all are dependent on Christ.

The ordinary and the mundane—particularly the reality of suffering. When we speak of the holiness to which we are called, the grace of spiritual maturity in Christ, we must speak of it as that which is fulfilled in the ordinary, routine and mundane rhythms of daily life. We can certainly affirm the extraordinary, and we will. But the point here is to say that formation of the human soul occurs not so much in the unusual but in the daily life of the Christian believer.

Then—and perhaps this is most crucial—we need to speak of difficulty: failure, disappointment and pain. A key thread that must run through any discussion of maturity in Christ is the formative power of suffering. In our lives and in our work we suffer with Christ as his joint heirs in suffering (Rom 8:17). And suffering will inevitably demarcate our relationships and our work. It is the context in which we live out our lives.

Glenn Tinder makes the observation that most cultures have a deep aversion to suffering.[10] No one in any culture wants to suffer, but what is unique in our time and context is our failure to see suffering as part of the human predicament due to our moral and physical imperfections. It is part of the finitude of life. It is a false hope to want to live in comfortable suburbia away from the painful reality of human existence with the assumption that technology will eventually ease all our pain.

Our theology of the Christian life must take account of how suffering, while an aberration in God's creation and not integral to what God has made, is for now—before Christ is revealed and all is well—a means by which God forms us and purifies us. Suffering will pass. But in the meantime it is inescapable, and so we must speak of pain, suffering and difficulty with reference to each dimension of Christian holiness. And we will do so, of course, the only way that can be done—with a hope that is possible only because of the cross of Christ.

These are the five perspectives that will undergird this study: trinitarian and christocentric, salvation within the order of creation, sin and the life of faith, the individual in community and, finally, the significance of the ordinary—specifically, the place of suffering in our lives.

THE APPROACH

Before we launch deeper into this project, here are several points about the approach we will be taking as we explore Christian maturity and holiness.

Biblical and theological. The vision that will be outlined in the pages that follow will be intentionally and explicitly "biblical." The consideration of union with Christ, for example, will include a focused examination of John 15. The call to wisdom will contrast and compare Proverbs 1 and Colossians 1. The call to love will in many respects be an extended reflection on Romans 12:9–15:7. Indeed, it should be evident throughout that each dimension of spiritual maturity is a reflection of the human vocation that is witnessed to in the Scriptures.

If our approach is biblical, it should be evident that the vision of righteousness found in the Old Testament will be foundational. We need to demonstrate how this vision is fulfilled, not abrogated, in Christ.

---

[10]Glenn Tinder, *The Fabric of Hope: An Essay* (Grand Rapids, MI: Eerdmans, 1999), pp. 134-40.

Consider, for example, the character of Christian worship. The shape of worship under the old covenant, including the sacrificial system, is not discarded with the coming of Christ but fulfilled in him. The difference between "discarded" and "fulfilled" is no small matter. And just as the shape of worship is sustained, so the shape of righteousness, holiness and justice is fulfilled in Christ. The Old Testament vision is fulfilled, not discarded.

While biblical, this vision will also be theological. Some will perhaps protest that if it is biblical it is necessarily theological and the only theology we want is that which is biblical. And yet the distinction I make between biblical and theological is important for two reasons. First, our approach will be theological in that we will seek a synthesis of the biblical texts and perspectives. We will ask, for example, what is the meaning of work? The answer will be more all-inclusive than a mere considering of individual biblical passages.

Second, "theological" also speaks to the heritage of the church—the witness of the Spirit through the journey of faith over the years, the experience and ongoing theological reflection that is central to the church's identity and work. We will learn from those who have gone before us.

Evangelical and ecumenical. Also, it will be clear that as the author of this work I am attempting to be explicitly evangelical and ecumenical. Being evangelical is not really an option for me. We all think and write from within some theological framework, and my own is undoubtedly the evangelical heritage that is heir to the great awakenings of the late eighteenth century and the formative voices of John Wesley, Jonathan Edwards and others.

A nonevangelical Christian reader has likely picked this up already; it will be evident in how questions are framed, what problems are addressed and how issues are illustrated. Most of all, it will be clear in how dimensions of the Christian life are nuanced and affirmed.

I do write with a particular concern for the way in which my own theological tradition thinks about and seeks the holiness of God. And I hope what follows will be compelling to evangelicals across the spectrum of this tradition—Reformed, Anabaptist, Wesleyan, Lutheran, Pentecostal, Holiness and more. An early version of some of these chapters was presented in a cosponsored lecture series in Baptist and Pentecostal theological seminaries in Romania. The lectures were well received and I was reminded that while there are significant theological differences, we can find substantive common ground even between Baptist and Pentecostal believers!

Yet I am hoping that what follows is also ecumenical—clearly written from within the evangelical tradition but drawing freely on contributions of other theological and spiritual traditions. While my primary audience is likely evangelical Christians, I hope that the discussion is also accessible to Roman Catholic, Orthodox and other Christians, and even those who are exploring the character of Christian faith, still not as yet having made a commitment to Christian identity.

So I write as an evangelical and will address the theme of maturity in Christ through this prism. But I will seek to do this in intentional conversation with other theological traditions.

Theological and practical. In this exploration of spiritual maturity and completeness in Christ, we need to ask what it means to be a Christian. Now, although it is easy to place a religious veneer on what is essentially a secular understanding of the human vocation, presenting spiritual maturity as a kind of psychological equanimity or balance, it is nonetheless valid to draw on the insights from other disciplines of study, including the thoughtful reflections on the nature of good work being conducted by those in the fields of business and contemporary psychology.

But what must ultimately define our vision of the Christian life is a thoroughly creedal and biblical theology. We need to foster a view of what it means to be a Christian that reflects the full purposes of God for the individual and for the community of faith. Thinking theologically gives meaning, substance and purpose to our lives. And because our lives are lived in the midst of complexity and challenge, with both blessing and suffering, we need a vision of the Christian life that can embrace the full scope of this complexity.

A theological vision will foster discernment: our capacity to read our culture and embrace the best it has to offer while also challenging those propensities that are not compatible with biblical faith. And fundamentally, it will mean a vision that is congruent with the pain and suffering that inevitably mark this life while also demarcated by a deep hopefulness.

It is often said that if we are being theological about something, we are not likely being practical. To the contrary: theology is very practical. Good theology fosters wisdom and thus the capacity to live well. We need a theological vision that can be translated into practice, that makes sense in the warp and woof of daily life. We need a theological vision that we can convert into approaches to spiritual formation. But the sequence matters. Our practice must be theologically informed.

Universal and particular. Then, finally, our approach will seek to be both universal and particular. Stephen Neill in his classic little study *Christian Holiness* makes an interesting observation: "Sinners are tediously alike. . . . Saints manifest a glorious variety. . . . No general terms cover them all."[11] We are always called to holiness in our own time and generation, and culture is certainly a factor in our understanding and practice of spiritual maturity. And yet as Neill himself points out, we can speak of "certain qualities" that are consistently found in all who seek maturity in Christ Jesus—from Norway to Thailand, saints in Christ will have some common qualities, indicators of living in the holiness of God.

Karl Barth, through his brilliant insights into the character of conversion and sanctification, makes a compelling case that while no two Christians are alike, there are certain boundaries and contours that make a Christian a Christian. We are called to one Lord; we are transformed—or, his word, "awakened"—by one Spirit.[12] We live in response to and are infused by the same Word. So we can speak of universals not to deny the particularities of our lives, but as a means to profile the common motifs, vision and hope we share on this road.

With our common vision of maturity in Christ, we also recognize that there will be remarkable diversity of expression. There is the diversity of personality; there is the diversity of culture. There are certain universals to the Christian life, but holiness is always lived out in unique contexts, in specific geographic and demographic settings, in particular

---

[11]Stephen Neill, *Christian Holiness* (New York: Harper & Brothers, 1960), p. 126.
[12]Karl Barth, *Church Dogmatics* IV/2, trans. G. W. Bromiley (Edinburgh: T & T Clark, 1958), pp. 499-612.

societies and communities. Maturity in Christ will therefore reflect both continuity and discontinuity with local culture.

No doubt at times readers may be inclined to respond negatively and perhaps even dismiss points that seem appropriate only to someone who is heir to the cultures of northern Europe. Asians, Africans, Hispanic Christians and others might conclude that what I present does not apply in their setting. That is fair. And yet in our exchanges across cultural lines let's not dismiss one another prematurely. Our perspective is consistently strengthened by conversation with those from other cultures and social contexts. We need to learn from one another. And we need to allow some of our most cherished ideals—elements that we might think are vital to our cultural identity—to be challenged by the way other Christians read the Scriptures.

Conclusion: An Overview of This Vision for Christian Maturity

We recognize a profound need for a theology of sanctification that undergirds and gives direction to the church on this distinctive commitment: to foster the capacity for growth in faith, hope and love, a capacity that will be evident in moral leadership, character, integrity and, quite simply, holiness—a reflection of the very character of God. We hear the words "Be holy, for I am holy" (1 Pet 1:16), and we ask, so what does this look like, this holiness?

In what follows, the reader will find a twofold proposal for what this vision of Christian maturity might look like. First, as the heart of the matter and the all-encompassing and defining vision, Christian spiritual maturity—the "perfection" to which we are called—will be described as union with Christ. With a full appreciation of the trinitarian character of God, I will speak of how the whole of the Christian life is found "in Christ." I will stress that this vision assumes a dynamic participation in the life of the ascended Christ Jesus—in real time. I will also emphasize that the Christian life is lived out of the fundamental experience of being united with Christ in his death and resurrection, the very meaning of a Christian baptism (Rom 6).

Second, I will speak of four distinct but deeply interrelated dimensions of Christian maturity. These are essentially four invitations.

- A holy person is a wise person.
- A holy person does good work.
- A holy person loves others in a manner consistent with how God has loved us.
- A holy person is a happy person.

Each of these invitations will be defined as a dimension of union with Christ. They are not all of a kind. Wisdom is foundational and is the basis for all other dimensions of the good life. Work and relationships represent two essential aspects of human life. And we are mature in Christ only when we know what it is to do good work and to live in love with others. And then, joy infuses the whole: joy in our work, joy in our relationships, the joy that arises from knowing and living in wisdom.

While the sequence of these four characteristics is important and intentional in the presentation here, there is an interactive quality between them. Thus, for example, we grow in joy as we grow in wisdom, in our capacity for good work and in our capacity to love others as we have been loved.

2

Union with Christ

The Essence of the Christian Life

Your throne, O God, endures forever and ever.
Your royal scepter is a scepter of equity;
you love righteousness and hate wickedness.
Therefore God, your God, has anointed you
with the oil of gladness beyond your companions.

Psalm 45:6-7

What is it that makes a Christian a Christian? For many evangelicals, the answer is simple: they have prayed a prayer or believed certain things to be true or "accepted Christ as Savior and Lord." While not diminishing the importance of believing in what Christ has done and accepting it as that which defines one's life, in what follows I will have a slightly different focus. I will stress that what makes the Christian a Christian is *participation* in the life of Christ Jesus, or union with Christ. One is a Christian because one is "in Christ," to use the recurring phrase of Ephesians 1.

This affirmation does not for a moment alter our deep commitment to a trinitarian faith and experience of God's grace. Our union with Christ is specifically a union with the second person of the holy Trinity.

The reality of the Trinity will be the lens and provide the contours for our understanding of the *telos* of the Christian life. The benediction of 2 Corinthians 13:13-14 is a touchstone reference: "The grace of the Lord Jesus Christ, the love of God, and the communion of the Holy Spirit be with all of you." And yet, there is a christological concentration to the Christian experience.[1]

IN CHRIST: THE ESSENTIAL CHARACTER OF CHRISTIAN EXPERIENCE

To know, love and serve Christ Jesus. Three of the Gospels—Matthew, Mark and Luke—clearly profile the identity of the Christian as that of a disciple, one who follows Jesus and then in turn lives under the reign of Christ, that is, the kingdom of God. This is the Christian's compass orientation; this is the fundamental alignment of a Christian life.

This was ably captured by the ancient medieval vision of the Christian life: to be a Christian is to know, love and follow Christ Jesus. In his *Spiritual Exercises*, Ignatius Loyola suggests that in our prayers we seek "an intimate knowledge of our Lord, who has become man for me, that I may love Him more and follow Him more closely."[2] Sometimes the third part of the triad—to follow—is expressed as service, obedience or both. And indeed, to follow is to serve and obey. So, then, to be a Christian is to be a disciple of Jesus, and a mature disciple is one who

- knows Jesus through the fruit of learning—specifically a learning that leads to intimate knowledge;

- loves Jesus such that Christ is the first love and the deepest love, the source of one's greatest delight and joy;

- serves Jesus such that all that one does is in response to Christ's call and an expression of allegiance to him.

Of course, the one we follow is the crucified, risen and ascended Lord, and thus discipleship is marked by the way of the cross and comes in

---

[1]I have borrowed this phrase from Michael Wecker in his study on the meaning of the Lord's Supper: *What Happens in Holy Communion*, trans. John F. Hoffmeyer (Grand Rapids, MI: Eerdmans, 2000).

[2]Louis J. Puhl, *The Spiritual Exercises of St. Ignatius* (Allahabad, India: St. Paul Publications, 1975), no. 104.

response to Christ's self-identification as the one to whom all authority and power are given. The passion, the deep longing and orientation of the mature Christian, is the resolve in love to live under the benevolent authority of Christ.

And so it is also for the church. To be the church is to be a learning community that seeks together in faith to know Jesus, to grow together in love for Jesus and to align our lives, mission and way of being in the world to the in-breaking of the reign of Christ. The salvation of God is found specifically as the one and the many come under the reign of Christ and participate in this reign. Thus there is no conceivable split between knowing Jesus as "Savior" and knowing him as "Lord." Indeed, the salvation of God is specifically the lordship of Christ.

Therefore, the life of the church, including her teaching-learning process (that is, her catechism), is rightly centered around this axis: to know him truly and intimately, to love him as the dearest possession of all and to serve him with alacrity. The church in her worship moves into a real-time encounter with her ascended Lord, who in worship is known and loved and who in worship calls us afresh to live in response to his benevolent authority over our lives and over the cosmos. From the encounter with Christ in worship, we move into the world as those who choose to live the Christ-way, following Jesus' example as the model of what it means to be fully human.

To be "in Christ." The phrase "to know, love and serve" is an immensely helpful baseline and aptly captures the call of Matthew, Mark and Luke. But as we probe further into the writings of the New Testament—notably the Gospel of John, the epistles of Paul and the book of Hebrews—what emerges is that the Christian ideal is not so much a life *with* Christ or *for* Christ, but rather a life *in* Christ. The whole of Christian life is derived from and understood in the light of this identity, this way of being.

We are called to live in and under the reign of Christ; there is no doubt that the kingdom motif provides a powerful, all-encompassing vision for the Christian life. But we must not miss that the Christian is invited not merely into the kingdom of Christ, but specifically into dynamic union with the one who reigns—Christ Jesus himself.

In John's Gospel. The Gospel of John speaks of a mutual indwelling, notably in the extraordinary words of John 15 where Jesus calls his disciples to "abide in me as I abide in you." Earlier in the Gospel we read of Jesus' promise that his disciples would know life abundantly (Jn 10), and what emerges in John 15 is that the abundant life is a life of dwelling in Christ as Christ dwells in us. This mutual indwelling is also the basis for his promise that the disciples would bear fruit.

What are we to make of this remarkable invitation? How is it even possible for us to live in Christ as Christ lives in us? To get at what Jesus means, we do well to note two things he offers. First, Jesus provides a metaphor and, second, he locates his call to mutual indwelling within some rich trinitarian theology.

The image or metaphor is that of a gardener who tends a vine and its branches. In this metaphor the Father is the gardener and thus the one from whom all life proceeds; the Father is the manager of life, one might say, the arbiter and fulfiller of what it means to be created. The Son, Jesus himself, is the vine—the bearer of life for the whole of creation. And we the disciples of Jesus are branches grafted into the vine. These branches live only insofar as they are "in" the vine. Only then do they bear fruit; only then do they live the life to which they are called by the Father.

This image of the vine and the branches is interwoven with another series of reflections on the life of the Christian and the life of the triune God. What happens here is simply breathtaking. Jesus begins by describing his relationship with the Father, which is an echo of his words in chapter 14 where he stresses that he and the Father are one and, later, that he abides in the Father as the Father abides in him. And then Jesus speaks of how our relationship with him is made possible through the ministry of the Spirit.

In chapter 15 he speaks of himself as the vine and the Father as the gardener in the opening verse, so we get a hint of what is to come—that the fruit Jesus bears through us is to the Father's glory (Jn 15:8). But then notice this: He speaks of his relationship with the Father—as the Father has loved me, so I have loved you (Jn 15:9), and he also stresses that he keeps the Father's commands—but then in the very same breath he speaks of his own relationship with his disciples. And he makes this staggering observation: just as Jesus abides in the Father, we are to abide in Jesus. In other words, the quality of life within the triunity of God is precisely the kind of life we can have in Christ Jesus.

This is what is intended by the call "abide in me as I abide in you." Christ himself, his very self, becomes our true home even as we ourselves, our embodied selves, are the home of Christ. Therefore we do not merely follow Jesus, though we certainly follow. We do not merely obey Jesus, though we certainly live as those who do his will. And we do not merely imitate Jesus, though without doubt we follow his example. Rather we participate in the life of Jesus—literally, not metaphorically. In fact, this is the very language we find in 2 Peter 1:4, where sanctification is spoken of as participation in the life of God, indeed, in the divine nature.

It must be stressed that our relationship with Christ is categorically different from Christ's relationship with the Father and the Spirit within the godhead. And yet Jesus himself clearly sets up a parallel indicating that while different—necessarily so in that the being of God is other than that of a human being—the quality of our communion with Christ reflects Christ's communion with the Father. Through our communion with Christ we have communion with the triune God, creator and redeemer of all things.

How is this possible, this participation in the very life of God? The answer is twofold. First, it happens through the work of the Spirit, who draws us into the life of Christ. Second, it is possible through the means of grace: the Word—specifically the Scriptures taught and preached—and the sacramental actions of baptism and the Lord's Supper. Both the priority of the Spirit and the power of the sacraments emerge in our reading of the Gospel of John. And both are a means of grace to the Christian and to the church through the ministry of the Holy Spirit. This is pivotal; there is no experience of Christ or participation in his life—no abiding in him as he abides in us—except through the grace of the Spirit.

But the bottom line remains. Our vision for the Christian life is not merely that we would be formed into the image of Christ—that we would be like Christ Jesus. Rather, the extraordinary vision into which we are called is that we would be drawn into the very life of Christ and thereby into the life of God. Our vision and passion is union with Christ, and in in our participation in the life of Christ we are drawn into the *perichoresis* of Father, Son and Spirit.

In Paul's epistles. Consider also the "in Christ" language of the apostle Paul, where a two-letter word—the word *in*—incorporates and means so much. It is the recurring line of Ephesians 1, where Paul continually speaks of our identity as "in Christ." In Colossians, he speaks of "Christ in you, the hope of glory" (Col 1:27), and at the conclusion of that section of the letter, where he speaks of his passion for his readers' spiritual maturity, he writes:

> As you therefore have received Christ Jesus as Lord, continue to live your lives in him, rooted and built up I him and established in the faith, just as you were taught, abounding in thanksgiving. (Col 2:6-7)

Then, in the autobiographical reflections of Philippians 3, Paul speaks of his identity in Christ as mediated through the experience of entering into the mystery of the cross.

> More than that, I regard everything as loss because of the surpassing value of knowing Christ Jesus my Lord. For his sake I have suffered the loss of all things, and I regard them as rubbish, in order that I may gain Christ and be found in him, not having a righteousness of my own that comes from the law, but one that comes through faith in Christ, the righteousness from God based on faith. I want to know Christ and the power of his resurrection and the sharing of his sufferings by becoming like him in his death, if somehow I may attain the resurrection from the dead. Not that I have already obtained this or have already reached the goal; but I press on to make it my own, because Christ Jesus has made me his own. (Phil 3:8-12)

Note that the Christian life is defined as knowing or gaining Christ, and this "knowledge" is not a reference to intellectual understanding but to an experiential encounter with Christ. Paul uses the language of *to know* the same way it is used to refer to intimacy in marriage—we know Christ intimately.

Note also that Paul makes a dramatic contrast between all other potential human aspirations and the single most defining aspiration of all: to know Christ. Paul considers all his personal advantages and speaks of them as nothing; indeed, they are rubbish in comparison with knowing Christ. Honor, position, accomplishments, wealth, power and influence are all discarded as so much detritus; they are potential obstacles to the only thing that matters—namely, "knowing Christ Jesus my Lord." All these are set aside that he might "gain Christ."

And then, third, we also recognize that this knowledge finds particular experience in identification with Christ in his death and therefore also in his resurrection. We know Christ only if we know him in the power of his resurrection, and we come to this through our radical identification with him in the cross. Thus when Paul speaks of a sharing, he means participating with Christ in his sufferings. Jesus' life, death and resurrection mark us; they are tattooed on our bodies, etched into our innermost beings. How to describe this? Paul actually creates a new word—the word translated here "becoming like him," meaning to conform oneself or make oneself like him in his death—is used nowhere else in the New Testament.[3] It involves imitation, but it means much more as well: we are drawn into the life of Christ; we are participants in his life; we are in union with him in his life, death and resurrection.

The pivot on which this all turns is the cross. For the apostle, the Christian life is one of active and dynamic participation in the cross of Christ. Baptism is burial with him in his death and new life with him in his resurrection. We cannot speak of union with Christ apart from the cross.

In the book of Hebrews. When we turn to the book of Hebrews, we have different angle on what it means to be "in Christ" and to abide in him as he abides in us. Like both Paul and John, the author of Hebrews is unquestionably trinitarian. But in this book there is also a profound christocentrism. The book of Hebrews is a book about Jesus, who became a high priest and whose work defines everything. Jesus is the central and defining feature of the gospel, of the God-story and thus of

---

[3]Gerald F. Hawthorne, in his commentary on the book of Philippians, notes that Paul creates a word to speak of something that is quite extraordinary: the apostle is "captivated by the staggering idea that he and all believers are caught up into Christ and are indissolubly linked together with him." *Word Biblical Commentary: Philippians* (Grand Rapids, MI: Eerdmans, 1983), p. 145.

the Christian life. Thus in the book of Hebrews, as a summary of what
the author has been stressing throughout, we read that we are to be:

> looking to Jesus the pioneer and perfecter of our faith, who for the sake
> of the joy that was set before him endured the cross, disregarding its
> shame, and has taken his seat at the right hand of the throne of God.
> (Heb 12:2)

Two things here. First, notice that Christian discipleship is marked by a
focus on Christ—Jesus fills our scopes and dominates our consciousness.
We look to Jesus. And, second, this verse is typical of the book of
Hebrews with its particular emphasis on the cross and the ascension.
Both, of course, assume the incarnation and the resurrection. However,
one gets the sense that the incarnation happened so the cross would be
possible and the resurrection is but the first stage of the ascension. The
one who is the focus of our attention is the crucified and ascended Lord.

This Jesus to whom we look is the pioneer and perfecter of faith:
pioneer in that he goes before us leading the way, establishing the path
and providing the example. We follow Jesus. But he is also perfecter in
that through his work he makes possible our following.

In other words, the whole book of Hebrews assumes that we are on a
journey, a pilgrimage; we are striving and indeed running a race. We
persevere (Heb 12:1) in this endeavor to follow Jesus and also—this is
crucial—to participate in the life of Jesus, the pioneer and perfecter. We
are striving and running toward a goal—the *telos* of our Christian
journey toward mature discipleship and transformation into sonship.

This transformation is possible because of what has been accomplished
in Christ Jesus. He is the high priest who goes before us and whose work
on the cross and as the ascended one is now the work of the one who has
been perfected by his suffering and obedience. He is ever before us, dy-
namically present to the world and present in real time to the church and
thus to each follower, each disciple. Jesus is priest and king in the order of
Melchizedek, with a very specific agenda: our transformation.

But what specifically is the content or meaning of this transformation? As Luke Timothy Johnson puts it in his commentary on
Hebrews—and this observation is pivotal; so much rests on this point—

the author of the letter to the Hebrews assumes that through the cross, through the sacrifice of Christ, the people are "perfected," but this perfection, this *teleiosis*, is not so much the fruit of an external transaction as it is an act by which followers of Christ are drawn into the very life of God. Yes, there is a departure from the way of sin and, yes, there is a cleansing of conscience (Heb 9:9), but as Johnson stresses, we need to speak not only negatively but positively about what is accomplished. We are freed from sin, but to what end? Clearly, it is to enter into the power and presence of God.[4]

And how is it that we are drawn into the life of God? Hebrews uses the language of *katanoein*, typically translated "consider," as in "consider that Jesus, the apostle and high priest . . . " (Heb 3:1), but the word *consider* does not quite capture the idea that Jesus is not merely an example to be followed. *Katanoein* speaks of contemplation, of the gaze that participates in, delights in and, yes, dwells in the other. We enter into the life of God as we "consider" Jesus—as we look to him and gaze upon him. Indeed, it is appropriate to use the language of contemplation, as Paul does in 2 Corinthians 3:18 when he writes, "And all of us, with unveiled faces, seeing the glory of the Lord as though reflected in a mirror, are being transformed into the same image from one degree of glory to another."

In other words, our transformation is both an external transaction, by Christ and for us, and also a participation in the life of Christ Jesus through him as pioneer and perfecter of our faith. Through him we are brought into the very holy of holies, into the very presence and life of God. Through the shed blood of Christ we are brought into the "sanctuary" (Heb 10:19).

This is that for which we long; this is our destiny, our vocation, our *telos*. It is that for which we have been created, and, of course, it is that for which we are redeemed. This is baseline stuff; all discussion of the nature and character of the Christian life needs to bring us back to this point of departure. Hebrews conveys little sense of a transaction happening outside of us that then is somehow imputed to us. Rather, char-

---

[4]Luke Timothy Johnson, *Hebrews: A Commentary* (Louisville, KY: Westminster John Knox, 2006), pp. 187-88.

acter formation and thus moral formation are the fruit of active, dynamic, contemplative participation in the life of the crucified and ascended Christ—made possible, of course, by the cross and by the continued reign of Christ, who is both high priest and king.

Christ is our high priest. He sacrifices for us and goes into the holy place, the presence of God, on our behalf. And yet this is not quite an accurate picture. As we read the book of Hebrews we are struck by a deep assumption: that we are drawn into the life of Jesus, who in turn draws us into the life of God. We participate in the cross through our sufferings and thus we participate in his ascended life, in the presence of God, as we are in turn taken up with him into glory—not just in the future, but here and now as well. In this life in real time we are in Christ even as Christ is in the "holy place," the presence and power of God.

Christ takes on our humanity—and our sin, a profound identification and intimacy—that we might in turn take on his life with the same profound identification and intimacy. Note that although spatial language is used, it is metaphorical: the holy place is the power and presence of God. We become, as Hebrews 3:1 puts it, "partners" in the heavenly calling of Christ Jesus.

This is what it means to live in the new covenant that God has established with his people, anticipated, as the book of Hebrews stresses, by Jeremiah's words (Jer 31:31-34), which spoke of a covenant written on the heart. This new covenant is not in discontinuity with the old covenant, but the purpose of the old covenant is now fulfilled in our hearts, in our inner beings, so that in Christ our relationship with God is direct and internal, immediate and intimate (see Heb 8:10-13).

The book of Hebrews uses a fascinating word to describe this participation in the life of God—namely, *sabbath* or *sabbath rest*. Intriguing. God created all things and then entered into his rest—into the sabbath rest—and the promise to his people is that they too will enter into this rest. And we are enjoined in Hebrews 4:11 to hurry, to enter eagerly into this rest. It may seem ironic to speak of "hurrying into rest," but the intent is to capture something significant: this rest comes not by human accomplishment but by active identification. Yes, there is a striving; there is a pursuit. Yes, we run the race that is set before us and we are called to perseverance. And yet what is accomplished in us is not ultimately the fruit of our efforts but rather that which is derived from our radical identification with Christ. And in this we rest. The whole of our life is lived, then, in grateful, restful, abundance—the life derived from union with Christ, from participation in his life and thus participation in the life of God.

So we naturally ask, how do we participate in the life of Christ? When we "consider Christ Jesus" and enter into his life, what is the essential content of this contemplation? The fascinating response of the book of Hebrews is that there is a parallel between what Christ did on our behalf and how we in turn participate in his ascended life—namely, through faithful obedience and, consequently, suffering. Christ learned perfection through faithful obedience, a recurring theme in the book of Hebrews. His obedience was the means by which our salvation was accomplished, and it was specifically an obedience carried out in the body—his body, his mortal flesh, a body in which he suffered. It was through this suffering that he himself was perfected; thus his body (that is, the incarnation) is the means by which we participate in the life of God. In like manner, then, we are called to the very same—a faithful obedience that will be particularly evident in suffering.

Taken together, the language of John in John 15, the apostle Paul's use of the phrase "in Christ" and his reflections in Philippians 3, and the witness of the book of Hebrews all highlight something about the essential character of the Christian life: participation in the life of Christ Jesus. Christ always remains other and distinct; the being of Christ is categorically other; through this participation we do not become "gods." But our union with Christ is so intimate, so organic, that our own lives are infused with and animated by the life of God. We are participants in—partakers of—this divine life.

We are not merely followers; we are not merely coworkers with Christ; we are not merely imitators of Christ. We are one with Christ, members of his body (Eph 5:29-30). We can and will speak of justification and sanctification, and of regeneration. But the baseline that ultimately defines and gives comprehensive meaning to the salvation of God is captured by the phrase "union with Christ."

This is the sum total of what it means to be a Christian and to be a mature Christian. Spiritual formation, then, is the cultivation of this union with Christ. It is not enough to speak of it as fostering "Christlikeness," for Christlikeness is derivative of this union. Without an emphasis on union with Christ, spiritual formation will be a frustrated effort to become like Christ. It will eventually become nothing more than self-development. The grace we seek is not so much to be like Christ as to live in dynamic union *with* Christ, abiding in him as he abides in us (Jn 15:4).

Let me return to what I spoke of above as the baseline for Christian believers. A Christian is one who, in response to Christ's call to "come, follow me," seeks to know, love and serve Christ. For many, to be a convert is to respond to this call and to choose to orient one's life in response to it. And this is good—very good. Yet our only hope for transformation is that we be drawn into the life of Christ such that we live our lives in him, in union with Christ individually and together with others who are growing up into him who is our head. As soon as we use this kind of language we alter the equation. We move, one might say, into a different order of being. And I am suggesting that we accept nothing less than this in our calls for transformation. This is the grace we seek.

While it may well be that a new convert views his or her life as primarily a life that has been reoriented and reconfigured in light of Christ and the Christ event, which is good and indeed very good, surely we should also be fostering within the new believer the capacity to move ever more consciously and intentionally into the life of union with Christ that is captured so cogently by the language of "in Christ" and "abide in me as I abide in you."

This is what our baptism speaks of and points to: a radical identification with the life of Christ. In and through the waters of baptism we are brought into dynamic union with Christ crucified and Christ risen (see specifically how this is described in Romans 6).

JUSTIFICATION, SANCTIFICATION AND FAITH IN CHRIST

The baseline observation, then, is that the heart and soul of what it means to be a Christian is to live in dynamic union with Christ. This is the central vision of the Christian life. From this, then, we can speak of two important theological categories, asking, what does it mean to be justified and, further, what does it mean to be sanctified?

The Protestant evangelical theological heritage has tended to emphasize that justification is the formal and, as some put it, forensic dimension of God's salvation. The counterpart to this is that a Christian is not so much justified in his or her own right but is rather justified "in Christ." In this sense the justified status or right standing is "imputed" to the Christian believer on the basis of Christ's redemptive work. It is often stated that our righteousness is an "alien" righteousness.

But what has happened is that for many the essence of God's salvation has been reduced to justification and, more specifically, to an exclusively forensic understanding of justification. Most evangelical Christians, it would seem, live with the assumption that one's salvation is transacted in and through an external event one believes in and trusts in.

This is problematic if this is equated with the gospel, if this is "it." There is indeed a forensic dimension to our relationship with Christ. In Christ we are vindicated; we are accepted and forgiven. And our right-eousness is derived from this state of being affirmed and accepted as we are incorporated into the benefits of Christ's redemptive work on the cross. This is acceptable, to a point. But it is a problem if our under-standing of salvation is reduced to an overly narrow understanding of justification. Salvation means more than justification, and justification means more than a right standing with God.

The gospel of Christ includes our transformation. Indeed, justifi-cation needs to be understood in light of the central and defining vision of the Christian life that has been articulated above—union with Christ. When salvation in Christ is reduced to justification, or even when there is an overemphasis on justification, it inevitably undercuts the call to transformation—the very purpose, ironically, of justification.

Justification *does* speak of our initial appropriation of the grace of Christ; conversion *is* the act of entering into God's justification of the sinner in Christ. Indeed, we need to sustain a forensic—a right standing—meaning of justification, that through faith in Christ we are positioned, made right, put in communion and relation with Christ and forgiven.

Our only hope for sanctification, for transformation in Christ, is this very justification. And yet to be justified means so much more. Justification is forgiveness, but it is also liberation from the power of sin and acceptance into communion with God—in Christ, of course. Further, justification and sanctification are intimately linked; they are distinct but inseparable. Justification is not merely forensic but effective; what is declared in justification is made experiential in sanctification. Thus they are logically distinct and sequential, perhaps, but not existentially so. They are the single act of God.

Thus conversion, as the appropriation of the justifying grace of God, is the launch of a journey of union with Christ, the incarnate one, in his death and resurrection. Nothing speaks to this more powerfully than baptism. And, further, our justification necessarily includes our appropriation of the gift of the Holy Spirit (see Acts 2:38), for the Spirit is the one through whom we enter into union with Christ.

In other words, we must affirm a strong link between justification and sanctification. If not, it makes God lie. How can he arbitrarily call the sinner a saint? God can declare us saints in Christ if and only if we are truly made into saints by the power of God from our position in Christ sanctified through and through (see 1 Thessalonians 5:23 NIV).

And that is the goal: union with Christ. Our righteousness is not self-produced but arises from our union with Christ, and thus our only hope is to be participants in or partakers of the life of Christ. He is the head of the new humanity, and the only righteousness we know is the righteousness found in and derivative of being "in Christ." So righteousness is not something external to Christ that is somehow "imputed" or sent our way; rather, we are in Christ and thus we know his justifying grace. We are united with Christ through God's justifying grace and we grow into union with Christ through God's sanctifying grace.

INTERLUDE: SPIRITUAL FORMATION AND MORAL FORMATION

What we are after here is a theology of Christian maturity—or, it could be phrased, a theology of Christian character. Often holiness or spiritual maturity is spoken of as character. This is likely the most common language used in evangelical circles. And this is appropriate in itself: people of spiritual maturity and depth are people of character. But the concern we could have is that character is often linked to morality. For example, Arthur F. Holmes wrote an influential book titled *Shaping Character: Moral Education in the Christian College*.[5] A decade later James Davison Hunter wrote about the "death of character" and also linked it directly in his subtitle to "moral education."[6]

Dallas Willard has made a cogent observation about evangelical Christians and churches:

> The current Evangelical understanding of salvation has no essential connection with a life morally transformed beyond the ordinary. Evangelicals are good at what they call "conversion." They're not good at what comes later because *what is preached by them as the gospel has no necessary connection to character transformation*.[7]

Are evangelicals good at conversion? The quotation marks suggest that Willard has some doubt. Of course, if we are not "good at conversion," we cannot expect to be good at what comes later. Conversion is but a good beginning; it is but an initiation into Christian faith. But the main question raised here is the link that all three authors make between what Willard first calls a life "morally transformed" and then speaks of as "character transformation."

The link between character and moral education is appropriate, but as all three of these authors know, we cannot make a one-to-one correlation between them. Both Hunter and Willard recognize the close affinity between character and understanding—character and creeds for Hunter and character and knowledge for Willard. This suggests that if we seek to foster the capacity for character we must begin by speaking more broadly of the nature of the spiritual life and particularly to consider the full scope of the Christian life.

The church has always failed in its articulation of the Christian life

---

[5]Arthur F. Holmes, *Shaping Character: Moral Education in the Christian College* (Grand Rapids, MI: Eerdmans, 1990).

[6]James Davison Hunter, *The Death of Character: Moral Education in an Age Without Good or Evil* (New York: Basic, 2001).

[7]Dallas Willard, "The Failure of Evangelical Political Involvement," in *God and Governing: Reflections on Ethics, Virtue, and Statesmanship*, ed. Roger N. Overton (Eugene, OR: Pickwick, 2009), p. 75.

when spiritual maturity has been equated with morality and when character formation is essentially *moral* education, whether at home, in the church or in the school. To speak of character and character formation, we must first ask, what is the essential meaning of the Christian life? What is it that makes a Christian a Christian? Then we also need to consider the full scope or the complete marks of a Christian—again, not reducing it to morality but rather locating morality within a more comprehensive vision of the Christian life. Thus we need to stress that spiritual maturity is not to be equated with moral maturity, though spiritual maturity most assuredly includes the latter. Rather, spiritual formation is the cultivation of a dynamic faith in Christ, and moral reform and renewal is derivative of this union with Christ.

And so, to summarize: To be a Christian is to be a follower, a disciple; it is to respond to the call of God on our lives, an obedience of faith wherein we are drawn into the life of Jesus and deny (set aside, put to death) the life of autonomy and independence from Christ. This is symbolized, re-presented to us, in our baptism. Baptism speaks of a transfer of allegiance reflected in the obedience of faith (see Rom 6). Now our lives are lived under the reign of Christ.

Further, our destiny is to enter into and share in the life of God. Thus we are invited into a life of radical union and participation in the life of Christ, a union made possible through the ministry of the Spirit. Through the Spirit we are drawn into the life of the triune God, specifically as we are filled and indeed baptized by the Spirit so that through and in the Spirit we might dwell in Christ. Thus I will be stressing below that the mature Christian is one who lives in consciousness and intentional response to the presence of the Spirit in one's life. And the baseline indicator or reference for the work of the Spirit is always this: that by the Spirit Christ is glorified in us and through us; we are drawn into union with the risen and ascended Christ.

This is our destiny, our calling; it is to this end that we are called by the Father Creator. This the dynamic center of our lives—we live in conscious and intentional awareness of Christ ascended. And we live in this reality through the grace and power of the Holy Spirit.

How do we participate in the life of the risen and ascended Christ?

The grand answer of the New Testament, of course, is faith: we are justified by faith; we are sanctified by faith. This is the defining answer for Paul, and it could hardly be more central to the book of Hebrews.

Maturity in the Christian life is maturity in faith. Nothing so marks faith as this: that a person recognizes and lives in the reality that there is another order of life beyond what we can engage with our five senses. To have faith is to live recognizing the reality of this world that cannot be seen and then living in light of its reality. Most central, of course, is the reality of the crucified, risen and ascended Christ. We live in dynamic communion with Christ in radical trust—that is, faith.

This is central to our experience of God's salvation. We are not merely justified by faith; the whole of our lives is one of growing in faith, in deeper dependence on God. Thus spiritual formation is the cultivation of union with Christ. And the leverage point in this formation is faith— faith being radical trust in the person and work of Christ, the faith by which we are drawn into his life.

THE MINISTRY OF THE SPIRIT, HUMILITY AND THE LOVE OF CHRIST

And yet while Christ is the focus and dynamic center of our experience, there is only one Christ, and it is the Christ Jesus who is in fellowship with the Father and the Spirit within the holy Trinity. We can speak of our union with Christ and Christian maturity, then, through this perspective only in light of the triunity of God.

Christ Jesus is the embodiment and quintessential expression of the grace of God. And with this we further affirm that the love of God, the love of the Creator and Father, is the love of one who reaches out for us— calling us, electing us to life in Christ Jesus. And it is by the Spirit that humanity is brought into fellowship with the Spirit and thus with God.

Christian spirituality is a spirituality of response to the electing grace of God in Christ, a grace that is communicated to humanity by the Sprit. The "christological concentration" of the Christian life is, then, is a thoroughly trinitarian vision of what it means to be a Christian.

On the one hand, as noted, it is through Christ that we are drawn into the life of the triune God. But further, we must profile not only that it is the will and call of the Father that we would be in Christ, but it is specifically the mission or ministry of the Spirit. John Calvin, the great Reformer, stresses this in his writings on the Holy Spirit in emphasizing that the Spirit is first and foremost "the bond that unites us with Christ."

Without the gift of the Spirit, the call to union with Christ would strike us as simply absurd. How can we be united with Christ Jesus, the second person of the Trinity? It is possible only through the gracious ministry of the Spirit. It is by the Spirit that we are participants in the life of Christ.

I need to express the following with great care and precision; few things have been so divisive to the church as how we understand and respond to the ministry of the Spirit. And for evangelical Christians in particular, where there are many points of division and potential division, nothing quite raises the fences as much as how we speak about the Spirit.

There is only one Christ Jesus: the Christ who is present to the world, to the church and to the individual Christian through the grace of the Spirit. And indeed there is only one Spirit: the Spirit of Christ. Thus a theology of the Christian life and of Christian holiness is in many respects a theology of the Holy Spirit.

This leads to two fundamental and defining questions: first, how do we appropriate or receive the gift of the Spirit? Or, to use different language, what does it mean to be filled with the Spirit? And then the second question: how do we appropriate the grace of the Spirit? The grace of the Spirit is known through what has aptly been called the "means of grace."

These two questions are closely interconnected. And yet they are distinct. The Spirit and the means by which the Spirit is known are not one and the same. We cannot reduce the Spirit's ministry in our lives to this "means," which is, as we shall see, largely the work of the church. And the church, through the means of grace, does not have final control over the work of the Spirit.

Mature and maturing Christians have learned to walk in the Spirit and to live in deep and intentional dependence on the Spirit. I stressed this already when I spoke about the interplay of sin and faith in chapter one. But we also need to ask, what does it mean to lean into the Spirit? It means very simply that we learn to receive the grace of God through the Spirit by consciously drawing on this grace as it is granted to us through the means of grace.

To profile this matter of the "means," I will speak of two great acts of the church. On the one hand I will speak of the Word—the Scriptures preached and taught. And, second, I will speak of the sacraments of baptism and the Lord's Supper. Both, as must be stressed, are located in the church. And so we must speak of the life and witness of a congregation, a faith community. We live in union with Christ through the grace of the Spirit as we live in dynamic communion with the church. Union with Christ must mean organic union with the church; the two are inseparable. Our faith in Christ is shared; thus we enter into the life of a faith community and participate in the faith of the church, the faith the church has in her living lord, and we draw our life (as a community) from the life of the head.

The church is the fellowship of the Spirit, and the central and defining means by which the Spirit draws us into union with Christ and sustains our union with Christ is through the Word preached and the sacrament celebrated. I will consider this more fully in appendix A, on the nature and ministry of the church.

Therefore, it should always be made clear that God is the beginning, the middle and the end of the Christian life. The Christian life is not something that is accomplished with a self-help guide or a path of personal self-fulfillment.

To profile this radical dependence on God, the New Testament speaks of the way of faith and the way of humility. Both speak of radical dependence on God and specifically on the Spirit to foster within us a radical, deeply rooted dependence on Christ. By faith one is united with Christ and thus spiritual maturity is in many respects the completion or maturity of our faith; maturity comes not as a self-construction project but rather through a life of complete dependency on Christ and on the Spirit of Christ in whom we live.

Human life is dependent life; thus the only way to live is in radical dependence on the other, on the Creator, on the author and being of life.

There is no self-dependence. And thus we never get beyond humility; it is the deep river that undergirds authentic Christian piety. There is no holiness without humility, and, indeed, some spiritual masters are convinced that in the end there is only one threat to holiness: pride—specifically the pride of self-autonomy and self-dependence. Thus we turn from independence to faith, from pride to meekness.

Humility, then, is basic to our human identity and thus a theme that runs through each thread of a theology of the spiritual life. Every dimension of our identity "in Christ" will be a means by which we live in humility. This humility is not an achievement so much as an aspect of what it means to live in Christ. To seek humility, then, does not perhaps make a lot of sense. What we seek is union with Christ, and humility is a derivative of this union with Christ.

This faith, this humility, has a particular orientation: the love of Christ. Faith and humility are critical marks of a life "in Christ." The whole of the Christian life is essentially a response to the love of God in Christ. And this is the intent of the Spirit in our lives. The interplay between the work and grace of the Spirit and the call to be rooted and established in the love of God is evident from the interplay of Ephesians 3:16 and the two verses that follow. We know the fullness of God and live in the power of the Spirit as we are rooted and established in the love of Christ Jesus.

Thus it could easily be said that nothing is so crucial in the Christian life as this: to know, to the depth and core of our beings, that we are loved—to know, as the benediction of Ephesians puts it, "the breadth and length and height and depth" that is the love of Christ, that is the fullness of God dwelling within us.

Radical dependence on the Spirit is evident in our appropriation of the love of God; we see this in this Ephesians text. The close interplay between the Spirit and the love of God is also evident in Romans 5:5, which speaks of the love of God poured into our hearts by the Spirit.

The fruit of this is precisely that we live not self-centered lives but lives that are, in the words of Rowan Williams, "de-centered."[8] We live not as though the universe revolves around us or depends on us, but we

---

[8]Rowan Williams, *Dostoevsky: Language, Faith, and Fiction* (Waco, TX: Baylor University Press, 2008), p. 183.

live with a dynamic freedom of knowing and dwelling in the reality that God is love, a love for us and for the world that is demonstrated in Christ and communicated to us through the Spirit, and this love in turn frees us to live in humble dependence on God. Each dimension of Christian holiness, then, will be animated by this dynamic awareness of the love of God in Christ.

EVANGELISM, SPIRITUAL PRACTICE AND SPIRITUAL FORMATION

What has been outlined so far has major implications for our approach to congregational life and witness. If Christian identity is first and foremost the experience of being "in Christ," then this is what we preach, it is to this end that we evangelize, and congregational life is oriented toward responding to this call.

Speaking of evangelism. This vision of the Christian life has significant implications for our understanding of conversion. While the process of coming to faith in Christ will surely include catechetical instruction—teaching and learning about the person of Christ—the experience of conversion is not ultimately a matter of knowing or even affirming certain truths about Christ; it is rather the fruit of an immediate encounter with the one who invites us to be disciples.

And so evangelism is about fostering and cultivating the opportunities for a person to meet Jesus: to meet Christ Jesus in real time. In the end it is all about Jesus. It is not about persuading them of certain truths or laws, or even about believing that Jesus has done something—that if they "believe" it will lead to their "salvation." It is rather about meeting Christ Jesus in person and in real time. Thus the church is nothing other than the place where there is a "Christological concentration": people who in worship and mission are about Jesus. That is their passion and focus and commitment. And as you join them in worship and in mission, in time you too will come to know this living Christ.

Yes, of course, we talk about Jesus; yes, there is of course teaching and instruction on the character of the Christian life and the meaning of God's salvation. We tell the story of Israel and the fulfillment of this story in Christ Jesus. But in the end, we are not merely talking about Jesus—as though conversion is in the end believing certain things about

Jesus to be true. It is rather about meeting Jesus and being welcomed into a real-time communion, a fellowship, with him.

Furthermore, it means that evangelism is not ultimately focused on or about the potential convert. Indeed the irony is that much seeker-sensitive evangelism and worship is about making the seeker the focus of attention: everything is designed or adjusted or aligned to make it so palatable for the seeker that he or she would come back next week. Is it any wonder that the fruit of this kind of evangelism frequently is church members who assume they are and should be the focus of attention? Should we not from the very beginning indicate that it is not about them? It is not about any of us. When we gather for worship, Christ Jesus is the passion and focus of our commitment and adoration. In mission, our commitment is to witness in word and deed to the reign of Christ. And evangelism is about learning that it is all about Christ. You are welcome to join us in worship and in mission, but only if you can appreciate that it is not about you. You are not the focus or the prime concern of this exercise. You are welcome to join us, but without any illusions or missing the point that this is all about Jesus.

The approach to spiritual formation. The essence of spiritual formation is precisely this: fostering the capacity, the orientation, the discipline of living in union with Christ. It is centrally and pivotally about cultivating an awareness of Christ Jesus, an appreciation for his love and a capacity to lean into the grace we know through his Spirit.

Spiritual formation is not ultimately about the pursuit of morality. Moral purity and orientation are important, but they are not what makes the Christian a Christian. As the rich young ruler of Luke 18 came to appreciate, the keeping of the law is not what counts in the end but rather responding fully to the call of "Come, follow me."

Spiritual formation is also about fostering the capacity to live in the dynamic captured by the great Celtic line "Christ before me, Christ behind me, Christ on my right hand, Christ on my left hand . . . Christ first in my heart." This is the passion and focus of spiritual formation. The heart of the matter is not character development or Christlikeness. Yes, Christ is formed in us, but not as the result of our personal resolve—"I *will* be like Jesus"—which is only an exercise in futility and frustration. Spiritual formation is all about learning to dwell in Christ. As we dwell in in union with him, he is formed—ever so incrementally, but surely—in us.

The heart of Christian formation is not ultimately intellectual belief in Christ resulting from doctrinal instruction. Nor is it teaching folks how to follow Christ's example—that is, teaching them to ask, "What would Jesus do?" It is rather fostering a dynamic communion with Christ as those who have been adopted by the Father and brought into union with Christ by the Spirit.

We cannot reduce holiness to morality, character or virtue; neither are these counterparts to sin. The essence of sin is not immorality; the essence of holiness is not morality. Thus the heart of spiritual formation is not moral formation. Rather, the essence of the Christian life is union with Christ fostered through a real-time encounter with him risen and ascended. Spiritual formation and all practices of the Christian life are necessarily structured around prayer and worship, the central practices by which our awareness of Christ and response to him is fostered.

When it comes to the development of character—when we ask the question so much on our minds and lips, "How is character formed?"— the answer is found precisely in the cultivation of faith in Christ Jesus. Spiritual formation is the fostering of faith, a deeper trust and more radical dependence on Christ.

Much teaching and instruction in the church aims to make us moral people. We confuse character with morality and then deliver sermons on being a good father, a faithful spouse, a generous giver, a just person and, of course, a kind and loving individual. The huge danger is that we foster the idea that the Christian life is self-constructed as we do our very best to live by the golden rule.

This kind of preaching is useless—perhaps worse than useless. Our root problem is not our morals or lack of character; the root problem is lack of faith. In good preaching, the Word proclaimed enables us to look to Jesus, the pioneer and perfecter of our faith, and as a result our faith in Christ Jesus grows, matures and deepens. All preaching, regardless of the text, is about fostering our capacity to see Jesus and trust him more deeply.

In speaking of faith, we must link it to obedience; it is by faithful obedience that we participate in the life of Jesus. Faith obeys or it is no faith at all. We are not called so much to be like Jesus, imitating him, as we are to obey him. This is what it means to be a Christian disciple. We walk in obedience, the liberating and empowering way of submission to the authority of the ascended Christ. Christ is Savior and Lord; these are one and the same and we know Christ's salvation as we come under the freedom of obedience to his benevolent authority. As the author of the letter to the Hebrews puts it—and it could no be plainer—Christ "became the source of eternal salvation for all who obey him" (Heb 5:9).

Now, the real test of faithful obedience is, of course, the way of suffering. And this is another recurring theme in the book of Hebrews: suffering is not only the way Jesus fulfills his mission, it is also the way a Christian disciple participates in Jesus' life and mission. Jesus suffered and died not so that we would no longer suffer but so that our suffering would have meaning—redemptive purpose. In the language of the apostle Paul, we are joint heirs with Christ in his sufferings (Rom 8:17). Suffering is integral to Christian discipleship, to character formation and thus to spiritual formation. Just as Jesus learned perfection through his sufferings, in like manner our "perfection" arises in part from our suffering. Hebrews 2:10 says that Christ brings many to glory, perfecting salvation through suffering. Christ himself learned obedience through suffering (Heb 5:8). And likewise we learn obedience through suffering. We do not have a theology of the Christian life, and we cannot speak of either character or spiritual formation, if we do not have a theology of suffering that informs our understanding of the Christian journey.

Now as I press on to the specifics of character and the nature of spiritual maturity, I perhaps need to highlight what I have done so far. I have sought to provide a christological foundation for our vision of spiritual and character formation. This is needed, I contend, because if evangelical Christians have failed to foster character development and true discipleship, it is largely because we did not view it as integral to the salvation of God. And for those committed to spiritual formation and spiritual maturity in the church, we must stress the following: we cannot build this house on a faulty foundation. We need to start from the ground up and begin by asking, what has Christ done? What is Christ doing? And how do we participate in the work of Christ?

Fundamentally, our baseline is that spiritual formation is the fostering of our identity "in Christ"; we live and work to this end, that we might abide in Christ as Christ abides in us (Jn 15:4). The work of Christ at the cross, into which we lean, translates into an active and intentional participation in the life of the risen and ascended Christ. And every dimension of the Christian life flows from or is the fruit of this life in Christ. Nothing so defines what it means to be a Christian as our relationship with a person—the person of Christ.

In all of this, we are of course affirming a fundamental principle of the Christian faith: that Christianity is not a religion of the book, as one might perhaps speak of Islam; rather, the Christian faith is ultimately about a person. It is about a real-time encounter with the risen and ascended Christ and a dynamic participation in the life of Christ.

Now, with this fundamental reference point, we can develop a complete theology of spiritual maturity. We begin with a call to wisdom.

3

HOLY PEOPLE ARE WISE PEOPLE

An Invitation to Sapiential Holiness

The law of the LORD is perfect,
reviving the soul;
the decrees of the LORD are sure,
making wise the simple;
the precepts of the LORD are right,
rejoicing the heart;
the commandment of the LORD is clear,
enlightening the eyes;
the fear of the LORD is pure,
enduring forever;
the ordinances of the LORD are true
and righteous altogether.

PSALM 19:7-9

THE WAY OF WISDOM IS ONE OF THE MOST compelling and
helpful ways to speak of the holiness of God, and the call to human

transformation in Christ is to speak of wisdom. A holy person is a wise person.[1]

This is not the only way to speak of holiness. What I am going to say here assumes that first and foremost, the spiritual identity of the Christian is one of union with Christ and that a full doctrine of sanctification would also speak of vocational holiness, the call to love others as we have been loved, and the ordering of the affections. And yet the witness of the Scriptures and the church's spiritual heritage make such a clear and profound link between the righteousness of God and wisdom that we can truly and simply say, a person who is mature in Christ is a wise person. This has significant implications for our approach to spiritual formation and to rites of initiation for new followers of Christ.

Wisdom and the Biblical Vision of Holiness

To speak of wisdom is to speak of life. Those who long for and seek wisdom are seekers after God and the ways of God. Wisdom is a powerful and tangible gift from God, and our pursuit of it is not incidental to our human identity; it is rather another dimension of our desire to fulfill our identities as those created in God's image. We have a palpable longing to discover and live in the truth, to know and walk in the light. This is wisdom. Each person longs to be wise, and all people long to see wisdom lived out in government, business and church leadership. Furthermore, the purpose of all formal education, from primary school through postsecondary studies, is that we would grow in wisdom and in our capacity for wisdom.

As a person grows older, he or she should by design and intent grow

---

[1]My primary conversation partners in the development of this chapter and the upcoming section on wisdom and higher education (appendix B) are Harry Blamires, *The Christian Mind: How Should a Christian Think?* (New York: Seabury, 1963); William P. Brown, *Character in Crisis: A Fresh Approach to the Wisdom Literature of the Old Testament* (Grand Rapids, MI: Eerdmans, 1996); David F. Ford, *Christian Wisdom: Desiring God and Learning in Love* (Cambridge, UK: Cambridge University Press, 2007), and his *A Long Rumour of Wisdom: Redescribing Theology* (Cambridge, UK: Cambridge University Press, 1992); David H. Kelsey, *To Understand God Truly: What's Theological About a Theological School* (Louisville, KY: Westminster John Knox, 1992); Jean Leclercq, *The Love of Learning and the Desire for God: A Study of Monastic Culture*, trans. Catharine Misrahi (New York: Fordham, 1961); and Daniel Treier, *Virtue and the Voice of God: Toward Theology as Wisdom* (Grand Rapids, MI: Eerdmans, 2006).

wiser. This is basic to what it means to be human. There are few things so tragic as an older person who is not wise; to grow older and not wiser is to live poorly, to fail to achieve the purpose for which one lives. It rightly breaks our hearts when we meet an older person who is foolish in understanding and ways of being. We wonder what happened that he or she did not grow older and wiser, just older. Something has been lost; a life has been, one might almost say, wasted. The implication of this is not that a young person cannot be wise but rather that wisdom is the particular mark of those who are older and that in the challenges of life, work and relationship, through both times of blessing and difficulty, part of the unique dynamic of life and one of the blessings of life is that one grows in the capacity for wisdom.

In consideration of a biblical vision for wisdom and the Christian life, it is helpful to consider two particular references in Scripture. First, the prologue or opening verses of the book of Proverbs, and second, the perspective on wisdom and sanctification in the first chapter of Paul's letter to the Colossians.

Bruce K. Waltke makes a compelling case in his exposition of Proverbs 1 for the profound link between righteousness and wisdom.[2] To be righteous is to be wise. While we cannot perhaps say that the essence of holiness in the Old Testament is wisdom or that there is a one-to-one correlation between righteousness and wisdom—though one could make that case—at the very least we can affirm this: a holy person is a wise person. God is wise, and to be like him is to therefore be wise. It is wisdom that arises as one lives in the fear of God.

Waltke observes that the book of Proverbs is really a full exposition of the Ten Commandments, so while wisdom and righteousness are not identical, you cannot have the one without the other. He writes, "Wisdom and righteousness denote different notions, but they are inseparable. If a person is wise, he or she is righteous; if righteous, they are wise." Later on in his essay, he turns it around and affirms that "in sum, if a person is wise, he or she is righteous."[3]

The opening verses of the book of Proverbs are among the most fre-

---

[2]Bruce K. Waltke, "Righteousness in Proverbs," CRUX 44, no. 4 (2008): 12-21.
[3]Ibid., 19-20.

quently read texts in holy Scripture, and rightly so: here we find a cogent, concise and compelling description of the way of wisdom.

The proverbs of Solomon son of David, king of Israel:

> For learning about wisdom and instruction,
> for understanding words of insight,
> for gaining instruction in wise dealing,
> righteousness, justice, and equity;
> to teach shrewdness to the simple,
> knowledge and prudence to the young—
> let the wise also hear and gain in learning,
> and the discerning acquire skill,
> to understand a proverb and a figure,
> the words of the wise and their riddles.

> The fear of the LORD is the beginning of knowledge;
> fools despise wisdom and instruction. (Prov 1:1-7)

While there is much in this text that merits attention, for our purposes here, three observations:[4] First, we note the close link between wisdom and teaching (or instruction). The focus of this instruction—and something integral to wisdom—is the capacity for understanding and insight. The impression is that a wise person is a learned person ("the wise . . . hear and gain in learning"); knowledge and prudence are intimately linked. Indeed, the whole book of Proverbs is essentially a teaching document, the words of a wise sage instructing a younger person. Wisdom is something that is passed on from one generation to another, and it is passed on through teaching or instruction.

Second, we also see that prudence is linked to knowledge; knowledge without prudence is no knowledge at all. Specifically, when speaking of character, we see that the triptych of "righteousness, justice and equity" are highlighted. I will be describing this below as "moral intelligence"; what strikes us here is that while the book of Proverbs and the wisdom literature of the Scriptures highlight many dimensions of character and morality, what is highlighted here, from the very beginning, is the link between justice and righteousness. There is no righteousness without

---

[4]Largely here following Brown, *Character in Crisis*.

justice. And, as is evident throughout the book of Proverbs and the words of the Old Testament prophets, there is no justice without economic justice.

Noteworthy also is that the demarcation of character—righteousness, justice and equity—is found not at the end of this description of wisdom but, one might say, at the heart of the text, in its center. We begin and end with instruction in knowledge (Prov 1:2, 7) for understanding, but at the literary heart of the text we have character. One could easily get the impression that the house of wisdom is maintained by teaching and learning but without character such learning caves in on itself. Without character development the center core, the very purpose for learning and instruction, is lost.

Third, what must not be missed—mentioned briefly here (Prov 1:7) but an abiding theme in the wisdom literature of the Old Testament and a recurring emphasis of the book of Ecclesiastes—is the close link between wisdom and the fear of the Lord. This is the defining intellectual capacity and commitment, the beginning and the conclusion of the way of wisdom. The language of fear suggests not anxiety or terror but rather humility, the realization that God is God and that human life and thus wisdom must be understood in light of the one who is the creator and source of all wisdom.

As a side note, we see also a reference to skill (Prov 1:5), which elsewhere in the Proverbs refers to the capacity for effective governance and wise leadership. Would it be pressing the point too far to conclude that all who are wise are "skilled" in the conduct of their work or vocations— in other words, a plumber is wise (that is, skilled) in the ways of how water moves through a home or office, a financial manager is wise (skilled) in the ways of the economic markets, the business person is wise in the ways of commerce, and the soccer coach is wise in finding effective ways to manage a team? I would maintain that this too is wisdom. Wise people are good at what they do, particularly at the tasks linked to their sphere of vocation and responsibilities in the world.

In turning to Colossians 1, we see the same themes emerging. This text speaks of wisdom in a way that seems to incorporate many—not all, but many—key perspectives that need to be considered when we speak of the relationship between wisdom and holiness. The apostle first celebrates the new faith of the Colossian believers (Col 1:1-8). It would appear that they have come to faith through the ministry and witness of Paul's colleague Epaphras, and it is through Epaphras that Paul learns of this new faith. In response, he writes:

> For this reason, since the day we heard it, we have not ceased praying for you and asking that you may be filled with the knowledge of God's will in all spiritual wisdom and understanding, so that you may lead lives worthy of the Lord, fully pleasing to him, as you bear fruit in every good work and as you grow in the knowledge of God. (Col 1:9-10)

Paul goes on in Colossians 1 to speak of his suffering and his preaching, stressing that he suffers, preaches and longs for them so they would know the goal, the *telos*, of their salvation, the end for which they have come to faith. This end is clearly and obviously "union with Christ" (see Col 2:6-7). He speaks of wisdom, but he clearly locates it within this call to know Christ and be mature in him. Wisdom and knowledge are found "in Christ" (in whom "are hidden all the treasures of wisdom and knowledge," Col 2:3). And he insists that he and his colleagues are "teaching everyone in all wisdom" specifically that they would be "mature in Christ" (Col 1:28).

And yet while the primary and foundational vision for holiness is "union with Christ," Colossians 1 demonstrates that we cannot speak of this participation in Christ's life without reference to wisdom and to the teaching ministry through which we are formed in wisdom. Colossians 1:9-10 delineates the character of Christian wisdom in a manner that is particularly helpful and accessible. As the end for which we are created and called in Christ, wisdom is a twofold experience of God's grace: it includes both understanding (Col 1:9) and practical goodness (Col 1:10). I will therefore speak to both understanding and practical goodness and consider the interplay between them.

Knowledge and understanding. Colossians 1:9 speaks of Paul's continual prayer that the Colossians would be filled with a knowledge of God and with all wisdom and understanding. This is picked up again in verse 10 when he speaks of growing in the knowledge of God. And this, of course, is the twin to what is mentioned earlier in the chapter, that the Colossians' knowledge of God is reflected by their faith in God (Col 1:4-5). Paul naturally insists on faith; it is a central characteristic and virtue of the Christian life. But what catches our attention is that faith is informed by understanding, by a knowledge of God and the will of God.

The classic Christian word for this is "theology": theology not as academic discipline but as a discipline of the church, which longs to know God and to know his will. Theology speaks of the pursuit of God and his will. And this all, of course, leads to an affirmation of the key place of teaching and learning within the Christian community.

Practical goodness. When we speak of understanding, we are referring specifically to the wisdom of knowledge that leads to action—the lived truth of a person who not only understands but then lives in light of that understanding. Wisdom is both understanding *and* practice. The common expression "practical wisdom" is often used to capture this particular vision of human life: a wise person is one who understands the truth and lives the truth, not as two distinct acts per se but as two parts of a whole, for we do not truly understand until and unless we live this understanding.

In Colossians 1, Paul prays specifically that his readers' knowledge of God and faith in God would be evident in love, a love expressed in bearing fruit (Col 1:6), which is further defined in verse 10 as fruit is born in every good work. The New English Bible translates this in an interesting way, speaking of this life in the world as an "active goodness of every kind." We see this also in Philippians 1:9-11: we cannot speak of wisdom without speaking of love and the close interplay between the two.

Behavior flows from understanding when we seek informed actions, a way of being in the world that is informed by the truth. The knowledge of God and of God's will is the necessary foundation for our lives in the world. To live in wisdom is to live theologically—in work, in relationships, in Christian community and in the world.

And yet the witness of the Scriptures and human experience suggests that not only is behavior informed and formed by understanding, but also behavior informs understanding. We cannot in the end speak of the priority of one over the other. Together knowledge of God and a life lived worthy of the Lord make for a life of wisdom. And this is life. What's more, it is life abundant. Indeed, the language of the book of Proverbs and also of the book of Ecclesiastes suggests a direct link between wisdom and joy. Wise people are women and men of joy; wisdom calls out, "Happy are those who keep my ways" (Prov 8:32). All of this speaks of the salvation of God, and thus it is no surprise that the psalmist prays, "Lead me in your truth, and teach me, for you are the God of my salvation" (Ps 25:5).

With this as our elementary framework, then—wisdom as understanding and practical goodness—let's stand back and consider the broader vision of wisdom that is spoken of in the Christian Scriptures.

THE WISDOM OF GOD: FATHER, SON AND SPIRIT

First, for this broader vision we must speak of the triune God. The Christian affirms that all wisdom comes from God who is the source of light, of life and salvation and as such is the source of all wisdom. God is wise, and God is the source of wisdom for all who would be wise. Thus the Proverbs speak of the fear of God as the beginning of wisdom, suggesting that to be wise is to let God be God, but more, it is to love God as God and to delight in God, who is the fountain of all life and thus of all wisdom.

Furthermore, Christ Jesus is the wisdom of God, the very embodiment of the Word, of God's wisdom; in Jesus we see the living, breathing vitality that is the wisdom of God lived out in the flesh. Surely part of what draws us to Jesus and leads us to doxological delight and trust in him is that Jesus is wise. He is a teacher whose teaching was one of leading his disciples, his learners, into this very wisdom that he embodied. Thus we seek a christological wisdom wherein Christ is the beginning and the end, the alpha and omega. Thus we can speak of the longing to know the mind of Christ (Phil 2:5-11) and the desire that every thought be captive to him (2 Cor 10:4-5).

And further, in speaking of Christ as the wisdom of God we are reminded that we must speak of personal knowledge—not ultimately information but the knowledge that comes from a personal engagement with Christ Jesus himself. Nowhere is this stressed more clearly than in the Gospel of John where Jesus is the "teacher" (Jn 1:38), but more, where Jesus as teacher is also the very one who is the giver of wisdom and life. Thus for the monastic tradition, which in many respects has sustained this vision more powerfully than any other (thinking particularly of the writings of Bernard of Clairvaux), liturgy and worship are vital to our teaching and learning process. We learn as worshipers; our study is informed by our prayers; a congregation is first a worshiping community and then a teaching-learning community.

But we also need to speak of the relationship between the Spirit and wisdom. In anticipation of his ascension, Jesus indicates to his disciples in John 16 that he has many more things to teach them but that they "cannot bear them now" (Jn 16:12). And so he is sending the Spirit who will lead them into all understanding (Jn 16:13). In other words, the ministry of the Spirit reflects a deepening outworking of the teaching ministry of Jesus. In Ephesians, this ministry is linked directly to wisdom, where foolishness is contrasted with wisdom and being filled with the Spirit (Eph 5:15-18).[5]

If the Spirit is so essential to true wisdom, what then of Christ? The wisdom of God, through the Spirit, remains radically Christ-centered. Our wisdom is Christ-centered rather than Spirit-centered. In 1 Corinthians 1:18-31 Paul challenges the Corinthians on this point: their wisdom is Spirit-centered rather than Christ-centered. In the grace of the Spirit, Christ must be the means by which we enter into the wisdom and salvation of God.

What then of teaching? Do we need teaching if we have the Spirit? There is no tension between the teaching ministry of the church and the

---

[5]There is some debate of whether the teaching ministry of the Spirit is "new revelation." Some see this text as affirming precisely that: Jesus has more to say (more than they can bear) and this will come through the witness of the Spirit and that revelation is not then limited to the teachings of Jesus. Others, in contrast, argue that the work of the Spirit is merely to help the original disciples "recollect" the fullness of Jesus' teaching because they did not get it all when he taught them (it was more than they could bear). We need a third way to speak of this: to affirm that Jesus and his teaching are axiomatic and foundational and that indeed in large measure the Spirit's ministry is one of continuing illumination of Jesus' teaching. But this is acceptable as a resolution of this tension only if we are able to affirm that the Spirit's ministry in the church will not contradict the original teaching of Jesus and the apostolic witness in Scripture. Still, it is new, and many teachings in the spiritual heritage of the church are essential to the life and witness of the faith community today.

work of the Spirit. In Colossians 1:9 the apostle prays that God would fill his readers with a knowledge of his will through all the wisdom and understanding. He speaks of this as either "spiritual wisdom," as some translations have it, or as "the wisdom that the Spirit gives," as it is expressed in other translations. Either is fine, though it is hard not to miss, given the earlier references in this chapter, that this is likely another intentional reference to the third person of the Trinity.

In Colossians 1:28 Paul speaks of teaching in all wisdom. This suggests that there is no inherent tension between receiving wisdom as a gift from God by the Spirit and teaching as a vital spiritual practice of the church. The two are mutually interdependent. It is surely in Christ and through the ministry of the Spirit that we are formed in wisdom, but this comes specifically as we participate in the teaching ministry of the church.

We will come back to the question of teaching; here I merely want to stress that in speaking of the Spirit I am not discounting teaching but rather insisting that the teaching and learning of the church must be located within the broader vision of the purposes of the triune God in the world. And yet what this does do is open the possibility of speaking of spiritual discernment and the witness of the Spirit as vital to our formation in wisdom—not at the expense of the teaching ministry of the church and not for a moment in contradiction of the Scriptures, but as an essential means by which the Spirit illumines our minds and equips us to respond to our immediate circumstances in light of the biblical witness. Thus below I will speak of wisdom and discernment and the witness of the Spirit.

The main point here is that we affirm that God is the source of all truth and wisdom and understanding and that "the fear of the Lord" is therefore the beginning of wisdom, understanding "fear" to be deference, submission and humility before God, the fundamental disposition for growth in wisdom. Christ is the embodiment of wisdom and we are ultimately wise only when we are wise in Christ. And growth in wisdom is given to us as a gift of the Spirit, who teaches, equips and empowers us to know the truth and live in wisdom. Thus nothing is so fundamental to our growth in wisdom as the cultivation of our relationship with God. And thus worship—specifically contemplative prayer and the liturgy—are the vital practices that ground and animate our growth in wisdom.

Just as worship and prayer are the means by which we sustain union with Christ, even so the call to wisdom finds expression in the central place of teaching and learning in congregational life, teaching and learning that is oriented toward obedience and wisdom and thus transformation.

THE CHRISTIAN MIND

We cannot speak of wisdom and of teaching unless we have a clear sense of the place of the Christian mind in faith formation. This is a particular challenge for those within the evangelical Christian tradition; I think particularly of Mark Noll's indictment in *The Scandal of the Evangelical Mind*.[6] For many of us, our revivalistic heritage was marked by a deep skepticism about all things associating with the intellectual life and the work of study and scholarship. These were viewed as a threat to true spirituality and devotion.

This perspective, though, is not unique to the West nor to the heirs of revivalism. The Chinese church has been deeply influenced by the writings of Watchman Nee, who was very suspicious of human intellect, suggesting that revelation is known through "intuition" and that reasoning, the use of the mind, might actually be an obstacle to our knowledge of God. Thus we must be deeply grateful to those voices that while in the minority have sustained a vision for thinking Christianly. One such voice has been that of Harry Blamires, with his classic mid-sixties study *The Christian Mind*. His perspective will serve as an inspiration for much I wish to offer here.

Working with the sequence we find in Colossians 1—and the assumption that a wise person is marked by the interplay of understanding and right practice—consider first that a wise person is a woman or man of understanding, a particular way of thinking, with a specific vision of God and of the world. In other words, our understanding is one that informs all of life from a Christian and, more specifically, a theological perspective.

---

[6]Mark A. Noll, *The Scandal of the Evangelical Mind* (Grand Rapids, MI: Eerdmans, 1994).

Everything—yes, literally everything—is viewed through the lens of the Christian or biblical vision of life, work and relationships. This perspective comes naturally to no one. It is learned. And this learning requires us to attend to God's self-revelation, notably in the Scriptures. This is not to suggest or imply that wisdom is Bible knowledge or that mature Christians are those who are biblically literate. It is rather that what emerges from our study and learning in the Scriptures is a theological vision of God and the world. Or, as Harry Blamires would put it, our way of thinking is Christian rather than secular. A secular vision is confined to the limits of the material, of life on earth; a theological and thus Christian perspective is informed by and one with Christ's vision of the world.

As Blamires insists, one can think secularly about sacred things and Christianly about mundane, earthly things.[7] We can have a secular perspective on the Lord's Supper and a Christian perspective on banking. In other words, we are not speaking here of religious versus nonreligious activities, but rather of cultivating a Christian perspective on, quite literally, everything. A wise person, a person who is mature in Christ, is one who through particular practices associated with the Scriptures has come to a theological vision of life, work and relationships. He or she has a Christian mind.

Blamires observes, "There is nothing in our experience, however trivial, worldly, or even evil, which cannot be thought about Christianly."[8] Indeed, part of having a Christian mind is insisting that all religious activities be judged from a theological perspective and not being content to consider any activity as good or worthwhile just because it is a religious activity. And further, having a Christian mind means that there is no aspect of life—absolutely none—that cannot be viewed through a theological lens, a way of seeing demarcated by the wisdom of sacred Scripture. Actually, *demarcated* is not the best word; it is not merely the contours, structure or outlines of our thinking that are transformed by the Scriptures. Rather, through immersion, through an engagement of mind and heart and will with the Christian canon, we are drawn into a way of thinking, into a vision that encounters the whole of reality

---

[7]Blamires, *Christian Mind,* p. 42.
[8]Ibid., p. 43.

through a Christian imagination. We could argue that this engagement of heart and will with the mind leads to clarity of thinking; precise and accurate thinking must be considered a feature of Christian spirituality.

What does it mean to have a theological vision or perspective on life? First, a Christian mind is a way of seeing and thinking that is demarcated by the grand narrative of God in the world, and nothing so captures this as the mantra most commonly heard in Reformed circles: creation, fall, redemption.

Creation. A Christian mind is one that sees the created order as brought into being by the power and goodness of God. The appreciation of the deep goodness, worth and significance of the natural order is matched in kind by a recognition of the worth, indeed the inestimable value, of the human person created in the image of God. A secular mind dismisses the created order or idolizes it; a secular mind dehumanizes the person, treating people as mere functionaries.

When it comes to the stuff of creation, a biblical wisdom or a Christian mind includes an appreciation of the sacramental character of the natural world, an appreciation that all of life is capable of being a means by which the glory and goodness of God are revealed.

Fall. A Christian mind is also marked by a profound recognition of the presence and power of evil. Though evil is foreign to God's world and will eventually be vanquished, it is real and it is powerful. Wise women and men are not naive to its power—in social structures and agencies, in the church and in the world, and in their own hearts.

Redemption. But then—and this is crucial—a Christian mind is marked not by despair or cynicism but by a deep and pervasive hope. It is to see and feel that sin has marred this good order of God but that in the mercy and goodness of God evil will be vanquished and justice will triumph. It is to refuse to despair in the face of evil and to view all things in light of the purposes of God in the world. To have a Christian mind is to speak of the life, death and resurrection of Christ Jesus and to see all things through the church's confidence in the future consummation of his reign. We can certainly see that evil is strong. A wise person is not naive to its power, and yet a wise person does not in the end give evil more than it is due.

To have this vantage point, to see this world through this lens, requires that we affirm the central place of the Scriptures in our formation in wisdom, for the Christian mind is essentially a mind formed, informed and reformed by the sacred text. Thus we will have more to say on the relationship between the Scriptures and wisdom.

MORAL INTELLIGENCE

Wisdom is marked by both understanding *and* behavior. Wise women and men do not only hear the Word; they *live* the Word (as James insists—see Jas 1:22); they walk in the light, in the way of truth. A Christian mind is matched by a Christian way of acting. True Christian spirituality is reflected in a dynamic ethic; there is a deep congruency between the interior life and ethics, between theological conviction and behavior. And for this we can speak of *moral intelligence*.

In the wisdom literature of the both the Old Testament and the New—thinking Proverbs, of course, but also the book of James and all the calls to wisdom that emerge in the teachings of Jesus, notably in the Sermon on the Mount, and in the writings of Paul—there are three distinctive character marks of the mature person. These three come up with remarkable frequency: finance, sexuality and speech.

Consider just one example: the magnificent call of Ephesians 4 and 5. Here the readers are called to be renewed in the spirit of their minds (Eph 4:23) as those who have "learned Christ" (Eph 4:20—a wonderful way to describe our transformation), and then Paul goes on to highlight what this looks like:

- They have put off falsehood and learned to speak the truth (Eph 4:25), turning from evil talk toward others, including slander, and turning to speech that "builds up" (Eph 4:29-31).

- They have given up stealing and devoted themselves to honest work, with generosity toward the needy (Eph 4:28).

- They have turned from fornication and impurity to thanksgiving (Eph 5:3-4).

This is just one core sample, of course; you will find these three emerging again and again as critical indicators of moral maturity. If we locate these attributes in our understanding of wisdom, we can rightly speak of them as signs of moral intelligence. The Ten Commandments tend to state these negatively—"Thou shalt not steal," for example—but in most wisdom passages of Scripture moral intelligence is stated both negatively and positively. We turn from slander to speech that is edifying; we turn from stealing to honesty and generosity in our finances; we turn from sexual impurity to thanksgiving.

Sexuality and speech are addressed back-to-back in the book of Colossians:

> Put to death, therefore, whatever in you is earthly: fornication, impurity, passion, evil desire, and greed (which is idolatry). On account of these the wrath of God is coming on those who are disobedient. These are the ways you also once followed, when you were living that life. But now you must get rid of all such things—anger, wrath, malice, slander, and abusive language from your mouth. Do not lie to one another, seeing that you have stripped off the old self with its practices and have clothed yourselves with the new self, which is being renewed in knowledge according to the image of its creator. (Col 3:5-10)

The new image, renewed in the image of its creator, is marked by transformation on these two fronts: misguided sexual desires and the lack of simplicity and purity in speech.

Putting it in a positive framework, a person of wisdom and moral intelligence is marked by a constrained sexuality—constrained by the limits of the good, the noble and the excellent, such that sexuality finds expression in and only in a covenant relationship (i.e., marriage), and more, that persons are treated with dignity and honor in all matters pertaining to their sexuality and gender.

In similar fashion, a person of wisdom and moral intelligence is marked by simplicity of speech, what James speaks of as the management or taming of the tongue—few words aptly spoken, words that edify and encourage, words of kindness and mutual understanding, and freedom from harsh words or speech marked by slander, gossip and sarcasm.

But we must also speak of finances. When it comes to moral intelligence and the evidence of wisdom in our lives, few things are so crucial as the way we live economically. There is no wisdom without financial and economic integrity, careful management, generosity and a profound commitment to justice and the economic well-being of all.

From the teaching of Jesus—who, when it comes to behavior, speaks about money and finances more than any other topic—to the witness of the book of Proverbs, the Old Testament prophets, the book of Hebrews ("Keep yourself from the love of money and be content with what you have," [Heb 13:5 NIV]), and the stern words of the book of James, self-indulgence and wages not paid those due them all speak to the pervasive sense in Scripture that wisdom and money are intimately linked.

In the fear of the Lord, a wise person knows that money is but a means to honor God, serve one's neighbor and meet one's basic needs for food and shelter. Wise people do not live in fear or anxiety but trust in God as their provider. They are similarly marked by a profound commitment to justice, equity and generosity in all of their financial dealings. They are characterized by respect for money rather than love of money, and this is evident at least in part in the careful management of the finances God has placed in their hands—for their stewardship.

Sexuality. Speech. Finances. Each speaks of wisdom in community; each is about living truthfully and wisely in relation not only to God but to others. A wise person is a responsible citizen, living and working in deep respect for the others in one's community and one's world, a respect evident in sexual integrity, simplicity and truthfulness of speech, and generosity and justice in all matters financial.

This is wonderfully summarized in the book of James when he writes, "The wisdom from above is first pure, then peaceable, gentle, willing to yield, full of mercy and good fruits, without a trace of partiality or hypocrisy. And a harvest of righteousness is sown in peace for those who make peace" (Jas 3:17-18).

Probably no voice has emphasized the relationship between wisdom and social responsibility as profoundly as that of the liberation theologians of Latin America. Jon Sobrino, for example, speaks of "political holiness."[9] Our vision of life, work and wisdom must be through the lens of the in-breaking of Christ's reign, Sobrino insists, and if we are

---

[9]Jon Sabrino, *Spirituality of Liberation: Toward Political Holiness* (Maryknoll, NY: Orbis Books, 1988).

discerning we will see that the God of all mercy, embodied in the radical mercy of Jesus, has what Sobrino and his liberationist colleagues speak of as a "preferential option for the poor," and that indeed the poor are the locus of God's presence in the world. Voices like that of Rene Padilla and other evangelical theologians from the Global South have rightly observed that when liberation theologians speak only of economic justice, they essentially present a half-truth. We need to speak of union with Christ but then match this with a commitment to act with integrity, with justice, in a deeply fragmented world.

These perspectives echo, of course, the vision of wisdom found in the book of James, which stresses that wisdom is pure and undefiled when it is marked by the visit to the orphan and the widow (Jas 1:27). The link between wisdom and matters of wealth and poverty comes up more than once in James (see also Jas 1:9-11; 2:1-7).

Finally, as I have stressed, when we speak of moral intelligence, it is imperative that we locate any conversation about moral character or integrity within its due context: union with Christ. The Christian life cannot be defined in the end as moralism or morality, as but another moral code. It is not about rules and regulations, as the apostle makes clear in the book of Colossians. The driving energy of the Christian life is union with Christ and the grace that comes through this union via the Spirit. Seeking moral formation can actually be a distraction if we are not careful. Many have sought morality as an end in itself and have defined the mature person as a moral person; many churches and seminaries in their passion for character formation have lost connection to Christ. Morality has the appearance of wisdom, Paul suggests, but it is a false wisdom leading to a false humility. True spirituality is a morality that is derivative of union with Christ. Thus the heart of the matter is not morality but the cultivation of this union. And therefore spiritual formation is never to be equated with moral formation.

WISDOM AS PATIENCE IN SUFFERING

We cannot speak of wisdom without speaking of suffering. Job, a major wisdom book of the Old Testament, speaks of wisdom and suffering extensively, and it is a critical theme in the New Testament

wisdom book James. Further, it is clear in the writings of the apostle
Paul that nothing so distinguishes the wisdom of the world from the
wisdom of God as the cross of Christ Jesus. We cannot speak of the
way of wisdom without speaking of the pain of the world and, indeed,
of the pain of God.

Wisdom and suffering. We are always in danger when we assume that
wise people suffer less than fools, and nowhere is this more dramatically
challenged than in the book of Job. Indeed, the book of Job, the tes-
timony of the Scriptures and the heritage of the church might suggest
that we are not wise until and unless we know what it is to suffer with
grace and patience, to be steadfast and generous even in the midst of the
pain. But more, it is also clear that we cannot speak of God and the
world and the way of wisdom until we learn how to speak of the suffering
of the innocent. It is a shallow wisdom, an incomplete picture, if we live
with the assumption that wise people live comfortable pain-free lives
and that fools suffer for their foolishness.

How do we live with wisdom and grace, with patience and perseverance, in the midst of suffering? It begins with denying the false
wisdom of Job's friends, who assume that Job must have done something terribly wrong and so brought on punishment for his sins. Part of
what we learn it is that it is not wise to make facile judgments regarding
the presence of suffering in the lives of others.

Gustavo Gutiérrez in his fascinating commentary on the book of Job
comes to the conclusion, "In the Book of Job, to be a believer means
sharing human suffering, especially that of the most destitute, enduring
a spiritual struggle, and finally accepting the fact that God cannot be
pigeonholed in human categories."[10] We have no wisdom, in other words,
if our way of wisdom is not informed by the suffering of the poor.

Wisdom and the way of the cross. Gutiérrez speaks through the lens
of the book of Job where God is above it all, relatively immune to Job's
suffering. Japanese theologian Kazoh Kitamori, writing about the
horrors of the Japanese experience during the World War II, speaks not
only of the pain that marks the human condition but also of the pain of

---

[10]Gustavo Gutiérrez, *On Job: God-Talk and the Suffering of the Innocent* (Maryknoll, NY: Orbis,
1987), p. 16.

God. Kitamori insists that the pain that demarcates the human condition touches the heart of God; he rejects the more static view of God in the West that resists any notion of "patripassionism"—the affirmation of a suffering God—and insists that God's love finds dramatic expression in his identification with the human condition.

Many, perhaps with good reason, feel that Kitamori overstates his case. And yet there is no doubt that the Scriptures speak unequivocally of the cross of Christ Jesus as "the wisdom of God" (1 Cor 1:24). And this has led Japanese theologian Kosuke Koyama to speak of a "crucified mind." This is his insightful and winsome (he does have a compelling sense of humor) way of describing wisdom as marked by the cross of Christ; a Christian mind is "captivated by the foolishness and weakness of God."[11]

But then, and most crucially, we are reminded of the words of Paul in 2 Corinthians wherein he clearly links his own experience of pain, suffering and setback to the cross of Christ. The wisdom of the cross is the insight that the grace of God is effected in our lives and in the lives of those we are called to serve when we appreciate that in our sufferings we are joint heirs with Christ in his suffering (Rom 8:17).

And this brings us back to the wisdom literature of the Scriptures: the patience and steadfastness of Job and the words of the epistle of James where the link between wisdom, suffering and patience is made explicit. Wise women and men are patient in the face of difficulty and trial.

This does not mean they acquiesce to evil and injustice. Witness the forceful words of Job and Habakkuk. But it does mean they learn to wait, to be patient and allow God to be God, doing his work in his time. And so a Christian mind and thus a Christian perspective includes an appreciation of this world as temporal, as only for a season. We do not dismiss the earth; rather, we hold an awareness of the transitory character of the earth as marred by sin and suffering. And the genius of the Christian gospel is that we see suffering as "slight momentary affliction" (2 Cor 4:17) in comparison with the eternal perspective. We do not suffer as those who have no hope (Rom 8:18-19).

---

[11]Kosuke Koyama, *No Handle on the Cross: An Asian Meditation on the Crucified Mind* (Maryknoll, NY: Orbis, 1976), p. 10.

I need to press one point here: while we are called to patience, we are not called to passivity. Martin Luther King Jr. had a rich theology of suffering that informed his life and spirituality, but this did not lead him to acquiescence; rather, his theology of suffering led him to a grace-filled, active solidarity with the sufferings of Christ in an identification with the sufferings of others. He aligned himself with them in their suffering and advocated for them in the face of injustice and systems of oppression.

WISDOM AND DISCERNMENT

Only with this as a backdrop can we speak of another crucial dimension of wisdom: the capacity for discernment. Philippians 1:9-10 makes the link explicit: "And this is my prayer, that your love may overflow more and more with knowledge and full insight to help you to determine what is best."

The basic conviction we bring to this consideration is the following: to speak of a wise person is to affirm the capacity for making good choices. Wisdom is evident, in part, in the capacity to decide well. Wise people are wise in the conduct of their lives, and this necessarily means that they are able to choose not only between good and evil, but also between two or more good alternatives. They are able to discern what is the best way to go or the best way to act in the midst of competing viable alternatives.

The immaturity of children is evident in that they have not yet developed a capacity to choose well. But over time, as they mature into adulthood, this should be evident in an increasing ability to make good decisions—in the use of time or money or in the choices they make about key relationships. A wise person makes good choices, decisions that are the fruit of wisdom.

And thus we can speak of prudence as a mark of wisdom—people who are wise in particular contexts, settings and circumstances, who are able to act appropriately and with courage in the midst of the options and opportunities before them. They are not reckless; their courage is informed by wisdom. But neither are they unduly cautious; prudence speaks of knowing what needs to be done and when it needs to be done. And doing it.

Many Christians at this point resort to either the Scriptures or the church as their referent for being prudent and making good decisions. They read their Bible so they know what they should do in this or that situation, or they insist that the church, through its teaching authority, will tell them how to live, how to make choices. But increasing Christians are affirming, and rightly so, that while the Scriptures and the faith community are foundational and basic—one cannot grow in wisdom except through the Scriptures and in the context of the church—the wise Christian has the capacity to choose "in Christ" through the inner witness of the Spirit.

This interior witness never comes at the expense of being immersed in the Scriptures and anchored in the life of the church; this discernment of the Spirit is never purely interior or subjective or unaccountable to the witness of the Scriptures or the need for accountability within Christian community. And yet what marks our holiness and thus our wisdom is a real-time relationship with the ascended Christ; we live and move out of union with Christ and in the fellowship of the Spirit. Wisdom comes through Jesus Christ not merely in a formal sense as a working principle but in the dynamic, existential life of deciding and acting with courage—we can choose "in the Lord." We can live our lives out of intimate and dynamic communion with Jesus and in response to the inner witness of the Spirit of Jesus.

The Proverbs pointedly stress:

Trust in the LORD with all your heart,
  and do not rely on your own insight.
In all your ways acknowledge him,
  and he will make straight your paths.
Do not be wise in your own eyes;
  fear the LORD, and turn away from evil. (Prov 3:5-7)

Growth in wisdom is reflected in greater dependence on God, not less, as it is often thought. It is not that as we mature in wisdom we are able to live with less of this profound truth—it is that we "trust in the LORD" with our whole beings. Thus an essential dimension of growing in wisdom is that we foster our capacity for discernment, for learning how to attend to the voice of Jesus, in our prayers and in the world, and in this learning develop the ability to recognize what is truly of God and what is spurious to the purposes of God in our lives.

CONCLUSION

In appendix A I will speak of a congregation as a teaching-learning community and specifically on the need for catechesis—how teaching is integral to evangelism and to an initiation into Christian faith. This means speaking about the connection between baptism and teaching. But for now, as I conclude this chapter, four observations.

The Scriptures and wisdom formation. In all that I have said and offered so far, it should be clear that for the renewal of our minds, pursuit of wisdom means we turn first and foremost to the Scriptures as the source of our wisdom and our understanding. This is forcefully profiled for us in the words of Paul in 2 Timothy:

> But as for you, continue in what you have learned and firmly believed, knowing from whom you learned it, and how from childhood you have known the sacred writings that are able to instruct you for salvation through faith in Christ Jesus. All scripture is inspired by God and is useful for teaching, for reproof, for correction, and for training in righteousness, so that everyone who belongs to God may be proficient, equipped for every good work.
>
> In the presence of God and of Christ Jesus, who is to judge the living and the dead, and in view of his appearing and his kingdom, I solemnly urge you: proclaim the message; be persistent whether the time is favorable or unfavorable; convince, rebuke, and encourage, with the utmost patience in teaching. For the time is coming when people will not put up with sound doctrine, but having itching ears, they will accumulate for themselves teachers to suit their own desires, and will turn away from listening to the truth and wander away to myths. (2 Tim 3:14–4:4)

These words reflect a theological assumption: that God forms us in wisdom through his Word, through his "self-communication." The Word is both revelation (thus intimately linked with the divine Logos), and it is the means of our sanctification and thus linked to the Spirit. The reference to the Spirit is important: the Scriptures have no transforming power in themselves as texts but only as they are linked to the Spirit. Thus the Reformed tradition rightly has stressed that we speak of the transforming power of Word and Spirit. In the end we do not trust the Bible; rather we trust the God who is revealed through the Bible. But in giving space to the Scriptures, in teaching and preaching the Scriptures, we are giving space to God in our lives; we are preaching Christ and him crucified (1 Cor 2:2).

And so the church is a community of the Word: studied, meditated upon, preached. While there is certainly more to congregational life, we cannot conceive of being the church without being a "fellowship of the Word."

Wisdom and the arts. I speak here very briefly on a topic of substantive importance. One of the urgent needs of our day is to recover an understanding of the interplay of wisdom with the arts—to speak to how the arts are vital to the formation of a Christian mind, the cultivation of a Christian imagination and the nurturing of a deep love for the good, the noble, the excellent and the worthy of praise (Phil 4:8)—or, as Jeremy Begbie puts it so well, to "show how artistic practices (and reflection on them) have their own distinctive and indispensable role to play in what we might call the 'ecology' of theology—the whole gamut of ways in which the wisdom of God comes to be learned and articulated."[12]

I will stress in an upcoming chapter that music in worship can juvenilize or alternatively cultivate an adult faith. In any art form, banality is the scourge of maturity in thought and character. Whether in music, fiction, the dramatic arts or the visual arts, we will come to see that formation in wisdom requires the gracious interplay of the artists and the teacher.

Wisdom and humility. We all long to grow in wisdom and thus in spiritual maturity in Christ. I am taken by the wonderful line in the ancient liturgy of St. Chrysostom: before the reading of Scripture, the holy book is lifted high and the one presiding calls out, "Wisdom. Be attentive." This call, which in today's liturgies is typically found in Eastern Orthodox services of worship, is a twofold call to humility and

---

[12]Jeremy Begbie, ed., *Beholding the Glory: Incarnation Through the Arts* (Grand Rapids, MI: Baker, 2001), p. xii.

joy: humility before the wisdom of God and joy in the presence of the God of all wisdom. And it is a reminder that, along the way, we should continually remember that the wise are humble and the wise are joyful.

Wise women and men recognize that wisdom is received as gift through the self-revelation of God. While we can pursue wisdom, we seek it as those who know that it is a gift given to those who seek it. Seeking does not make us wise. Rather, in humility the wise recognize their folly, their urgent need for wisdom, truth and understanding. In humility we recognize the authority of another voice; we know that we are not wise in ourselves but rather in submission to God and to the means by which he enables us to know and live the truth, namely the Scriptures.

Knowledge in itself easily "puffs up" and also leads to dogmatism. True wisdom is evident in humility, a gracious humility that acknowledges our human limitations—the boundaries of our knowledge, our perspective. We do not have or see all the truth; we are ever learning, ever open to correction and new understanding. David Ford speaks of how the wise know something of what they know while also recognizing what they do not know. Thus humility is a "supporting virtue" in the pursuit of wisdom.[13]

We learn from our seniors; we learn from our children. We learn from those who agree with us and from those who differ with us. Indeed, true wisdom is marked by humility and charity toward all, most notably those with whom we differ. The answer to evangelical anti-intellectualism is not dogmatism; we can have conviction regarding our beliefs as long as these are matched by generosity and the capacity for continuous learning. Or as David Ford puts it so aptly, "We seek a hopeful pursuit of wisdom . . . magnanimity without presumption, humility without despair."[14]

Wisdom and joy. Regarding joy, we do well to remember the wise words of the book of Ecclesiastes, which remind us that the pursuit of wisdom is itself not meant to be burdensome. We may well be diligent in our study and learning; we will indeed need to learn how to think deeply and thoroughly. But let this never so weigh us down that we lose

---

[13]Ford, *Long Rumour of Wisdom*, p. 26.
[14]Ibid., pp. 20-21.

a sense of humor and that we forget what it means to be present to the moment. The words of wisdom suggest that we always remember to enjoy the gifts of eating and drinking and the gift of good work:

> There is nothing better for mortals than to eat and drink, and find enjoyment in their toil. This also, I saw, is from the hand of God; for apart from him who can eat or who can have enjoyment? For to the one who pleases him God gives wisdom and knowledge and joy. (Eccles 2:24-26)

Wise women and men know that the creation is infused with the glory of God and that we are thus called to revel in the beauty and in the goodness revealed through what God has made. We delight in good food, the joys of marriage and friendship, good books, poetry, music. For myself, at this stage of life, I relish the sheer joy of being a grandfather. We celebrate the gifts of God for today, and this is wisdom.

4

CALLED TO DO GOOD WORK

An Invitation to Vocational Holiness

Let the favor of the Lord our God be upon us,
and prosper for us the work of our hands—
O prosper the work of our hands!

PSALM 90:17

WHEN WE SPEAK OF HOLINESS and spiritual maturity, we need to consider our work. We need to reflect on how our work—our duties and responsibilities at home, in the workplace, in the church—is an integral dimension of our relationship with Christ and thus of our experience of the holiness of God. Eugene Peterson has introduced into our theological lexicon the intriguing idea of vocational holiness.[1] What might this mean—vocational holiness?

When we read the Gospels, we are struck by Jesus' wisdom, his depth of spiritual insight and, of course, his love and compassion for others. But also, we are taken by the simplicity and focus of his work. He knew his calling; rarely if ever was he rushed or anxious about his ministry. He knew what he had to do and was prepared, quite literally, to die for what

---

[1]Eugene H. Petersen, *Under the Unpredictable Plant: An Exploration in Vocational Holiness* (Grand Rapids, MI: Eerdmans, 1992).

mattered. In the end, he was able to say those remarkable words: "I glo-rified you on earth by finishing the work that you gave me to do" (Jn 17:4).

What grace! To be freed from anxiety about our work and from the frenetic fear that we are not doing all we could do or feel compelled to do or want to do. Just simply and clearly at the end of one's life to say, "I completed the work that was given me." This is vocational holiness—that on any given day or week or year or chapter of our lives, we are able to say, "I glorified God and completed the work that he gave me to do." To be able to say that for this day I have completed the work God as-signed to me.

We can think of this in terms of assignments or responsibilities—to parent these two teens or manage this small business or teach this course or attend to this garden. At the end of a day or a week or a life, we aim to know we have completed the work God has given us to do. Few things matter more than knowing in the depths of our heart how the Creator and redeemer is calling us to live our lives. What is the work to which we are being called, work that we receive from God and then offer back to him as an act of thankful praise?

When we use the language of vocation and vocational holiness, we assume two things. First, the language of vocation suggests that we live in *response* to a call. We need to be freed from any idea that we are driven; we are not herded but invited and summoned. The biblical vision of vocation is that it is an invitation. We live not self-constructed lives. Rather we live in response to divine initiative, to God's personal call. Consider the invitation to Moses to lead the people of Israel, to Mary to be the mother of the God-child, to Paul to proclaim the gospel to the Gentiles. Yes, there is command, certainly, but, most of all, their engagement in their work was an act of response to God's invitation.

Second, the language of vocation assumes that more is not neces-sarily better. We need to speak about vocation against the backdrop of a generation of Christians who are driven by hectic activity and inclined to assume that the busier you are, the holier you are. I think of the standard mantra of my own religious heritage: pray more, give more, serve more! This is exhausting! And it causes us to think we are always underperforming, always coming up short, never able to rest.

We tend to assume that important people are busy people and that devoted people are even busier. But vocational holiness means embracing what we are called to do and graciously declining that to which we are not called. We learn to say "yes" and we learn to say "no." Actually, we will likely say "no" more often than we say "yes." And, when we say "no" it is specifically and precisely so that we can say "yes" to that to which we are being called.

We can come to this grace, this way of thinking and being, only if we foster the capacity to think theologically about our work and engage the spiritual practices that foster this very grace. For this we can turn to the remarkable wisdom that has emerged from the spiritual writers and theologians of the sixteenth century. I am thinking of the insights of both the northern Reformers typically associated with the Protestant Reformation and of the southern Reformers who were part of the Catholic Reformation. In the north, the key voices were John Calvin and Martin Luther; in the south, insights emerged from Ignatius Loyola, agent of reform within the church of Rome. This dependence on the sixteenth century will be evident at numerous points in these reflections—not in terms of direct quotations but in terms of our basic approach to the character of our work.

THE THEOLOGICAL VISION FOR VOCATIONAL HOLINESS

The wisdom of the sixteenth century is particularly evident in this: it helps us cultivate a theological vision for good work. This theological vision assumes that freedom comes not in a self-determined or self-constructed life but in a life of deference—we could even use the word "submission," for these are hard boundaries and points of reference—to three realities:

- The work of God in the world as Creator and redeemer—we live within a biblical theology of God's work.

- Our selves as agents who respond to the invitation to participate in the work of God. We live in deference to who we actually are, not who we wish we are. We learn to read ourselves accurately, which requires a maturing self-knowledge.

- Our world—the actual situation of our lives, the arena into which God calls us, which suggests that we give careful attention to our circumstances and see them as God sees them.

As a rule it can be said that if people do not discern vocation well, it is due to a lack of a vital theological vision on one or more of these three points of reference. They either have a faulty understanding of the biblical meaning of work and God's work in the world, or they do not have a maturing self-knowledge, or they have not developed a grace-filled read of their context. They are not living in reality. Each is crucial and merits focused attention; we begin with speaking of God as Creator and redeemer.

Creator and redeemer: God's work and our work. Our first reference point, and we must begin here, is the work of God. Vocation is a matter of discerning—seeing, understanding and appreciating—the purpose of God in the world. Our work is a participation in the work of God. Thus it is important that we get a read on what it means to appreciate the work of God.

Our longing is to do *good* work, and nothing so defines the character of good work as the work of God. God is a worker; the Scriptures portray God as one who creates and redeems. There is no other way to speak of God except through the lens of this remarkable reality. The Bible opens and closes with the celebration of the work of God. And the narrative that is the Christian Scriptures is the story of the work of God, who created all things and redeemed all things. One psalm after another celebrates God as either Creator or redeemer or both. When we gather for worship on Sunday, central to our adoration and praise is the celebration of the good work of God, who has created all things and is redeeming all things.

We revel in this; we delight in the glory of God's creation; we recognize that God spoke well when at creation in speaking of all that was made as good. The counterpoint to that celebration is the doxological celebration of God's work in Christ, who was incarnate, lived, died, rose and is exalted and who pours out his Spirit on all and who will one day make all things well.

Between creation and redemption we are given work to do, and one of the deep longings of our hearts is the yearning to do good work—

with talent and joy, with skill and diligence. We long to make a difference. In the language of Genesis 1 and 2, we long to "till the earth" and "name the animals"—to embrace that which was given to our human parents—and then, in Christ and in the anointing of the Spirit, we long to be instruments of the peace of God—to heal, to restore, to rebuild that which has been torn down, to be the means by which the shalom of God is manifest and the prayer "thy will be done on earth as it is in heaven" is fulfilled.

To speak of good work is to speak of both the *nature* of the work and *how* that work is done. Good work by definition is work that reflects the purposes of God in the world. And so it is work that meets a genuine need; it is work that brings delight to God and to the created order; it is work that alleviates suffering and brings healing.

And this leads me to two axiomatic affirmations about our work and the work of God. First, our work is a *participation* in the work of God. The farmer participates in the work of the true Grower, who is the Creator; the doctor knows that she is no healer but only a participant in the healing purposes of God.

This is no less true of the redemptive work of God. We worship a God who is redeemer, healer and reconciler. And the language of vocation signals that we respond to the Creator and redeemer who invites us into a participation in this larger work: first, as co-creators, and second, as co-redeemers and ministers of reconciliation. We create; we heal. In both cases, we are coworkers with God.

Second, when we speak of the work of God and thus our work, the sequence of creation and redemption is important. We truly speak of redemption only when we do so in the light of the creative work of God. When we use the phrase "good work" we must begin with creation: what did God intend when we were invited to be co-creators with the Creator? Work is part of the created order, not merely the order of redemption. Work is a gift; it is inherent in creation and integral to what it means to be a person, a human being. We are called to do good work as a means by which we bring glory to the Creator.

Yes, we do need to speak of sin, and yes, our understanding of work needs to include a recognition of how work has become a curse through sin's fragmentation of our world. But it is essential to stress that work is not part of the order of the fall—of sin—but of creation. To appreciate the close interplay between sanctity and work we need to consider the place of work in the original, creative purposes of God.

Without this backdrop we too easily fall into the temptation of viewing some forms of work as inherently superior or more sacred than others— somehow more holy. Rather, the creation-redemption sequence opens our eyes to the wonder that God calls women and men into every sphere and sector of society. And it is this calling that makes their work sacred.

Surely one of the most powerful demonstrations of good work in the Scriptures is that found in chapter 31 of the book of Proverbs. While this passage is typically viewed as a portrayal of a noble woman and more specifically a married woman, it is also a stunning portrayal of good work. And it is almost doxological in its celebration of this work.

- She manages her home and is a buyer and seller in the marketplace.

- She works with her hands and is creative and attentive to beauty.

- There is a public side to her work, but she also works in quietness and obscurity.

- She is celebrated for the mundane and ordinary of her life and work, not merely the grand or heroic.

What must not be missed is that she is a businesswoman. And the very accessible vision of work described in Proverbs 31 needs to form the backdrop as we consider the meaning of work in light of the Christ event.

One way to test is whether we truly believe this—and feel the force of it—is to ask whether we believe in the value of two expressions of work in particular: the calling to business (the production of goods and services) and the calling to the arts (the cultivation of beauty in homes and places of work, worship and learning). The first tends to be viewed askance by anyone who considers money a bit suspect. The second is questioned by anyone whose pragmatic bent leaves them wondering if the arts are "useful."

Do we celebrate and preach in our churches that God calls artists, businesspeople and educators into every sector of society to participate in his work as Creator and redeemer? Indeed, God calls farmers and electricians, carpenters and lawyers, doctors and, yes, even dentists— with their drills!—to be the means by which he brings about the peace of the city; and God calls theologians and teachers to provide religious leadership for congregations and to equip and empower all these people, in all walks of life, through word and sacrament to fulfill their God-given callings.

God is a creator, and thus we consider our work from the perspective of God as Creator. But we are soon caught up short and reminded that no one works in an ideal world, only one that is marred by sin and profound fragmentation. We were designed for joy in our work, but with the fall work too easily becomes a toilsome burden.

And yet all is not lost; sin does not have last word. Now, in light of Christ's work of redemption, work is viewed not only through the lens of creation or through the lens of sin, but also in light of the Christ event—most notably the cross—and the gift of the Spirit.

Through his death and resurrection, Christ Jesus is now the ascended Lord. All authority has been given to him, and through the Spirit he is fulfilling his redemptive purposes in the church and the world. With the outpouring of the gift of the Spirit on the day of Pentecost, all Christians now live out their lives and thus their work with reference to the Christ event.

Paul in Colossians and Ephesians celebrates the cosmic scope of the work of Christ, and especially in Ephesians he speaks of the church as a means by which the kingdom purposes of God are fulfilled. That "means" finds particular expression in the language of Matthew 28 with the mandate to "make disciples of all nations."

This suggests that all work—from the garden to the accounting firm, from the work of plumbing to the work of preaching—can and must be viewed through the lens of God's mission in the world. We do our work now in light of the Christ event. It is Christ himself, the crucified, risen and ascended Christ, who calls us, and it is the Spirit who animates and empowers us for this work.

But we must not miss the fact that the redemptive purposes of God are as wide as his work of creation. In the name of Christ and the power of the Spirit, women and men are now called into every sphere and sector of society as witnesses to the reign of Christ. And crucial to this vision of work is that we are co-creators and co-reconcilers with the Creator and redeemer.

Of course, there is only one Creator. A gardener knows he is not a creator or grower. Only God makes things grow; the gardener or the farmer is but a participant in the work of the Creator God. And a doctor knows she is not a healer. Such a thought would be ludicrous. Rather, a doctor participates in the work of the only one who can be called healer, namely God. Likewise, God is the ultimate worker, and our work is that of participants in the work of the one who is Creator and redeemer.

What on earth is God doing? God who has created all things is now reconciling all things to his very self. And we are invited to join the program. This is vocation: to respond to God's invitation to participate in this extraordinary work of creation and redemption.

This suggests that since God is the Creator, all of us are on some level called to reflect the glory and beauty of the Creator in our work, such that we live out our vocations—regardless of the specific work we do— in a way that honors and cultivates the beauty and order of God's creation. God will not call anyone into work that violates or destroys what he has made. Some, of course, are called specifically into fields such as marine biology, which is focused directly on the preservation of the created order. But all of us need to attend to what it means to live out our vocations in a manner that is faithful to the mandate to be stewards of God's created order.

Furthermore, this suggests that all of us be also attentive to the redemptive side of the work of God—the God who in Christ is reconciling all things, making disciples of all nations, establishing Christ's reign of justice and peace. Thus, for example, just as a preacher needs to believe in and support the work of the marine biologist, so the biologist needs to attend to and support the work of those who are called to teaching, preaching and other vocations more obviously aligned with God's redemptive purposes.

And both need to be attentive to the vision of God to establish his reign of justice and peace. God is a God of justice and compassion, and his deep commitment will necessarily shape the heart and contours of every vocation. The Old Testament prophets—notably Isaiah, Amos and Micah—make it abundantly clear that in God's redemptive purposes, peace and justice will embrace; the shalom of God will mean the triumph of justice. There is no righteousness without justice, and there is no justice without economic justice. Thus everyone's vocation needs to take account of this agenda: in word and deed, we witness to the God whose justice will be revealed.

Holiness and self-determination. Vocation is discerned at the intersection of three realities. The first, as we have just discussed, is the vision of work in the Scriptures, specifically the work of God and his invitation to us to participate in that work.

The second reality is our very selves as agents, as called ones. Here we need to attend to the significance of the human person and, more, the significance and particularity of our own selves as actors on God's stage. We ask, what does it mean to be stewards of our lives in light of what God is doing in the world? As we walk down this road, testing and seeking to understand what it means to be a human person created in the image of God to do good work, we begin by recognizing the significance—indeed the power and glory—of the human person as an actor.

Affirming human agency. A familiar contemporary expression is partly right and partly wrong, and as such it is really not that helpful. It is the refrain "There is no 'I' in team." This is cute, perhaps, as a way to speak of how personal egos can too easily undermine the capacity of communities and organizations to achieve their mission. And yet it is not really a helpful way to speak of the interplay between the individual and the community and ourselves and God. The "I"—the person in each team or community—is never lost; the individual always matters and always remains an "I."

We must speak of ourselves as individuals who are self-directed and recognize that we truly act with integrity in the world only when we act in a way that is consistent with our selves. And for this, we must affirm that each human person matters. The key players in the redemptive purposes of God—as revealed in the biblical narrative, for example—are individuals with extraordinary egos: think of the personal force of a

Moses or an Elijah, or think of the way that Paul celebrates in Romans 16 the variety of people with whom he was able to partner in his work and ministry. Indeed, one is struck by the personal force and power, the charisma, of the apostle Paul himself. But Paul and others did not confuse themselves with God. God always remained God. They did not see themselves as the center of the cosmos.

Ironically, what we fear is not a strong ego but a weak ego. A weak ego is controlling. It must always be appeased; it is easily hurt or offended; a weak ego needs to be pandered to, insists on loyalty and longs to be liked; it yearns to be affirmed and thanked.

Perhaps my resistance to the idea that "there is no 'I' in team" arises in part by the discounting of the human person that has typified my religious heritage. We tend to sing such songs as "More and more of Jesus; less and less of me," all on the assumption that the "me" in question is a threat to the glory and honor of Christ—since Christ wants all the glory and there is only so much glory to go around, the less of us—you and me—the better. We can certainly overstate the significance of the human person and fail to see the human person as a creature dependent on God and living in glory to God. But it is equally a problem to discount ourselves, to disparage or dismiss the significance of our own lives.

I have an image etched in my mind: I can picture my four-year-old granddaughter, Charis. With her family we were on a picnic in a beautiful meadow by the sea. Charis had wandered off and I was struck by how she was quite some distance away. She was aware of us, but she was also in her own world. I watched her *striding* upon the earth, out on her grand walk along that grassy meadow—a tiny little person, but the world was hers. And I could not help but think that my joy was shared by her Creator.

To speak of vocational holiness is to insist on the extraordinary significance of each human person *striding* upon the earth. Each one is created in the image of God and as an image-bearer is doing the work they know in their souls they must do. A healthy ego is one that firmly but gently presses to this end, toward the fulfillment of one's identity in response to the call of God.

Of course, this personal call and determination must be tempered by the messiness of life and the needs of others along the way. We fulfill our work within a host of constraints. But let us not come to those constraints prematurely; we need to first consider what it means to speak of the remarkable beauty and power of each person created by God.

Vocational integrity and self-knowledge. Affirming the significance of each human person leads us to an appreciation of the uniqueness of each person. The continuity between creation and redemption means that the redemptive purposes of God in our lives and in the world will call us back to the question, how has God made us? And this means that vocational holiness is a matter of being in the world in a manner consistent with how we have been made—not generically but specifically and particularly as individuals created by God. There is no such thing as a generic person, someone who is a mere pawn in the purposes and mission of God.

Therefore, vocational holiness requires that we attend to the specifics of our own lives. Self-knowledge and self-awareness are an essential aspect of spiritual maturity and wisdom: we need to know ourselves but then, of course, also come to a gracious acceptance of how God has made us. We see ourselves in truth, and, more, we are grateful for the life we have been given. We move toward the freedom that comes with no longer wishing we were anyone other than who we are. We let go of envy and resentment and embrace the life that has been given to us.

The Christian spiritual tradition has a distinct thread of continual affirmation that this perspective on self is humility—I am thinking here notably of such voices as Catherine of Siena and Teresa of Àvila, both of whom speak to self-knowledge as the precursor to genuine humility. A humble person, a truly mature person, is one who embraces the life one has been given—to know and accept and live within one's body, one's skin, this life that one has been given. Of course, those in abject poverty may feel the force of what strikes them as nothing but a curse on their lives. And there are certainly also those who have suffered deeply, perhaps as children, who wonder who would want this life. And yet that is part of the mission of the church: to foster the capacity for economic equilibrium and mental health such that each person can give thanks and grow into the life for which they were created. This is the passion of the church: to see each person as an individual of extraordinary worth, significance and potential. Part of getting to this point requires that we give each person the spiritual and emotional resources to see themselves in truth and begin to live in this truth.

Those who do not live in Christ can come to a remarkable level of self-knowledge and self-acceptance—a sign of common grace—and yet the Christian spiritual tradition also consistently affirms that true self-knowledge is inexplicably linked with intimate knowledge of Christ. It is in knowing Christ and particularly the knowledge of the love of Christ that we are freed to see ourselves in truth. The knowledge of the love of Christ frees us from pretense, from living the facade, from being anyone other than the very one who is loved by Christ Jesus. Christ calls each of us by name, reflected in Christ's knowledge of us and his acceptance of the very life that has been created through him.

Self-knowledge is expressed in two notable ways. First, to know oneself is to be attentive to one's deep passion or joy. The second expression of self-knowledge is a gracious acceptance of one's strengths and limits. First, regarding passion, self-knowledge includes the capacity to respond to such questions as, what do I want and what matters to me? Both get at the heart of the matter (pun intended—the heart of a person and who he or she is as created in the image of God). A mature person knows his or her heart and then orders one's life accordingly. We tend to distinguish between "what God wants" and "what I want to do." This is helpful and appropriate to a point; we do need to challenge our propensity for an ego-centered life. But we also need to recognize that the movement of our hearts is part of the way that God has made us. Furthermore, our deepest joy is congruent with how we have been made and how we have been called.

This is all an attempt to get at what Henri Nouwen and Annie Dillard are after when they speak of lives that are lived "according to [one's] necessity."[2] As Dillard stresses, this necessity is not something superficial to our identity but resides at the heart and soul of who we are. To

---

[2]Annie Dillard, *Teaching a Stone to Talk* (New York: Harper and Row, 1982), pp. 12-16; Henri J. M. Nouwen, *Reaching Out: The Three Movements of the Spiritual Life* (New York: Doubleday, 1975), p. 27.

fail to acknowledge this necessity is to deny how God has made us. Mature self-knowledge is evident in the capacity to speak of our deep joy. Joy is not generic; it is grounded in our particularity as human persons. For each of us joy is found in our own personal orientation and desire.

It is very common when organizations interview prospective candidates for positions for them to ask a rather standard question: what are your strengths and what are your weaknesses? The assumption seems to be that this will provide insight into how a person might perform a particular job or assignment. It is a fair question to a point, but it might actually distract us from the heart of the matter. For what matters most *about* this person is what matters most *to* this person. To know someone is to know what it is they care about and care about deeply; to know someone is to know his or her necessity.

What, for example, makes a person angry—not in the sense of loss of temper or irritation when she is crossed, but rather the anger she feels when her heart is aligned with the purposes of God in the world. What breaks the heart of God—for this person? Putting it more positively: if God longs to give us the desires of our hearts when we are aligned with the good, the noble, the worthy of praise (Phil 4:8), what is it we long to do more than anything else? What is it we *need* to do?

This is not to say talent does not matter. It is rather that talent and ability are at the service of our necessity. We master a craft—whether it is public speaking or surgery or woodworking or business administration— so that we can fulfill our calling, so that we can do what matters (to us). Talent does not equal calling; rather, talent is at the service of calling.

Then also we need to consider self-knowledge as an awareness of strengths and limitations. For these observations I am particularly indebted to two writers: James Fowler and Parker Palmer.[3] Both in distinct ways circle back in their writings to the idea that our vocation is fulfilled as we learn to embrace our strengths and accept our limits.

While strengths matter, they do not determine vocation. I have just

---

[3]See especially James W. Fowler, *Becoming Adult, Becoming Christian: Adult Development and Christian Faith* (San Francisco: Harper & Row, 1984); and Parker Palmer, *Let Your Life Speak: Listening for the Voice of Vocation* (San Francisco: Jossey-Bass, 2000).

stressed the priority of joy and living according to our "necessity." Indeed for some people, their capacities and strengths can get in the way of their true passion. These capacities actually derail them from what they have been called to do. So we need to distinguish between our deep passion and our strengths. But strengths matter. Perhaps what we should stress is that we need to identify and cultivate those strengths and capacities that open up the possibilities of fulfilling our deep passions. These are the strengths that matter.

And these strengths merit cultivation: we need to nurture the talent, to develop the capacities, to learn the art by which our deep passion is fulfilled. We master a craft not as an end in itself, but because that mastery allows us to fulfill our calling. We excel not because we are perfectionistic, but because something else matters to us, the very thing that our mastery allows us to do. If something reflects our calling, our deep necessity, if it truly matters to us, this will be evident at least in part in a resolve to do it well—to do our best, to master the art.

If we are teachers, we need to master the art of classroom instruction. If we are administrators, we need to understand how organizations work and how we can work within them. If we are carpenters, we need to revel in and develop the skills to work the wood. Our passion is driven not by ego or dominance but by a love of beauty, a caring for people, a longing to see the outcome for which we have been called to make a difference for God and with God.

But to embrace our strengths means that we also accept our limits. A crucial sign of vocational holiness and maturity in our life and in our work is the gracious acceptance of our noncapacities. I stress that I am not speaking here of "weaknesses." While we certainly all have our weaknesses, a limit, a noncapacity, is not a weakness; it is merely a nonstrength. No one is all things to all people; we each bring certain strengths to the table, and our limits are the points where we learn to live in dependence on others.

A good writer needs a good editor; they both need a good publisher. And the folks in marketing are good at something that neither the writer or the editor know how to do well. We need each other. And we all need gifted booksellers.

Limits are not a problem; they are an opportunity for us to focus, to truly embrace our calling. Furthermore, our limits bring us to interdependence with the strengths of others, allowing the synergy of our strengths to produce an outcome that is beyond—perhaps way beyond—both of our individual capacities.

Now, as a quick aside, we do need to be aware of false notions of our limits. Some of us need to learn how to live within our limits; others of us, out of fear or for other reasons, have claimed "limits" when the real issue is laziness or lack of willingness or courage to do what we are called to do. Think for example of Moses, who resisted the call of God by putting up false notions of limits, a kind of false humility. Or I think of the day when I claimed as a limit that I did not know how to do "fundraising," only to be challenged by a colleague and friend who asked, "Are you willing to learn?" Is this really a limit, or is this a reflection of unwillingness or fear of growth and new learning?

One more point here: all of this implies that the individual human person has significance and a calling or vocation in his or her own right. We all rightly believe in the force and power of the church's calling or mission. And I will speak to this later in this chapter. But in this section I am emphasizing that the collective mission of the church does not co-opt the vocation of each person. We are *each* called to be participants in the work and mission of the church in the world, and we are each called to faithfully respond to God's calling on our own lives. In appendix A I will outline how these two intersect and how they are complementary—the mission of the church and the vocation of the individual Christian.

Knowing our circumstances: seeking hopeful realism. Vocational holiness is found at the unique intersection of (1) the purposes of God in the world, (2) the way God has made us personally and (3) the circumstances in which we find ourselves. Thinking and acting theologically about vocation involves attention to the intersection of these three realities: God and his purposes of Creator and redeemer, ourselves as actors on God's stage, and the actual context or setting in which we live and work.

The third critical reference in discerning vocation is found in careful attention to our circumstances. We are providentially located in time and space, thus "vocation" is never just about us and God, about God's mission in the world and our identity in response to that mission. It is also about the social circumstances and historical "accidents" in which we have been placed—what Douglas Schuurman has so aptly referred to as how we are "providentially situated."[4]

Naming reality. As we consider this third critical factor for vocational discernment, we begin with a crucial affirmation: the calling of God is always specific to a time and place; it is always historical. We are called to be present to our circumstances, our world—to be agents of peace and justice in the world as it actually is rather than as we wish it were. This means we turn not only from pretense (wishing we were someone else or acting as though we are someone else) but also from wishful thinking and illusion regarding our circumstances.

If I am called to be the executive director of an agency, the principal of a school, the pastor of a church or the manager of a business, I lead by naming reality. I ask, what is the actual set of circumstances that lie before me and around me? And the point of departure for discerning vocation is always today. We start here and now. No nostalgia, no regrets, no illusions.

This means that we do not live emotionally in a previous time. We have no patience with "the good old days." They are long gone. We discern in light of what is actually the case today. This also means we do not engage in wishful thinking. In other words, we do not dwell on what we wish were true but on what is actually true. We do not need to overstate; there is no need for melodrama. And we certainly need to move

---

[4]Douglas J. Schuurman, *Vocation: Discerning Our Callings in Life* (Grand Rapids, MI: Eerdmans, 2004), p. 28. Schuurman is a good counterpart resource to Frederick Buechner, *Listening to Your Life* (San Francisco: Harper and Row, 1992). I have suggested there are three points of reference: the work of God in the world, our selves as agents and our circumstances. Buechner emphasizes two of these, and in response to him, it seems important to also stress that we have to see how God is at work in the world. Schuurman emphasizes two as well: the work of God (a major theme for him) and also how we are "providentially situated." He seems to resist the idea, so strong in Buechner, that self-knowledge is critical. One almost has a sense in Schuurman that we simply need to do what needs to be done. I propose in response to both that it is all three. In response to Buechner I stress the need for a theological vision of God's work as a crucial reference point; in response to Schuurman I insist that there are no generic people and that wisdom and good work require a mature self-knowledge.

on from self-pity or a propensity to bemoan our circumstances. But mainly the genius of effective vocational holiness is that we are present to our world, our circumstances and the specific realities and challenges of our situation.

Thus vocational integrity includes the capacity, to use golfing language, to play one's lie: to proceed without complaint about the weather, the depth of the rough, the capacities of the groundskeeper, the noise of the children in the nearby backyards, the quality of the conversation in your foursome or the refusal of other golfers to turn off their cell phones. We just play the shot. This is real life; we do not have the option of picking up the ball and finding a better spot from which to play. We play the lie.

We live in the world as it presents itself—no nostalgia, no pining for an earlier golden age. We are not waiting around for good fortune to suddenly and finally hit us. We stop investing emotional energy in "what-ifs," and we get on with it.

All of us are called to such a time as this. None of us are ahead of our times, and no one is born too late and able to complain that opportunity passed us by. Rather, we are each invited to respond to the call of God for this day.

This commitment to realism is not oppressive, however difficult our circumstances might be, because we face our circumstances with a confidence in the power of God and the ultimate triumph of goodness. By this I do not mean we engage in naive optimism, nor again do I mean we spend time on wishful thinking. What I mean is that we have a clear, level-headed read on our situation and we see it through the lens of the purposes and grace of God. We are reminded of the extraordinary benediction of Ephesians:

> Now to him who by the power at work within us is able to accomplish abundantly far more than all we can ask or imagine, to him be glory in the church and in Christ Jesus to all generations, forever and ever. Amen. (Eph 3:20-21)

This perspective on our circumstances means that no situation is inherently hopeless; each context and setting is filled with the possibilities of God's goodness and grace. We are women and men of hope; this is an imperative under which we live. We let go of despair and cynicism. We see this day and this set of circumstances in the light of the ultimate purposes of God and our confidence that in time—perhaps not soon, but eventually—goodness and justice will win the day. We attend to this day and engage this chapter of our lives with the confidence that one day Jesus will make all things well.

But more, this perspective also means that no situation is inherently hopeless: our circumstances are also an opportunity for us to consider the possibilities of God's grace and the intervention of his mercy and power into the complexity and messiness of our situation. We all know that if we could write the script it would be different; our situation would not be like this! But in naming reality we are not crushed by it; rather we see it though the lens of the gracious power of God.

Opportunities and constraints. Just as a read on ourselves means we recognize both our strengths and limits, a read on our circumstances requires the capacity to recognize both opportunities and constraints. Vocation is fulfilled as we learn to respond to opportunities but also graciously accept the constraints of our lives. Taken together, our read of our opportunities with our constraints reflects how we are living out the call to hopeful realism.

One side of the equation is that we fulfill our vocations when we see openings, recognize invitations of the Spirit, step out in new ventures that may involve some risk. There is no growth, no faithfulness to vocation, without moving one step away from that which has been a source of security, confidence and comfort to us—whether it is home and parents, the familiar routines of a job situation or an occupation that provides the false comfort of good salary while not being deeply congruent with the calling of God.

The other side of the equation is just as crucial: that we learn to accept and to live graciously within the constraints that God has placed around us in his invitation to fulfill the divine call on our lives. In fact, courage demands that we attend to constraints. We all have them—the constraints of our family or our social location. For example, we might decline a job opportunity because of a spouse's failing health, or we might be called in this chapter life to be present to a child with a mental disability. Or perhaps we accept the limits of our own health, graciously acknowledging that while there may be an opportunity, the limits of physical strength require us to say, "No, thank you." Perhaps there are constraints placed on us by our social context; perhaps there are even cultural constraints on what we are able to be or do—the constraints of a culture on what a woman can do, for example.

Now consider three essential perspectives on the meaning and significance of constraints. First, a constraint may seem to be something that limits us and thus limits God. But constraints are always opportunities for the grace of God. Thus we naturally respond eagerly to opportunity, but we also learn to accept limits or constraints as ways in which we might be surprised by divine grace. We keep attentive to how God, through the constraints, calls us into deeper dependence on him, knowing that how God works in our lives can be attributed only to divine grace.

We tend to bemoan the limits of funding for a project or perhaps feel the pinch of constraints that come with marriage or children or the health of parents. And yet each is also an opportunity to witness and experience the possibilities of God's grace.

Second, we must also ask, is this constraint real or assumed? Some constraints are quite real: the constraint of time, for example. At other times, we are capable of creating assumed constraints. Consider the account of Elijah in 1 Kings 19. Was Jezebel a true constraint or an assumed constraint? Elijah was inclined to rail against God and insist that he, Elijah, needed to remove her from her throne. And he was frustrated with God because he was alone in the battle. However, God called him not to revolution but to the quiet faithful work of a priest and a prophet. God called him to accept the presence of Jezebel—a constraint, for sure—as the context of his prophetic work.

In another example, Numbers 13 describes the reports of ten scouts who were sent by Moses into the land of Canaan to assess their prospects. These ten spoke of fortresses and giants and not only the difficulty of taking the land but the impossibility. For them, these factors constituted a constraint. But those of us raised in Sunday school know that for Joshua and Caleb this was an opportunity. Their response is a reminder that sometimes we accept a constraint because it is actually easier than embracing an opportunity. Is fear—perhaps fear of failure or the fear of what others will say—the real issue? We need to be careful of using "realism" as a cover for a lack of courage, creativity or commitment to a just cause.

Perhaps here it is also appropriate to speak of the danger of victimization. Many times we feel overcome by the ways we have been wronged by others or limited by them. We feel like victims who are straightjacketed by what others have done or are doing to us. And all too frequently, what dominates our attention is self-pity. Quite possibly we are true victims, and naming that reality is important—to know how we have been wronged and what implications this might have for our emotional, physical, social and spiritual well-being. And yet we cannot allow these wrongs to define us; we cannot overstate the degree to which we are constrained by these wrongs. Rather, in accepting the limits that these have created for us, we must be alert to the possibilities of grace.

Third, when it comes to constraints, we also need to appreciate that God will lead some to respond in one way and others to respond differently. There is no template. One person might quit his or her position at a company to spend extended time caring for aging parents; someone else might choose a different arrangement so that the parents are adequately cared for but without the requirement of a job change. In Cuba, some church leaders live graciously and quietly within the constraints of the government system; some choose to work against that system and view any acquiescence as a compromise of faith and allegiance to God.

Surely part of spiritual maturity is knowing when to accept constraints and when to press against them, when to see opportunities rather than closed doors. When are we called to accept the health needs of a loved one as a constraint? And when are we to insist that our sense of call requires us to make alternate arrangements for them? Perhaps the church needs to equip all of us to effectively discern when we have a true opportunity and when we are called to graciously accept constraints, all the while recognizing that God will not call each of us to respond in the same way to similar circumstances.

And it must be stressed: nothing in these comments should suggest that we be unduly resigned to constraints. We need have no patience with a false sense of limits. The wise woman or man learns to press against these limits—to press beyond what our culture or religious heritage might think appropriate or the way our family system underestimates us or how perceptions of aging lead us to being prematurely sedentary because we perceive ourselves as "old."

The key, of course, is that we be freed from any tendency toward self-pity and while raging against the limits learn when it is time to see the possibilities of grace within those limits. We will all face it at some point, that point when we are aged and our bodies can do little. And those who are aged have the daily potential to witness to the possibilities of God's grace in the midst of significant constraints. They become teachers for all of us to this kind of attentiveness to God's goodness and grace.

Living in time—with time as a gift. One constraint that is truly and surely a constraint is the limit of time. There are only so many hours in a day and days in a week. One sign that we truly do appreciate the possibilities of God's grace within our constraints is that we know how to live in time. As already indicated, our vocations are always located in particular time and place. But it is also important to recognize that time is a gift, not a curse, and that to live in faith and gratitude is to graciously accept the limited hours and days of our lives. We learn to stop complaining about time as though God did not give us enough (if it is a gift, it is not something about which we complain). And we come to accept that hurried, hectic, frenetic or anxious work is a sign of a lack of vocational holiness.

The grace we seek is to live within the time that has been given to us: to accept the limits of a six-day workweek and a twenty-four-hour day. We do not need to be impressed with those who overwork. We get over being impressed by those who pretend to flourish and be superior human beings because they get by on four hours of sleep a night. We accept that every day will hold surprises—a flight is delayed, the dentist is held up because of a nasty problem with the patient just ahead of us in her schedule, our four-year-old has a crisis that requires the immediate presence of a parent—and we learn to wait. We learn to keep enough margin in our day and week to respond to that which cannot be foreseen.

Living within the limits of time means we learn to not overcommit ourselves. If we say we will do something, it means we have the time to do it. We keep our word. Yes, there will be those unforeseen developments that occasionally derail us, but as a rule, friends and colleagues know that we live with a measured approach to life and work and that if we agree to a project or a responsibility, we are not overcommitting ourselves.

And we complete our work in a timely fashion. If we live graciously in time, we are not forever struggling with deadlines, frustrated with the vagaries of life, but are able to do what we are called to do and care for what needs to be done because we accept the limits of the hours in a day. We will certainly have those days that leave us scrambling in the face of unforeseen developments. Of course. But living graciously in time means that the norm of our lives is an ordered pace to our day and our work. Timely work means also that we do not procrastinate; we do today what needs to be done on this day.

Living in time also means that we do not live in the past or become overly concerned about the future. We are present to God's call and grace for today. And we recognize an important principle: God leads us one step at a time. We do not make assumptions about the future; we live in response to God's call on our lives for this day and this chapter without presuming to know the long-term implications of how God is guiding us.

We might wish that God would give us a blueprint, an outline of the coming ten or twenty years, but it is not for us to know these things. We cannot see around the next bend of the road that is the journey of our lives. And so today we might engage in medical studies, with the obvious thought that we would practice medicine. But who knows how this might actually play itself out in our lives? We discern and embrace the calling of God for today, within the limits of time and other constraints of our lives, always with attentiveness to the ways of God in our world and with faithfulness to how God has made us. And we trust God for the future.

Living in time also means that each day we learn to give attention to those things that truly matter to us: if we are artists, we know we have to preserve a certain minimum time each day to be in the studio. If we are writers, we learn to protect the quiet time and space that we need for writing. The nineteenth-century British novelist Anthony Trollope is famous for his rigorous schedule: he produced more than forty novels in his lifetime by writing only in the prebreakfast hour before heading off as an employee of the postal service.

If we are in business, we know that our time is our greatest resource and so we choose carefully how we invest it. All of us learn to turn off the phone so we can attend to something that matters. The phone can too easily be an interruption to our day from someone who is perhaps unwittingly taking time from where our focus needed to be. And we learn to turn away from immediate gratification, be it a computer game or a phone call from a friend—easily justified but which we know, if we are honest with ourselves, will keep us from that which matters to us most. This is all part of attending to our propensities toward procrastination, which is nothing other than failing to live well in time, failing to do what we are called to do today in this fullness of time rather than later perhaps under duress.

FIVE VARIABLES THAT QUALIFY OR CONDITION VOCATION

We discern our vocations at the intersection of three realities: the work of God as Creator and redeemer, our own identity as individuals and a gracious read of our specific circumstances. Alongside these three reference points there are five variables that shape this discernment of vocation.

Embracing the cross of Christ. First, we discern and live out our vocations as those whose lives have been marked by the cross. The cross marks all three of the key reference points. It is the centerpiece of the work and mission of God. It marks our own lives as we take up our cross to follow Christ. And the cross marks our world: we speak of Christ's sufferings, our suffering and the suffering of the world as variables without which we cannot accurately discern our callings.

We speak of the *via negativa* as the way of the cross; it is an identification with Christ, the very one who calls us to a life of radical self-emptying service. We need to find a way to speak of the integrity, worth and self-determination of the human person while also speaking of the call to lay down our lives for the sake of Christ and others. We need to speak of being true to ourselves while at the same time affirming the call to honor others, defer to others, and generously if not sacrificially give of ourselves for the sake of others. This is a dynamic tension for the Christian: we are called to be faithful to ourselves and our own identity and at the same time live the cross of Christ.

We recognize that our work is marred and thus marked by the fall and the presence of sin; work becomes toil. It will not always be happy and easy and successful. And our own identification with the fragmentation of our world will include an embracing of this fragmentation—not as resignation but as an act of identification. Work is participation in the reign of Christ as agents of reconciliation (2 Cor 5). The apostle uses remarkable language to speak of his own identification with the cross: he says that death is at work in him even as life is at work in the lives of his hearers. His work, his vocation, was an act of radical participation in the cross of Christ. And Christ is our example: he gave of himself for the sake of others. The hymn of Philippians 2 is a hymn to the vocation of Christ, and it suggests that vocation for all involves a self-emptying and self-giving for the sake of others.

The perspective of the cross also is a means by which we recognize that life is messy and filled with setbacks and disappointment. Our failures can be an essential element of our vocational development. This is part of the problem with the popular book *The Seven Habits of Highly Effective People*.[5]

On the surface, there is good wisdom here; I appreciate the point about "first things first," for example. But the problem with this overall vision of work is that there is no place for suffering in the "seven habits." There is no place for failure. Success, we are led to believe, is the fruit of good practice, discipline and due diligence, of hard work, well-managed time and radical self-determination. There is no cross.

I am inclined to think this is a book that could have been written by Job's friends. Within the context of contemporary Western society, it implies that we live in a (potentially) ordered world if we can just get our

---

[5]Steven R. Covey, *The Seven Habits of Highly Effective People: Restoring the Character Ethic* (New York: Simon and Schuster, 1989).

act together—if we can just change our habits. It is an instrumental or pragmatic view of the universe. Right technique or habit will, it is assumed, lead to a predictable outcome. In this view of life and work, we are in a sense vindicated by the ordered quality of our lives and the quality of our work.

But a biblical understanding of vocation recognizes the importance of suffering and failure, of the deep ambiguity of much of our lives and our work. I might also add that the historic Christian witness recognizes work that is done in obscurity and quiet, as contrasted with *Seven Habits,* which affirms accomplishments that garner wide praise and affirmation.

In speaking of the cross, we are of course recognizing that our vocation is a means by which we fulfill our baptismal identities as those called in Christ into lives that witness to his reign and his purposes in the world. And nowhere is this more evident than in this: that through baptism we enter into union with Christ in his death and resurrection (Rom 6); this finds expression at least in part through the ways that in our work we bear the cross of Christ.

Work and the wind of God. Even though we stress the importance of mastery of our craft, of being good at what we are called to do, in the end what sustains and animates us is not our capacity. What finally energizes us is not our passion or drive. Rather, the Scriptures clearly testify to this: that our vocation is given to us by God, and the animation to complete that vocation is similarly provided by God.

Yes, we can speak of the importance of self-mastery and self-discipline, but these must be located within the powerful interdependence to which we are called within community (my next point) and the radical dependence on God, specifically the Spirit of God, as the source of life and calling.

We are anointed and set apart for service by the Spirit (2 Tim 1:6-7). We are not self-empowered but animated by the "wind" of God. We are driving not a powerful motorboat where we have control of the motor, but rather we are riding the waves in a sailboat, subject to the winds and moving ahead only when we learn how to read and respond to the wind (of God). The genius of a Spirit-directed and empowered life is the existential realization that our lives are infused with and dependent on the grace of God.

Too easily do we get caught in the trap of justifying ourselves by our work. It is a constant temptation: to vindicate ourselves through either the quality or the amount of our work, to prove ourselves to ourselves, to another (perhaps a parent) and ultimately to God. But we are justified in Christ, specifically in the cross of Christ, and our work is not an act of vindication but of resting in power of another, namely the Holy Spirit. And it must be stressed: to lean into the Spirit, into the wind of God, requires that we learn how to appropriate this grace, and this necessarily means that we learn what it means to participate in the means of grace (which I will speak to more fully in appendix A).

Living in community. A third variable that intersects the ways we discern vocation and live out our calling is this: that vocational holiness reflects our lives in community, in an intentional intersection of our lives with the lives of and the work of others. We do not navigate this road alone.

There are a number of ways in which community is a variable in the reference points of vocational holiness. First, we remember that God has created us to live in community and that his mission cannot be appreciated except through recognition of the vital role the church plays as a witness to the reign of Christ.

Second, we cannot know ourselves except as those who live in community. Yes, we see ourselves in truth when we meet and know Christ (which I will stress below), but we also know ourselves only through the interplay of our common lives. The language of "take a sober look at yourself," as found in Romans 12:3, can be appreciated only in the context of the observation that follows in Romans 12:4—that we are members of a body, and no one person is all things to all people. This does not mean community determines or imposes its corporate will on us; it is rather that our self-knowledge emerges as we see ourselves as those who live in the interdependence of community. Our vocations are negotiated in community: we know ourselves through our interplay with the strengths and callings of others.

Third, vocation is always about others. Our calling comes from God, but it is always for the sake of others: others for whom we care, for whom we work. We are called to love our neighbor as ourselves. While we are not ultimately beholden to others since we do our work for Christ, nevertheless all vocations—literally all—are an act of service for another.

Fourth, we do our work with others. No one fulfills vocation alone—no exceptions. For all, vocation is fulfilled in deep interdependence on others. And thus one of the key elements of our vocational development is the fostering of our capacity to work with others.

And finally, we need one another. We will not be able to fulfill our callings without the encouragement, support, teaching, mentoring and blessing of others. We cannot discern vocation alone; we are too prone to self-deception. We need others in our lives who believe in us, know how to listen to us, love us without flattery and provide essential feedback on our vocational musings and encouragement when it is time to act. But more, we need others not only for our discernment processes but to support us as we seek to fulfill that calling. We need the grace that comes to us through others. We need the companionship of the other to both discern and fulfill our vocation.

As implied, though, we need to note that while the community is essential and invaluable to the discerning and embracing of our vocation, it is also likely a major threat—we too easily get caught up in fulfilling the expectations of others rather than living true to our calling and to our God. And thus while community is a variable in our discernment process, it is not the defining factor in vocation: for this, as we will see below, we must speak of the voice of Jesus.

But the main point here is that there is always a communal character to Christian vocation. We each come to our calling through the help of those who walk along side us. Thus in discerning call, the focus on the self is not a sign of either narcissism or egocentrism. We do need to take a "sober look" at ourselves. Rather, the danger is isolation—isolation from the community of faith and from the communal dimensions of life that are integral to our identity and our capacity for good work. My emphasis in this chapter on the particularity of the human person must not lead to any conception of the human person as one who can be known in isolation from others.

The justice of God. Any reading of the Old Testament prophets makes it abundantly clear that there is a fourth variable: the mission of

God and thus the purposes of God in the world are inexorably linked to the justice of God. Righteousness and justice are virtually synonymous for Isaiah, Amos and Micah, and by justice we necessarily mean economic justice.

This suggests that a deep commitment to justice—by which we mean justice for all—demarcates all good work. We all are called to do our work with an attentiveness to the poor, the marginalized (those without advocacy or access to the levers of power) and the vulnerable. We do not through our work enrich ourselves at the expense of others (see Is 58). Rather, we recognize that advocacy for the cause and needs of others, particularly the poor, needs to be inherent in each vocation—whether business, art, education or preaching. It involves seeing our world and thus our work through the lens of God's commitment, as evident in the oracles of the prophets, to justice.

The stages and phases of an adult life. A fifth variable that demands our attention arises when we listen to the wisdom of adult developmental theorists—I am thinking of key voices like that of James Fowler and Erick Erickson.[6] Their observations about the character of an adult life are a reminder that we engage our work in a way that is consistent with our life stage. We discern vocation differently as young adults, as middle-aged adults and as we move into our senior years. And vocational integrity or holiness requires that we be attentive to the rhythms of an adult life. Briefly summarizing this wisdom, we note the following.

For young adults, perhaps the most crucial question is the matter of differentiation—will they find their own identity before God in response to his call? Will they have the strength and blessing to "leave father and mother" and embrace an adult responsibility for their own life? Our twenties and thirties are typically those years when we "find ourselves"—fostering an awareness of our deep necessity, to use the phrase introduced earlier in this chapter—and come to understand our strengths and limitations. But crucial in this is that we find some separation from our parents or our parental figures; we are no longer children but adults, taking adult responsibility for our lives. And for the Christian this also

---

[6]Fowler, *Becoming Adult.*

means we affirm that our primary allegiance and loyalty is to the God who calls us to do good work.

For those in midlife—in most people's experience, the forties and fifties, though it will of course vary within cultures and as influenced by other factors—the issue at hand is twofold. First, will we embrace our deep necessity, recognizing what it is that truly matters to us and learning to live out of this heartfelt passion? Will we have the courage to do that which we are being called to do? And, second, will we eagerly embrace and live out of our strengths and graciously accept our limits? This may not be an easy chapter of our lives—the mid-adult years can be traumatic as we face our limits and thus feel our mortality—but they can also be profoundly rich years as we live out our lives in a way that is congruent with our deep identities.

Our senior years bring new limits but also new opportunities. We face the limits of physical and emotional vitality, but this comes with opportunity to be a source of wisdom and blessing for the next generation, to find ways to bless those who will succeed us as leaders within the church and society. As many have noted, moving into our eldership— our sixties and seventies and perhaps into our early eighties—means we learn to let go of formal structures of power and office and do our work at a different pace. It means we learn to do more by doing less, for with less energy and within the limits of our bodies we may be forced to discern what truly matters most to us. But in letting go of formal roles, we have greater influence as those who learn how to bless a younger generation and be present as a voice of wisdom and counsel when this is invited and called for.

I speak of three transitions: into our young adult years and then into midlife and then into our senior years. But is there perhaps a fourth—a move from our senior years to our senior-senior years, when we are truly aged? Most people in their seventies and many into their eighties are not aged, really; they are healthy, relatively strong and often very engaged. But then there is a chapter of life when we are hardly mobile, feeling keenly the limits of our bodies, our mortality, and the fact that death is near.

These are years of relinquishment. And yet as Paul Wadell notes, they are still and indeed must be years of vocation, of responding to the calling of God.[7] Deep within our cultural and religious psyches is the assumption that the older we get the less we are oriented toward vocation. We are, thankfully, beginning to recover a sense that our senior years are for vocation as much as any other chapter of our lives. The goal for the Christian is not a work-free retirement when all we need to do is play golf. And Wadell's observations take this a step further. He notes that the Christian vision of vocation suggests that we are always under the call of God. The inevitable limits of our older years will no doubt alter the contours of our work and our engagement in the world. And yet even with powerful limits—including decreasing strength, limited mobility or a loss of hearing or sight—a sense of vocation is not necessarily diminished. It just finds different expression. This expression is constrained, of course, but no less significant in the eyes of God.

Learning to accept our limits earlier in life is all part of anticipating and preparing us to accept the inevitable limits that will come as we get older. All along we learn to embrace the call of God within the actual limits of our lives. Graciously.

One more point here. One of the crucial signs of vocational integrity and maturity is the capacity to *leave* well when it is the time to leave. Life is full of departures and leavings—whether it is leaving home as a young adult, leaving a job position when one is either released or chooses to move on to a new assignment, or when it comes time to retire, whether we want to retire or not. Either way, we learn along the way to leave well: to move on without acrimony or a need to control our legacy. We leave and let go. We bless those who follow us. This is not easy. I have often

---

[7]Paul Wadell, in "The Call Goes On," *Christian Century* 128, no. 8 (2011), states, "The language of vocation confirms that at no time in our lives are we exempt from responsibility for others. Our children may be raised and we may have retired from our jobs long ago, but we never stop being called to share in the creative and redemptive activity of God through lives of thoughtful and faithful discipleship. As we grow older, a common temptation is to narrow our circle of concern, to be more selective in the neighbors we choose to love and perhaps, in our insecurity and fear, to be more mindful of our needs than we ought. But to see aging through the lens of vocation reminds us that the elderly, even as their physical and mental abilities diminish and their energy lags, are still called to imitate Christ by the witness of their lives. Calling rescues us from being mere victims to the losses, sorrows and occasionally painful humiliations of aging by alerting us to all the ways we are still, in religion professor Douglas Schuurman's wonderful phrase, 'providentially situated' to do good."

been struck by how, when we leave an organization thinking our gap will be hard to fill, in retrospect it feels like a finger pulled out of the water. The gap fills in quickly. And yet this is as it should be. We are not indispensable, and the organization needs to move on and engage the future without us. Our holiness is expressed at least in part in our acceptance of these changes and in our capacity for a gracious leave-taking.

We will not manage this gracious leave-taking unless we are at peace with the fact that we are not our roles. We take up a role as a means by which our vocation is expressed. But we do not own the role; we are not ultimately defined by the role. We take it up and we let it go in due time. We make a deliberate effort to distinguish our self from the role—not as a way to minimize its significance but as a means by which we take it seriously insofar as we actually have it. We are not first a mother so that we relate to our children only as their mother. We are not first a pastor so that in every context we expect to be received as a religious leader. We are not first a president of a company. For in time we will let it go, with all the trappings of the office, and move into a pattern of life where the power and prestige of the office are gone but where we ourselves are not diminished.

The Contemplative in Action

All this might seem quite impossible. How do we see the work of God in the world—comprehend it, take it in in all its scope? And then how do we truly see and understand ourselves? We are prone to self-deception, to self-illusions, to either thinking too highly of ourselves or discounting ourselves. How can we see ourselves truly and have the grace to accept who we are, to not wish we were anyone other than who we are? As the cross of Christ intersects our life, how can we recognize it? And when Christ is truly inviting us to bear his cross, how, oh Lord, can we learn to bear it graciously?

How can we come to a gracious acceptance of our circumstances and to see the possibilities of grace within the situation into which we are called? How can we discern when a constraint truly is a constraint and when we are just assuming it to be so? How can we learn to live in radical dependence on the Spirit and in interdependence on the community of fellow believers? And yet, while in community, how can we learn to be truly attentive to the ways the community might distract us from the call of God? When it is time for us to make a transition, how can we have the grace to discern this and then graciously move to our leave-taking?

The weight of our spiritual heritage and tradition suggests that the only way forward is to embrace a distinct appreciation of how our work, our vocation, is the sphere of our formation and transformation in Christ. But more, discernment will come as we learn to attend to the voice of Jesus—the defining element of our lives and thus of our vocations—in the midst of the emotional turmoil of our hearts, the multiple demands around us and our own longings and aspirations.[8]

Vocation and transformation; joy in the world. First, it is important to highlight how the Scriptures affirm that our work is a sphere of God's transforming work in our lives. Indeed, service is not merely our duty; it is a vital way by which we identify with Christ and his cross. And thus we can even speak of work—our engagement with our world—as a means of grace. We grow in faith, hope and love not merely so that we can be faithful in our work; our work is a very means by which that growth in faith, hope and love will happen.

This requires then that we be attentive: where is God in our world? How is the Spirit present and active in the circumstances of our lives and the work to which we are called? What dimensions of our vocation are God's present means of cultivating within us greater faith, growth in love and a deepening of our hope? God is not just present in the prayer chapel; we do not view the world as a godless space with no redeeming value. To the contrary, God goes before us and the Spirit is present and active in our world. Wise Christians, then, learn to be attentive to the

---

[8]To speak to this, I find it immensely helpful to draw on the theological and spiritual tradition that has most effectively responded to this range of questions. We will find wisdom in many, many places, of course, and we must be attentive to the witness of the Spirit through the Scriptures. But if there is one such stream of Christian thought and practice that has given particular attention to these matters, it is that of Ignatius Loyola, the founder of the Society of Jesus. The comments that follow arise directly from the wisdom of the Ignatian spiritual heritage or they reflect the ways of thinking about vocation, work and career that tend to arise in conversations between those of us that have been formed by this tradition. And yet I offer these comments in conversation with the perspective of John Wesley.

Spirit not merely in their own hearts and in the life and worship of the church, but also in the world—specifically the world into which they are called to exercise their calling in faithful work.

Two things stand out here. First, our work is an identification with the work of Christ. It is the completion or expression of our baptismal identity. I will be stressing this further when I speak of rites of Christian initiation: that our baptism is a grace in which we appropriate the forgiveness of God. But more, it is also a grace wherein we identify radically (to the root) with the mission and purposes of God in the world, resolving to align our lives, meaning our sense of call, with Christ.

And second, this also means that it behooves us to live with joy in the world, even in the midst of fragmentation and perhaps deep suffering. We learn to live the grace that marked the apostle Paul's life when he was able to say to the Corinthian believers, "I am filled with consolation; I am overjoyed in all our affliction" (2 Cor 7:4). Or, as it is found in another translation, "In all of our troubles, our joy knows no bounds" (TNIV).

Consider the following: When our lives in the world are oriented about the reign of Christ and the ultimate triumph of goodness and justice, we see and feel the world differently. We still see the fragmentation, and we still feel the pain of a dislocated universe. And yet the emotional contours of our lives and our hearts are not ultimately shaped by these circumstances but rather our confidence that this fragmentation is only for a season. This too will pass. The consequence of this confidence is the capacity to live and work with joy even when so much is wrong, even when that wrong intersects our lives. And the transforming value of our work as a sphere of God's grace requires a deep confidence that, in the recurring words of St Julian of Norwich, "all shall be well, and all shall be well, and all manner of things shall be well."

Vocation and the contemplative vision. And now, to the heart of the matter: we come to that which more than anything else defines us and our work; we come to the source from which our vocation arises and the grace by which our calling is sustained. We come to Christ. Jesus stresses to his disciples, "Those who abide in me and I in them bear much fruit, because apart from me you can do nothing" (Jn 15:5).

Vocation flows from union with Christ; it is an integral dimension of living in Christ, abiding in Christ and identifying with Christ. And our only hope for navigating the complex world of vocation, work and career is to have a prior commitment to and practice of dynamic communion with Christ. I speak not of a commitment to live from the idea of Christ—not a Christology, not a conviction about Christ or about the truth or about right and wrong. It is not truth or even truth about Christ that compels us; it is Christ's very self.

This is demonstrated clearly in the experience of the early church. In Matthew 28, the first disciples receive the commission to make disciples of all nations. And yet what must not be missed is that this commission flows from their worship. They first meet Christ on the mountain and they worship him. Or take the example of John 21, where Peter hears those words: feed my sheep. Here too his call, his vocation, flows from his intimate and dynamic encounter with Christ at breakfast on the shore of the Galilean Sea. And we cannot explain the vocation of the apostle Paul—the heart of his work and ministry, his remarkable passion and energy—without appreciating the contemplative vision of which he speaks in 2 Corinthians 3:18—the vision of Christ's glory, of Christ's very self, that sustains him in ministry.

What our theological and spiritual heritage in the church commends to us, then, is this simple principle: that mission flows from worship just as much as mission leads to worship. In the vocation and work of the individual Christian the same principle applies: our work in the world flows from our communion with Christ in our personal prayers even as our work leads us to prayer. We learn to live from the rhythm of prayer and work, with each informing and sustaining the other. We worship and pray as those who are faithful in our work, and we work as those who are faithful in worship and prayer.

Our worship and our prayer are not escapist; we pray as those who are eagerly engaged in our world. And then, conversely and oh-so-critically, we are in the world as women and men of worship and prayer. With the apostle Paul, through prayer and worship we seek to know Christ and grow in our love for him that we might with joy and generosity serve Christ in the church and in the world.

Our capacity to be in the world but not of the world and to see the world from the perspective of the risen and ascended Christ requires—we must insist on this—some distance: to step aside in retreat and worship so we see Christ and thus our world more clearly. The contemplative vision, in worship with the community of faith or in personal prayer, is not ultimately about disengagement but about informed engagement. The contemplative sees the things of this world more clearly and with greater discernment. It is those caught up in the hectic pace, who lose themselves in their obsession with more and more work, who are confused and bewildered by what they are facing. We cannot hope that all ambiguity will be erased; it is only that greater clarity about our lives, our situation and our calling necessarily arises when we learn to pray—to step aside for worship, communion and encounter with the risen and ascended Christ.

Practices of engagement. Thus our prayers are the most fundamental practice of the spiritual life. And yet we must speak of other practices—spiritual disciplines—that foster an awareness of God's work in the world, an identification with the cross of Christ and a dependence on the animating grace of the Spirit.

There are certain practices that foster our engagement with the world. The prayer of Jesus recorded in John 17 speaks of how his disciples are specifically called to be in the world, even if they are not "of the world." Here, then, are the spiritual disciplines of engagement—each of them a classic means by which the faith community has responded in Christ to our world.

First, our lives in the world should be marked by the intentional practice of hospitality. Regardless of our vocation, hospitality is a mark of Christian presence in the world. I will be speaking more about hospitality in an upcoming chapter, but here I simply suggest that it is integral to vocational holiness.

Second, our lives in the world and our identification with the mission of God will also be evident in the practice of what John Wesley aptly called "works of mercy." This perspective is certainly not limited to the Wesleyan or Methodist Christian vision, of course; it is basic to the witness of the Scriptures. We are called to feed the hungry, clothe the naked, shelter the homeless and visit those who are sick and in prison. Regardless of our vocation, God would never give us so much to do that our lives could exclude works of mercy. And these works of mercy are, in the Wesleyan ideal, a means of grace to us, not merely to those we serve. They are grace to us because they are practices by which we are aligned with the heart of God for the world.

Third, it is clear from the Scriptures that generous giving—specifically in our finances—is a key marker of our identity as Christians and the work to which we are called. We do not work for the accumulation of wealth; we work to meet our basic needs, but as God provides for our needs, a key means by which we identify with his work in the world is through financial generosity.

And fourth, we are called to intercessory prayer. Regardless of the character of our vocation, we are called to intercede for others—as often as not, we keep in our prayers those with whom we live and work. Prayer for others is a key means by which the church is called to serve the community and the world. The prayers of the people in Sunday morning worship are an essential means by which we feel the link between our worship and our world. We also serve through our intercessory prayer. For the individual Christian, prayer is a vital and typically quiet means by which we enter into the work of God for his world—praying for those with whom we live and work, praying for our customers and suppliers if we are in business, our parishioners if we are in pastoral ministry, our students if we are teachers—without fanfare, without continually announcing that we are "praying for you," but in quiet.

The practice of disengagement. Finally, when we speak of the spiritual contours of our work and consider it in the light of John 17—the implied call that we are to be in but not of the world—we must stress that sabbath observance is crucial to vocational integrity and holiness. This is one of the central commandments of our Judeo-Christian heritage; the witness of the Scriptures suggests that rest is part of the rhythm of God's creation and thus of God's work. And as we participate in the work of God in the world, it makes sense that we learn to disengage and intentionally practice, one day in seven, a sabbath rest.

This is a practice that limits our work; it is a practice in which we affirm that God is God and that our work does not ultimately define us or validate us. It keeps us from idolizing our work or from being consumed by it. We learn to rest.

And in our rest, our work is put in perspective: it belongs to God. We are but stewards of our lives, and the quiet of sabbath disengagement confirms the parameters of good work. It is essential to our lives and our work: the fact that sabbath observance is included in the Ten Commandments suggests as much, and Isaiah 58 and other texts profile just how essential it is to the character of good work. I will speak more of sabbath in chapter six, where we will consider the interplay between joy and sabbath rest.

5

LEARNING TO LOVE

An Invitation to Social Holiness

*How very good and pleasant it is
when kindred live together in unity!
It is like the precious oil on the head,
running down upon the beard,
on the beard of Aaron,
running down over the collar of his robes.
It is like the dew of Hermon,
which falls on the mountains of Zion.
For there the LORD ordained his blessing,
life forevermore.*

PSALM 133

IT IS NEVER A STRETCH TO SPEAK OF HOLINESS and love in the same breath. The Scriptures could not be more clear: we are called to love God and neighbor; this is the human vocation. Jesus, when asked about the "greatest commandment," responds with the call to love God and to love the neighbor as one's self (Mt 22:37-40). Then at the conclusion of his earthly ministry, in the discourse in the upper room, he insists that if his disciples are to remain in him and in his love, they must love one another (Jn 15:17). When it comes to the apostle Paul, almost a quarter of his magisterial letter to the Romans is essentially an extended exposition of the call to love one another—beginning with Romans 12:9 through the end of Romans 15, if not actually through to the end of the letter.

Thus we cannot speak of transformation into the image of Christ without embracing the call to love one another. To be mature in Christ is to be a person who loves the neighbor, the other. A Christian community is marked by worship, learning and witness, and all of these actions are tied up in the fellowship of the Spirit, which is the fellowship of mutual love. To be the church is to be a community of the mutual giving and receiving of Christian love. Indeed, we know from 1 Corinthians 13 that without love, our learning, our worship and our witness to the world are all vacuous.

As Christians and as Christian communities, we eagerly seek the way of truth so that we are marked by wisdom and understanding. But the pursuit of wisdom, learning and understanding has meaning only if it is governed by the law of love. When the pursuit of truth is not marked by and infused with love, compassion and mercy, it lacks the essential generosity that makes it a Christian practice.

Furthermore, the church as a whole and we as individuals are called to do good work. It is not an overstatement to say that all our service, or work—the work to which we are called, individually and collectively— is but a set of tasks and responsibilities given us so we might fulfill the law of love: to love God and to love our neighbor.

COMMUNITY AND HUMAN IDENTITY

The call to love one another can only be appreciated against the backdrop of the social nature of human experience. No one is an island; we cannot speak of life without reference to the profound interconnectedness each person has to each other person.

God is not a solitary being; rather, the divine being is a union of three persons bound together by the mutuality of love. In like fashion we affirm and celebrate that the human person is not a spiritual monad but a being designed to live in interdependence and communion with others. Adam was created in the image of God to be in communion with God, but Adam was not created a solitary or isolated being. Genesis 1 celebrates the deep goodness of the created order, as is evident from the recurring line "and God saw that it was good."

But then we have one of the most extraordinary declarations in all of Scripture when God says of Adam that it is not good for him to be alone. This speaks of Adam's need for the other as well as his responsibility for the other. With Adam, we need one another for comfort, encouragement, strength and the meeting of our basic needs, and in like manner we are called to be that to others—comfort, encouragement and strength and the very means by which their needs are met. We can rightly speak, then, of our profound interdependence with other human persons.

One of our deepest human longings is to be in communion with God, whose love is revealed to us and embodied in Christ, who in turn loves each of us to the very core of our being. This is matched by our profound yearning to love and be loved, to live in mutual love with our neighbor, which is actually a reflection of God's love for us. Thus our first calling is to dwell in the love of God. I will conclude these reflections below by stressing this very point and some of the implications of this connection. But first I will attempt to address this topic comprehensively and draw on the wisdom of our spiritual fathers and mothers. Second, I will give some content to the call to love one another, asking specifically what it means and how we can learn to do it.

All of this will be based on the simple assumption that we are designed to live in mutuality with others, a mutuality governed by, informed by and infused with love. In many respects, the genius of community is precisely this capacity for mutuality. From this perspective, the effects of sin are evident in the severing of interdependence—sin is alienation from others, thus the salvation of God must include restoration of this interdependence. And the church is the embodiment of this hope—a living entity that illustrates mutuality and interdependence made possible by love. This interdependence is both an expression of God's salvation and a means by which the church witnesses to this salvation.

Before I speak about the nature of love, I perhaps need to add an additional comment about the nature of community. We need to speak of both the importance and the limits of community, and in speaking of the limits of community we must speak of the dangers of community. The biblical vision is for the individual to thrive in community and in mutual interdependence. This suggests that we need to be alert to the potential for the community to overwhelm the individual, to rob the individual of life and authentic individuality. The Christian vision is for diversity in unity and diversity with interdependence. The constant danger is that the community would squelch the vitality and power of the individual rather than equipping and empowering the individual to thrive within the community.

Different words might be used to describe this phenomenon, including the word *tribalism*, which has recently been used to refer to the potential for the community to oppress the individual. True community is threatened by communalism (or tribalism) as much as it is threatened by individualism. True community is not about control or compliance; it is about interdependence that includes the capacity for each one to both offer and receive love.

LOVE AND THE LAW

In speaking of love one of the ongoing challenges we face is that the language of love has been coopted within our social context by two trends or propensities: the sentimental and the erotic. Much of the language of love within our social context makes one or both of these mistakes. And this is likely most evident with the rather strange social practice known as Valentine's Day.

Love is too easily spoken of as nice feelings that one might have for another, such as someone we think of as affectionate, nice and even sweet, a delightful personality that we enjoy being around because he or she makes us feel good. What is too often lacking is an appreciation of the deep substance of love: both its close relationship with the law and how it is fundamentally a matter of service. The Old Testament prophets, Jesus and the apostle Paul were all living witnesses to what it means to love, and they assuredly were not always nice or sweet or affectionate. Similarly, our social context consistently confuses love with sex; love is eroticized, reduced to physical passion and sensuality.

There is some truth in both associations, of course. Affection matters, and kindness is an essential dimension of what it means to love another. Furthermore, there is also no doubt that sex is designed by God to be located within the loving union of husband and wife, whose relationship is nurtured by what is appropriately called "lovemaking," such that, ideally, children are the fruit of this union of love.

And yet both the sentimental and the erotic can easily distract us from an appreciation of the true nature of love and the fundamental marks of a relationship that is governed by love. What we urgently need is to see that both the sentimental and the erotic are given substance, grounding, depth and strength when they are governed by what we might call the law of love, which is, of course, the law. We teach love by teaching the law.

The apostle Paul speaks to the close affinity between the law and love in Romans 13 when he observes that the one who loves fulfills the law. In speaking of the interrelationship between the law and love, he identifies four of the Ten Commandments, likely by way of illustration in that he immediately adds, "and any other commandment." What he reveals to his readers is that the law is the content of this love for our neighbor. Love is marked by justice and truth. Love means faithfulness in marriage. Love means not only that one does not murder but also that one does no wrong, that one does not intend any evil against the other (Rom 13:10). It means that we honor the possessions of the other and do not covet or delight in the misfortune of the other. The point is clear: the law is deeply relevant to those who seek to fulfill Christ's call to love their neighbor, for it provides the content and substance of—the parameters and guidelines for—the fulfillment of this call on the life of the Christian.

All of this finds expression in the immediate relationships of our lives—for me personally, in the call to love my wife, my children and my grandchildren and then also to love my parents and siblings. And it guides my relationships with colleagues and members of the community where I live. Also, during the course of the day it shapes the way I do business in my buying and selling and the way I navigate traffic in my car or the way I use the public transport system to get to and from work.

But the neighbor is not merely the one who is seen. Loving my neighbor includes all of those who are in any way affected by my life, by my actions and reactions. Surely my voting in a federal election is shaped by my call to love all of those who live in my country. And surely the call to love means I have a direct concern for justice not only for myself and my family and my clan but for all. The call to love for the Croat transforms how he thinks about the Serb; the Israeli Christian is actively concerned for the Palestinian. In the language of the apostle Paul, this is our continuing debt to one another (Rom 13:8). It is never fully paid. It is our continual and constant posture toward the other.

And it is not easy. It is not easy. The deep challenge that we all face—and I stress all, for the call to love comes easily to no one—is that our hearts are bent on independence, self-sufficiency and autonomy. No one is naturally "loving." For no one can it be said that they have a personality type that is more inclined toward or more capable of genuine love. For all of us this is a learned practice; indeed, Rowan Williams suggests that if we are going to get beyond just being nice, beyond sentimentality, it will only be as we realize that "love is something painfully learned."[1]

Not only does love not come easily, it is learned not before we enter into relationships but in the furnace of the joys and sorrows, challenges and limitations that come in our multiple and complex interactions. We learn it not in the classroom but in the encounters with others that fill our lives each day.

Family is for most of us the first space and place where we learn how to live with others. The faith community, the church, is also a venue where we learn love. And we learn love in the context of the market-place—our spaces and places of work.

But the heart of the matter when it comes to the call to love is recognizing that nothing so threatens our mutual love, the awareness of our interdependence, as our propensity to view the world as something that revolves around us. For the child, this self-centeredness is cute and not entirely inappropriate; the child is incapable of seeing the world and his

---

[1] Rowan Williams, *Dostoevsky: Language, Faith and Fiction* (Waco, TX: Baylor University Press, 2008). Williams observes that we can love those who are different or difficult only when we appreciate that each one deserves to be loved. And this is only possible, he suggests, if we "embark on a process of decentering the self (a better phrase than 'emptying' or 'denying' the self)," p. 183.

or her own needs except as all-encompassing. But growing up means appreciating that we are not the center of the universe and that the universe is not at our beck and call. The ego-centered person is essentially the child who has grown up but never come to an understanding of a fundamental feature of life: that we live in deep interdependence, that we need one another even though none of us is indispensable, that we cannot live with a feeling of entitlement and that we have been created to love others and serve others. This is captured wonderfully by the words of the apostle Paul in Philippians 2:3-4, where in speaking of the call to love, he urges his readers, "Do nothing from selfish ambition or conceit, but in humility regard others as better than yourselves. Let each of you look not to your own interests, but to the interests of others."

Paul does not discount or deny the legitimacy of our own needs or "interests"; it is merely that our needs and interests now must be considered in light of the needs and interests of others. We typically speak of the need for "self-denial" as the key to love, and in some respects this way of speaking is helpful. But the interplay between our interests and the interests of others that Paul profiles in this text suggests that there is no absolute denial of the self and our own interests. The issue at heart is to see ourselves in context, to see that we are not the center. Thus we come to a full appreciation of the call to love one another only when we know the grace of what Rowan Williams calls the de-centered self.[2]

The call to love, then, alters everything. It means we treat the other on their own terms rather than how they make us feel or how they meet our needs. Too often we "love" others so that they will love us in return, so that they will meet our needs. We do have real needs; we do need to be loved. But the paradox of the Christian call to love is that we know the love of God and the love of others by giving freely of ourselves rather than by using or controlling others, by demanding their affection or love.

THE WISDOM OF THE CHRISTIAN SPIRITUAL HERITAGE

The call to love is a recurring theme in the history of the church. By way of illustration, I highlight three voices or perspectives.

---

[2]Ibid.

The church fathers. First, going all the way back to the early church and the perspective of the church fathers, I will summarize the insights into the teachings of the church fathers and mothers by Roberta C. Bondi in her book *To Love as God Loves.*[3] Bondi makes the following observations:

> First, for the early desert spiritual writers the call to perfection, to completion or maturity in Christ, is intimately linked to love commandment. St. Anthony and others heard the call of Christ "sell your possessions, and give the money to the poor . . . then come, follow me" (Mt 19:21) and took this call not only seriously but literally. They pursued perfection, the way of salvation, resolved that nothing, least of all their possessions, would stand in the way. But what marks this "perfection" is the awareness that to be perfect is to love; the call to perfection is intimately linked with the parallel command: to love the Lord your God and your neighbor as yourself. In other words, for Anthony and the other early church writers, perfection is the love of God and neighbor; love for God and neighbor is the goal of the Christian life. Thus love of others is to be pursued at all costs.

The church fathers also insist on the close connection between love and humility. There are two aspects of humility pertinent in this discussion. First, humility is a disposition of heart that affirms that one is not the center of the universe; it is the antithesis of self-centeredness. Second, humility is the posture of complete dependence on God for the grace to live the Christian life. Humility is the antithesis of self-dependence. But also, humility is the vision of heart that recognizes that we are all on the way, all in need of divine grace, such that no one has any right to judge or condemn the other. It is humility that enables us to love rather than judge our neighbor.

Finally, early church writers affirm something that will be a recurring theme in the history of the church: the close connection between spiritual maturity, humility and, to use the ancient phrase, the ordering of the affections. The greatest threat to our capacity to love, whether to love God or to love the other, is our misguided desires, longings and aspirations. Desire is not wrong! Passion is not wrong. Rather, our affections,

---

[3]Roberta C. Bondi, *To Love as God Loves: Conversations with the Early Church* (Philadelphia: Fortress, 1987). Bondi draws on biblical wisdom and the experience of the early church to lay out practical guidelines for growing in Christian love.

our deep desires and longings, are misdirected, disoriented and not rooted in the good, the noble, the excellent and worthy of praise (Phil 4:8). And when our affections or passions are disordered, we are blinded; we are not free. Freedom, including the freedom to love the other, can come only with the ordering of the affections

John Wesley. Consider also the perspective of the great eighteenth-century evangelist and teacher John Wesley. It is Wesley who introduced the language of "social holiness" into our theological lexicon, affirming that "Christianity is essentially a social religion" and that thus there is "no holiness without social holiness."[4] Like the early church fathers, Wesley preached perfection: the call of each Christian to grow in grace and in response to the call of God, the work of Christ and the empowerment of the Spirit. For Wesley, this call to maturity or perfection, this doctrine of sanctification, could all be summed up in one word: love.

First then, for Wesley, perfection in Christ is perfection in love, and by this Wesley means not merely actions that reflect love but love as a way of being—first the love of God and, with it, the love of one's neighbor.

Second, Wesley speaks of the link between faith and love. Faith is crucial to the Christian life as the foundation or wellspring from which the Christian lives; faith is oriented toward Christ and the work of Christ. The fruit of this faith is love; faith is a means and love is the end. Thus for Wesley we grow in love and in our capacity to love as we live in deep dependence on the grace of God, appropriated through the means of grace. This too speaks of our deep dependence on God and that our love for others is derivative of our conscious awareness of God's love for us. Our love for others is the fruit of God's love spread abroad in our hearts by the Spirit (Rom 5:5).

And third, Wesley's teaching on love is intimately linked to his understanding of the law; he highlights the points from Romans 13: that the law of God is fulfilled in love. You get the clear sense in reading Wesley that the law of God—specifically, for example, the Ten Commandments—is an essential guide to the Christian life, and yet what governs

---

[4]In his preface to his shared publication hymns and poems with his brother, Charles Wesley. See J. Ernest Rattenbury, *The Eucharistic Hymns of John and Charles Wesley* (London: Epworth Press, 1948).

our thinking and our way of being is the law of love. It is not the law so much as love, which is the fulfillment of the law, that infuses and informs our lives.

Dietrich Bonhoeffer. A more contemporary voice on this subject is that of German theologian Dietrich Bonhoeffer. His insights on this topic are found throughout his writings but most notably in his exposition of the Sermon on the Mount and his extraordinary reflections on Christian community in the book *Life Together*.[5]

First, Bonhoeffer's observations on love make sense only in the context of his teaching on Christian community. In this regard one is struck by how, for Bonhoeffer, the greatest of God's gifts to us are found in the other, the one with whom we are privileged to be in community, whether it is in the faith community, the congregation, the home or in personal friendship. The other is gift, nothing but gift, and we enter into our common life together not as demanders who complain but as those who are grateful recipients.

Second, in *Life Together* Bonhoeffer distinguishes between what he calls "self-centered love," which is love for the other but for one's own sake, and love that is for the sake of Christ and for the sake of the other. The first is an oppressive love. It loves the other not as a free person but to win, conquer and control; it loves only for the love one hopes to get in return. But genuine love for the other, what he calls "spiritual love," has Christ Jesus as primary reference; we love the other "in Christ." Spiritual love desires to serve; spiritual love can and will love the enemy; spiritual love is liberating rather than controlling—all because it is offered out of one's identity in Christ.[6]

And third, for Bonhoeffer the love we have for the other is expressed concretely in specific practices that flow from our common commitment to Christ. I will be speaking of these practices below, with observations that are highly dependent on how Bonhoeffer speaks of the call to listen to one another, to bear one another and to serve one another.

---

[5]Dietrich Bonhoeffer, *The Cost of Discipleship*, rev. ed., trans. R. H. Fuller (New York: MacMillan, 1963); and Dietrich Bonhoeffer, *Life Together and Prayerbook of the Bible*, Dietrich Bonhoeffer Works vol. 5, trans. Daniel W. Bloesh and James H. Burtness (Minneapolis: Fortress Press, 1996).

[6]Bonhoeffer, *Life Together and Prayerbook of the Bible*, pp. 42-44.

What It Means to Love: It's Not (Just) About Being Nice

Now we come to the heart of the matter: what does it mean to love one another? What is the specific content of this love, this way of being toward our neighbor?

On this matter we need clarity. We need to speak about love in ways that transcend mere sentimentality and civility; we need to distill the teaching of the New Testament in a way that helps us speak simply and clearly about how the call to love can inform our relationships. We need a guide to love that has substance and content, that is practical and realistic, that inspires us toward a robust approach to love within Christian community. It is not enough to exhort our children to be nice to other children—or urge adults to be civil to their neighbors.

The challenge to love your neighbor as yourself is qualified by two intriguing phrases that the apostle Paul uses in Romans 12. First he stresses, "Let love be genuine" (Rom 12:9). And then he writes, "So far as it depends on you, live peaceably with all" (Rom 12:18). Both of these calls can be misused. Some people are so scrupulous about the need for authenticity that they are rude toward those with whom they have a complaint. Others, going by verse 18, refuse to confront a wrongdoer or address the presence of underlying conflict because they want to be "peaceable."

And yet these two phrases do provide us with a helpful way forward. I suggested earlier that if we are going to learn how to love, we need to get beyond the distraction of our social context that sentimentalizes and eroticizes love. Romans 12:9 suggests that, further, we also need to get beyond pretense (which, of course, includes hypocrisy). What we ask of God is the capacity for genuine love. So what does "genuine" love mean? What is the content of this love?

With reference to verse 18, we can also ask what the limits are—the "so far as it depends on you" qualification. While this verse suggests that there are limits—that it "takes two to tango"—it also offers a powerful reminder that we are called to be active, proactive and intentional, doing all we can to foster authentic community through the demonstration of love.

In what follows, I draw on the comprehensive teaching of Paul as found in Romans 12:9 through the end of the epistle to the Romans.

That will be my primary reference in these observations, though I will draw on other New Testament sources as well. It is my abiding impression that men and women who love others display three specific characteristics in their relationships. These are not so much qualities as they are actions or practices.

Each provides content to the call to love the neighbor. For me personally, this is what it means to love my wife, my sons and their families, my neighbor, my sisters and brothers in Christian community, my colleagues and those I serve through the work to which I am called. And, as we all long to know the grace of genuine friendship, this is what it means to be a friend.

Radical hospitality. First, we begin with hospitality. At the conclusion of the section of Romans that begins with 12:9 and the call to "let love be genuine," we come to Romans 15:7, which along with 12:9 serves as a kind of bookmark to this section in which Paul is providing his readers with an exposition of the meaning of love. And the bookmark of 15:7 is an apt counterpart: "Welcome one another, therefore, just as Christ has welcomed you, for the glory of God."

Hebrews speaks of love and mutuality. "Let mutual love continue," we read in Hebrews 13:1. This mutuality is marked by a mutual hospitality. But this passage also includes the line "Do not neglect to show hospitality to strangers" (Heb 13:2). Hospitality is a mark of mutual love within Christian community, and then we are enjoined to take it beyond the walls of the church to the world, to the stranger and even, as the author puts it in Hebrews 13:3, to those in prison. To offer hospitality is to welcome the other, to accept and receive the other. It fundamentally refers not so much to something offered in our homes (though it surely includes this), but rather to our own disposition of generosity toward our neighbor. When we drive a car, we can be hospitable to other drivers; when we use the earth's natural resources, we can be hospitable to those who may not even be alive yet. We can consider their lives, their space, their perspective. The other is not a bother, not an impediment, not a competitor. In receiving the other we receive Christ. And for the prisoner who cannot come to us, we go—we take our hospitality to the other, so to speak. First Peter also makes this link between love and hospitality.

"Above all," the author writes, "maintain constant love for one another, for love covers a multitude of sins. Be hospitable to one another without complaining" (1 Pet 4:8-9).

This welcome of the other does not discount the legitimacy of private space; it does not mean unquestioning compliance, that we can never say "no," or that there are no boundaries. It means we welcome the other on his own terms rather than asking him or her to conform to our expectations. I say all of this within the limits, of course, of civil society and our need to share space—whether we are sharing water, food, roads or other resources.

In this I am particularly struck by the way Dietrich Bonhoeffer speaks of the priority of listening as essential to this radical hospitality. He suggests:

> The first service one owes to others in the community involves listening to them. Just as our love for God begins with listening to God's Word, the beginning of love for other Christians is learning to listen to them. . . . We do God's work for our brothers and sisters when we learn to listen to them. . . . Listening can be of greater service than speaking.[7]

Those who are resolved to live in a community marked by and infused with love are those who, in the words of James 1:19, are "quick to listen, slow to speak." They recognize that nothing so marks hospitality toward the other—nothing so takes the other seriously and gives him space—as listening to him. Listening is a fundamental means by which we honor the other and fulfill the call to honor others above ourselves (Rom 12:10).

Of course, listening means not only that a person is noticed but that he is heard; he is attended to. One is not multitasking—either with one's hands or in one's head—but granting undivided attention to the other, attending to what he says rather than anticipating what one will say in reply. This is surely what is intended, at least in part, by Paul's call to weep with those who weep and rejoice with those who rejoice (Rom 12: 15). Our listening includes an identification with the emotional contours of the other's life, with the joys and sorrows that mark our shared human experience.

We all long to be heard, and there is nothing that so marks our hospi-

---

[7]Ibid., p. 98.

tality toward the other, our concern for the other and thus our love for the other as that we listen. We love our children and we listen. As leaders we listen to our colleagues and those we are called to serve. As neighbors we listen to the story of the one next to us. In business we listen to our clients. As doctors and dentists we listen and listen carefully before we diagnose. As government leaders we learn that our first responsibility is to listen, and this is equally as crucial for those in religious leadership: pastoral leadership is first the act of listening to God and second, as Bonhoeffer suggests, the act of listening to one's parishioners. In families, to love is to listen—spouses find that they are heard and children know that this is a safe space where they can speak and be heard. Few things are so powerful in the formation of a child as that the child knows early on that she is given space and that her parents listen to her. For married partners, perhaps it could be said that the mark of love in marriage is that "s/he listens to me."

If we are marked by sincere or genuine love it is evident in this: that we listen more and talk less. Perhaps a good rule of thumb in any relationship is that we resolve to listen, at the very least, twice as much as we speak. And we listen, essentially, that we might fulfill the call of the Scriptures to welcome one another in the Lord (Rom 15:7).

Hospitality also means that we do not impose ourselves upon the other—we give the other their space. I am thinking of those who speak when the person next to them longs for silence, or of those who wear heavy and intense perfume that invades the aromatic space of the other. You might say that rather than giving space they invade the other's space. It is not true hospitality for a church greeter to overwhelm a newcomer and demand that he feel "welcome" when all he seeks is to quietly slip in and perhaps test whether this is a place where he can worship. The true greeter-welcomer is one who can gauge what is required as a person ventures into the intimidating new space of a church building and allows him to come at his own pace and on his own terms.

One more side note: Romans 15:7 and the call to welcome one another surely applies to the whole of our disposition and attitude. What is noteworthy, however, is that this comes at the conclusion of an extended session where Paul speaks of our need to be gracious regarding those areas in which we differ on substantive matters. While there are serious issues on which we will disagree and perhaps need to part ways, the teaching of the apostle suggests that to love the other with genuine hospitality is to allow the other to differ and to respect the other in those differences; we do not demand that the other agree with us before we love or expect that other to agree with us because of our love. Our love for the other can include a profound respect for the freedom of the other to differ with us.

The call of 1 Peter 2:17 to honor the other—indeed, Peter stresses that we are to honor everyone—is surely expressed in this radical hospitality. With enemies, with those with whom we significantly differ, indeed with those whose views are actually offensive to us, we are called to show honor. I suspect that Peter's intent here is that we honor even those who commit evil: we honor not what they do, perhaps, but we always honor the person who has been created in the image of God.

Thus there is never any justification for torture or for despising another or for demeaning or debasing another with speech or actions. We never slander the other but always maintain a distinction between the action and the other's inherent dignity as a human person.

Patience, forbearance, forgiveness and the resolution of wrongs. Then also we cannot love until and unless we graciously come to terms with the imperfections and failures of others. In many respects it is as simple as that. This will include at the very least that we are patient with others, that we bear with and forgive each other. This is the sequence found in Colossians 3:12-13, where we read that those loved of God and clothed with compassion and meekness are to be marked by patience, bearing with one another and forgiving one another, with the concluding affirmation that we are to clothe ourselves with love. Patience, forbearance and forgiveness.

Patience is closely linked to hospitality, only now our hospitality is that of those who accept rather than demand, whose hope and aspirations for the other are not oppressive but grace-filled. We let God do God's work in the life of the other in God's time. Patience is a key indicator of our trust in God, a sign that we live by faith as we let God be God to the other.

Forbearance is the twin sister of patience, one might say. Romans 15:1 calls us to "put up with the failings of the weak." While there is no doubt that if we love another we long for her maturity and wholeness, but in the meantime our love accepts and puts up with her limitations, weaknesses and, yes, failings. This mark of compassion and generosity signals not tolerance of evil or wrongdoing but the reality that all of us are on the road to transformation and none of us has yet arrived.

Forgiveness is, of course, utterly foundational. We will be wronged. Every relationship and every community will be marked by failure, disappointment and betrayal. And just as the love of God for the world is marked most specifically by God's resolve to forgive, to love while we were yet sinners (Rom 5:8), even so our love for others will just as surely be evident in forgiveness. Indeed, this may well be the quintessential mark of love for the other.

We will be wronged by our parents and by those in authority as we move through our youth and early adult years. We will be wronged by colleagues, by spouses, indeed by friends. Sometimes it is merely a matter of learning to bear with the other's limitations and foibles, but often there is no other word for it: the other has wronged us and the only possible way we can respond is to realize that we are called to forgive even as God has forgiven us.[8]

Now we must make some crucial affirmations about forgiveness. Forgiveness does not mean that we forget, necessarily. Usually that is not even possible; wrong—deep wrong, in particular—will leave its mark. And yet it does mean that we do not rehearse in our minds again and again how we have been wronged, feeling again and again the pain of the wrong as though it happened yesterday. To forgive means we let it go; we no longer hold it against the other. We bless the other rather than curse the one who has wronged us.

And yet, it is important to stress that forgiveness does not mean passive compliance; it does not mean we tolerate physical or emotional

---

[8]When I was working on an early draft of this chapter, I was simultaneously in e-mail correspondence throughout the day with my mother, and we were reflecting together about a situation over which we shared a concern. As I paused while working on this section, I received an e-mail from her with this line: "I've lived a long life but of course there is much about living that I do not know. But I do know that one never regrets having forgiven."

abuse in the home or a violation of due process or an abuse of power in the workplace or in government. Forgiveness will be accompanied by the love of justice and the pursuit of the good and the noble for the sake of each party involved, including the one who has done the wrong.

Which leads me then to the counterpoint, the flip side of the call to patience, forbearance and forgiveness: the proactive resolution of wrongs. Not only will others wrong us, we will wrong others—by what we say or fail to say, but what we do or fail to do. We will not be all that we could be to our children, parents, spouses, colleagues or neighbors. Sometimes our misdeeds will be cruel and premeditated. More often they will be unintentional or the result of simple carelessness, the fruit of actions that were not wise. Sometimes with good intentions we say or do something that in retrospect was not the right thing to say or do.

Good people, wise women and men, those who pursue the way of love recognize that such words and deeds have the capacity, when left unaddressed or unresolved, to poison a relationship. They recognize that there is a need for intentionality in rebuilding the relationship through confession, apology and restitution. They make things right as best they can; they seek peace and the restoration of the relationship. In the case of a more minor offense, they are eager that it would not be allowed to fester and undermine the relationship. Without being overly scrupulous, they recognize that relationships are fragile and that bridges often need to be rebuilt. They monitor the health of their relationships and are willing to take the initiative, as the way of love, to either assure the other that all is well or, if necessary, to seek reconciliation through confession, apology or, as appropriate, restitution.

The way of patience, forbearance and forgiveness begins at home, of course. As we grow up we learn to forgive our parents; in most cases they are the ones who first wronged us. But it continues with those we live with each day. And it is so very imperative that the church community be marked by this mutual forgiveness. It is one of the premier signs of life in the kingdom of God. Christian community is a place of real people in real relationships, and this necessarily means there will be differences, even conflict.

Yes, there will be conflict. Real families and real Christian communities will have real conflict. Paul's whole assumption in Romans 14 is that real and substantial differences exist in community, and he does not lead them to premature resolution. Learning to love means learning to live with conflict that does not divide or destroy but calls for hospitality, patience, forbearance and, likely, mutual forgiveness.

Finally, one more point. To forgive is to let go of the need for vengeance. We do not repay evil for evil; we do not harm; we live peaceably with all. Indeed, if the enemy is hungry, we offer food and shelter. We respond "in Christ," which means we respond with generous service. And this leads me to the third point—the call to service.

Generous service. To love is to serve. This is manifestly evident in the love of God and God's self-offering in Christ, whose radical service for the world is the heart of the gospel. This interplay between love and service is powerfully evident in two texts in particular.

In John 15:12 the call of Jesus is to love one another. This is followed quickly in the following verse with Jesus' observation that to love is to lay down one's life for the other. Another text where this link between love and service is evident is Ephesians 5, where the apostle is writing of the love of a husband for his wife: "Husbands, love your wives, just as Christ loved the church and gave himself up for her" (Eph 5:25). He goes on to stress this fundamental meaning of love: that husbands are to love their wives as their very own bodies, much as Christ loved the church through sacrificial self-offering. This is what it means to love: to listen, to forgive and then also to serve.

Specifically, to serve the other is to respond to genuine, concrete need. If I ask you how I can serve you, it is synonymous with the question "What do you need?" When we love we develop discernment: what is needed by this person or by this community or by my neighborhood, and how can I respond?

We respond with generosity. This is crucial. It is not a calculated pseudoservice given with the expectation of something in return; it is not the service that leads to a feeling of entitlement or that obligates the other. Simone Weil puts it well when she observes that true service "is as instinct and immediate as it is for oneself to eat when one is hungry.

And it is forgotten almost at once, just as one forgets yesterday's meals."[9]

So to give some content to this "service"—just what does it mean? First, it is important to stress that our generosity is always a generosity "in Christ." Our reference point is not so much that we serve the other as it is that we respond to the needs of the other in Christ and in his name. This means that a need does not determine a call; we cannot respond to every need that arises. Furthermore, it means that we do not necessarily respond to the demands of the other. Rather, our response is always in Christ for the other.

Second, "in Christ" also means that our acts are never to our own merit or honor; we can and must learn how to serve quietly without seeking recognition or thanks for the simple reason that we do it in Christ and for Christ. Our contributions to a charitable ministry are always done quietly, without fanfare; our service is carried out without a need for acknowledgment. The best work we do might very well be done in obscurity, but it is offered consistently as that which we do for Christ and in response to the needs of the other. True service is offered without the assumption of an obligation or debt of any kind due from the other to the one who serves.

Love and service do not create obligation or dependency. Our service on behalf of our children does not create in them an obligation toward us. Our service on behalf of the church does not establish for us a feeling of entitlement. Our service on behalf of the world is given freely without the assumption that the world now owes us something.

Third, to love is to actively seek the welfare of the other. We are called to love; therefore our way of being in the world is always one of attentiveness to the well-being of all. And thus there is a close affinity between love and justice.

But, and this is so very important, our love is not merely for those who are near. It always has universal application. I do not love my family at the expense of others, my country at the expense of other nations or my generation at the expense of generations to follow. I do not accept that my nation will know wealth at the expense of others, nor can I seek

---

[9]Simone Weil, *Gateway to God*, ed. David Roper (New York: Crossword, 1982), pp. 82-83.

the welfare of my nation at the expense of other people. When patri-
otism is confused with love it is a distortion of the biblical ideal.

Glenn Tinder stresses the need to speak of the close affinity between
love and political responsibility. He observes that political responsibility
is an act of love, of being attentive and "consciously present to one's
fellow human beings, and this requires paying attention to them—to
what they are doing, suffering, and saying—all over the earth."[10] This
attentiveness is an act of political responsibility to the other, and thus it
is an act of love. To love is to ask, what does it mean to live with political
responsibility toward my neighbor? How can I listen well, serve well and
seek reconciliation? How can I seek my destiny in the light of the well-
being of the other? How can the sufferings and needs of the other shape
my life and my destiny?

And on a national scale, how can the very genuine needs of other
people groups and nations shape the way I act responsibly as a citizen of
my own country? When it comes to matters of personal and national
security we ask, what are the needs—the genuine and personal needs—
of those who have committed crimes? We do not allow our need for safe
streets to be the only criteria by which we decide who goes to prison and
for how long. We ask even for the criminal, what does it mean to love
this person and to be of service to him or her? A longer prison term is
rarely the most redemptive response to the wrong that has been done.

Fourth, one of the most powerful forms of service is intercessory
prayer. We serve one another by praying for one another. It is done
quietly and without fanfare; it is offered in secret as an act of service for
our neighbor, our friend, our world.[11] The church is in active service for
the world when on Sunday morning through the "prayers of the people"
we come before God not only with prayers for our immediate needs and
ailments, but for the needs of the world, including the needs of other
Christians in other denominations and women and men in other religious traditions. We serve by praying; indeed, I wonder if it could be
said that we are not truly serving another if our acts of service are not
accompanied by solitary, private, "secret" prayer.

[10]Glenn Tinder, *The Fabric of Hope: An Essay* (Grand Rapids, MI: Eerdmans, 1999), p. 151.
[11]Bonhoeffer, *Life Together and Prayerbook of the Bible*, pp. 86-87.

Finally, to speak of service is also in the end to speak of a fundamental kindness. True service is offered in hope, patience and joy. Our service for the other is not a burden or an oppressive duty but a gift freely given such that it is a gift as much to the giver as the one who is served. It is an honor to serve the other, for in so doing we participate in the service of Christ for the world. And so we serve with hope, with patience and with joy.

And, as we have already discussed, to serve is to respond to the need of the other. To love is to ask what is best for the other rather than what is convenient or preferable to me. It means a parent might enjoy having a child stay home, but as the child moves into adulthood she is freed to move on to new challenges and opportunities. Or a pastor recognizes the need to move on to another assignment and does not allow the deep affection for his church to stand in the way of needed growth—growth that might only come through a successor. We do what is best for the other. Rather than staying in a position where we have job security and comfort, we let go and move on for the sake of the community, the church or the organization where we have been of service. It is a kind of severe mercy where we do what is best for the other.

This is most evident when the deep disposition and manner of being that informs our lives in the world is one of kindness. Whether the other, the neighbor, is attractive or compelling or worthy of love or admirable or not, we respond with kindness.

It means we are kind even to those who may have offended, hurt or oppressed us. Rosa Parks is often referred to as the mother of the civil rights movement—this quiet, strong and resolute woman who refused to give up her seat to a white man on a bus in Montgomery, Alabama, in 1955. But one of the qualities that most impresses us about her is that she refused to curse the man or the people who were so cruel to her. She knew the system was unjust, but she was never harsh. Even though we could easily accept it if she had lashed out, it was this quality of kindness that marked her as much as her resolve against injustice. What she demonstrated is that we must resist the temptation to curse those in power.

The other side of this is how we speak of people when they are not in our presence. If we are in positions of power we tend to think we can get away with it even when the person is right there in front of us. We can mistreat the waiter or yell at the flight attendant because we assume we have some power in the situation—we're paying, after all. But even when we're on the other side our words can be harsh—against our boss and coworkers, or the people we had to carry on the bus all day if we're a bus driver. Or if we're a waiter we go over and over in our mind the sheer delight of "accidentally" spilling the whole meal on that man's lap—the man who was so rude. The call to kindness applies to even those who least deserve it.

SPIRITUAL FORMATION AND SOCIAL HOLINESS: WORSHIP, TEACHING AND EVANGELISM

In all of this it should be patently evident that the call to love is a necessary and integral dimension of spiritual formation. We make disciples as we learn together what it means to fulfill the call to love one another in Christ. Since learning how to love is so vital to the Christian life, it is an essential focus of the approach to spiritual formation within a congregation.

All of this assumes something that merits repetition: we do not love community; we love the people who make up community. We do not, in the end, love an ideal. We love our neighbor. We truly love the church only when we love those who compose the congregations of which we are a part. We must beware of the temptation to be frustrated with people because they somehow unsettle our ideal of Christian community. We are called to love these very people with whom we live and work and, in the case of the church, worship. Bonhoeffer believed in the importance of Christian community and of the priority of learning how to love one another. But he also stressed that we do not love community per se or treat community as our highest value. For indeed, the danger is that we would ask the Christian community to be to us what only Christ can be to us.[12] Put another way, our love for God is always primary. And our love for others is but an expression of our love for God. We love others in Christ.

---

[12]Ibid., p. 27.

How can we learn to do this? We begin where each dimension of Christian holiness must begin: with worship.

Worship—prayer, liturgy and spiritual formation. Spiritual formation that fosters our capacity to live in mutual love surely begins with worship. This is so because fundamental to our love for others is our capacity to dwell in the love of Christ.

Søren Kierkegaard uses an apt image when he speaks of our love for others. Where does our love for others come from, he asks. Well, it does not originate in our own hearts; rather, it is revealed to us by God. And like a lake that goes dry without a spring that continually feeds it, our love for others will go dry if hearts are not fed by the stream of God's love.[13]

His image reminds me of the words of Romans 5:5, which says the love of God is poured into our hearts by the Holy Spirit. Specifically, this love is the love of God demonstrated in Christ, who loved us while we were yet sinners (Rom 5:8).

As I have stressed and will continue to do throughout this book, worship is fundamental to our formation in Christ. And worship is crucial when it comes to our capacity to love one another. We can love only as we humbly grow in our proclivity to live de-centered lives, lives that are oriented around, first, the centrality of Christ in the cosmos and, second, the love of Christ for each one of us.

Worship gives us perspective. Through worship we see the big picture and we actively cultivate an awareness that it is not all about us but about Christ and his purposes in the world. We are not the center, but in humility we see, appreciate and indeed celebrate that Christ is the center of the universe. But also—and this is important—in worship we enter into and dwell afresh in the wonder of the gospel: that Christ loves each of us and indeed that Christ loves the whole world.

I have valued the formative role of the spiritual exercises of Ignatius Loyola—formative in my prayers, but also in how from prayer we move into the world of action, through community and in generous engagement with the world. And Ignatius picks up these very themes midway through the exercises. We read, "Love ought to manifest itself

---

[13]Søren Kierkegaard, *Works of Love: Some Christian Reflections in the Form of Discourses*, trans. Howard and Edna Hong (New York: Harper and Row, 1962), pp. 26-27.

in deeds rather than words," and then later in the same section we are reminded that "love consists in the mutual sharing of goods."[14] Ignatius is clearly echoing New Testament references to the call to love one another. But then we naturally ask the question, how can we learn to love in this way? And the answer is that this love for others arises from an awareness of the love of God for us—a sensible appreciation of God's favor and blessing offered specifically and particularly to us.[15]

It is implied if not actually stated: our love for others is derivative of our experience of the love of God for us. And for Ignatius, it is an affective awareness of the love of God, or, as Karl Rahner puts it, it is "felt knowledge." We cannot fulfill the call to love except the love of God be poured into our hearts, until and unless we experience this love, knowing how long and high and wide and deep it is for us in Christ (Eph 3:18-19). Worship cultivates this humility and awareness of the love of God. Nothing is so spiritually formative. Of course, this is the case only when worship is Christ-centered—not seeker-focused, not dumbed down so that it is all about our needs, which essentially makes it ego-centered rather than Christ-centered. When it is Christ-centered, we experience the crucial reality that our love for others is a dimension of our love for Christ.

In this regard, nothing is so powerful or formative as the Lord's Supper, which is an encounter in real time—Christ present to his people at the table—with the one who loves us and welcomes us and forgives us.

Public worship, the shared liturgy of the church, also needs its complement: our personal, private prayers, the solitude that is essential to the faith journey. Our personal prayers alone with Christ are an essential counterpoint to our lives in community. We put first things first: our relationship with Christ. And we in prayer dwell in the love of Christ and know the grace of this love being poured into our hearts by the Holy Spirit (Rom 5:5). Thus both the worship of the church and our daily prayers are the essential "formation" of the hearts and souls of those who hear the call to love their neighbor.

Teaching and preaching. Furthermore, all of this suggests a need for

---

[14]Louis J. Puhl, *The Spiritual Exercises of St. Ignatius* (Allahabad, India: St. Paul Publications, 1975), nos. 230-31.
[15]Ibid., no. 234.

intentionality. As I noted above, love comes naturally to no one. It is, for all of us, something that is learned. Our preaching of the Word and our teaching of parishioners of all ages needs to include not only the call to love one another but specific content that illuminates what this means.

What does it mean to offer hospitality, to be patient, to forgive and to serve? In the context of Christian community, it must be said that many congregations are deeply conflicted. In too many situations we have come to accept underlying conflict as the norm rather than recognize its toxic effect on our common life. Thus preaching and teaching must include instruction and guidance on how we approach matters of substance when we differ and, most notably, when we have wronged one another.

We urgently need clear and specific teaching that illumines for us the contours and character of the Christian call to love the other. If we don't, the word *love* will be filled with content that comes from the advertising industry.

But it must be stressed that teaching and preaching need to be embodied—lived out, illustrated and evident in our common life. We learn through both instruction and experience; the Word is preached on the need for mutual forgiveness and it takes root in our hearts as we see and experience the power of two brothers in Christ being reconciled to each other after a deep wrong or misunderstanding.

Here, too, the Lord's Supper is properly preceded by the ancient greeting of the "passing of the peace," such that this holy meal not only symbolizes our common identity and union in Christ, but also fosters and cultivates our common faith, our shared commitments and our love not only for Christ but for each other.

Evangelism and catechesis. Finally, to speak of evangelism and catechesis of course reminds us of the extraordinary words in the prayer of Jesus recorded in John 17, where we read that the world will know Christ Jesus is sent by the Father and the Savior of the world if it sees and experiences the unity of the Christian community.

This is a reminder of a recurring theme in the Scriptures: the relationship between the truth—specifically the truth proclaimed—and love. On the one hand, we are reminded that there is no love without wisdom; we love in truth and wisdom. We love by living in wisdom and by acting wisely toward one another. And thus the sequence is intentional and important: wisdom is the basis for love.

But the principle here can be reversed. Just as there is no love without truth and wisdom, there is no truth, no wisdom, that is not proclaimed and taught in love and evident in the love and unity of the church. Wisdom provides the contours and grounding and content of love. And those coming to faith require a catechetical process by which they learn what it means to be the church, a community marked by the commitment to hospitality, patience, forgiveness and service. But those coming to faith in Christ need not only to hear these words but to see them lived out in the church. More specifically, they feel the force of these words, of this teaching, in their own experience of the Christian community.

6

JOY AND THE ORDERING
OF THE AFFECTIONS

An Invitation to Emotional Holiness

You have turned my mourning into dancing;
you have taken off my sackcloth
and clothed me with joy,
so that my soul may praise you and not be silent.
O LORD my God, I will give thanks to you forever.

PSALM 30:11-12

NOW WE COME TO THE CAPSTONE, the ultimate mark of a person who is mature in Christ. We speak of joy, along with a call to emotional maturity and the ordering of the affections. Alexander Schmemman, an American Eastern Orthodox theologian, made this observation in his journals:

> I think God will forgive everything except the lack of joy; when we forget that God created the world and saved it. Joy is not one of the "components" of Christianity, it is the tonality of Christianity that penetrates everything.[1]

---

[1]*The Journals of Father Alexander Schmemann, 1973-1983*, trans. Juliana Schmemann (Crestwood, NY: St. Vladimir's Seminary Press, 2000), p. 137. See also Schmemann's *For the Life of the World* (Crestwood, NY: St. Vladimir's Seminary Press, 1998), pp. 25-26; joy is a recurring theme

What does this mean, that joy is the tonality of Christian spirituality and thus of Christian maturity? What does it mean that joy it is not something incidental or a nice extra to the Christian life but fundamental to our experience of knowing the fullness of the work of the Spirit in our lives (Acts 13:52)?

One of the primary indicators and fruits of faith is joy in midst of a confusing and broken world. But, as we must insist, the genius of the biblical call to joy is that we come by this joy honestly: as those who speak the truth, who name the pain and suffering of the world and who thus know joy in the midst of it all, a joy that is the foretaste of the kingdom yet to come.

In the comments that follow, it should be clear that joy arises from a life lived in wisdom, with a vision and passion for good work and with a resolve and capacity to love as we have been loved. Most of all, I will speak of joy as the fruit of or the evidence of our union with Christ. But in all of this, my point will be that joy matters and that indeed it is the capstone, not merely icing on the cake but an integral dimension of our identity as maturing Christian believers.

To speak to this, we must address why the emotional life matters when we speak of spiritual maturity, and then we need to anchor these reflections in ancient wisdom, evident particularly in the attention we will give to the "ordering of the affections."

EMOTIONAL MATURITY AND SPIRITUAL MATURITY

In Isaiah 35 the prophet makes an extraordinary declaration, opening with these words:

> The wilderness and the dry land shall be glad,
>   the desert shall rejoice and blossom;
> like the crocus it shall blossom abundantly,
>   and rejoice with joy and singing. (Is 35:1-2)

And the prophetic oracle ends with these words:

> And the ransomed of the LORD shall return,

---

in this book, with particular attention given to the Eucharist as the expression of this joy and the means by which it is sustained.

and come to Zion with singing;
everlasting joy shall be upon their heads;
    they shall obtain joy and gladness,
    and sorrow and sighing shall flee away. (Is 35:10)

The line "they shall obtain joy and gladness" would be better translated that joy will overcome them—they will be overcome with joy rather than with bandits and evil.[2]

Inherent in this prophecy is a deep assumption that the coming of the Messiah will bring about the fulfillment of the longing of the human soul to know the joy of God. This joy is not incidental to the purposes of God in the world but at the heart—no pun intended—of the mission of God. It will overcome us.

With this backdrop, then, we can consider the words of Jesus in John 15 and 16 (John 15:11; 16:16-24). In the very text where Jesus makes the initial call "Abide in me as I abide in you" (Jn 15:4), he also declares that he has come and that through him and through his work in our lives our joy will be made complete (Jn 15:11).

Many religious subcultures have a residual ambivalence regarding the emotional side of our human and Christian identity. And one of our urgent needs as we speak of spiritual maturity is to recover the deeply biblical view of the vital place of affect, of emotion, of "heart" in the life of the Christian. This recovery is really about the interplay between head and heart, intellect and emotion. It is not a matter of one over the other. The answer to cerebralism and the discounting of emotion is not sentimentality. To discount the mind is as misguided as the denial of the vital place of affect in our Christian life. Thus this chapter on joy assumes the earlier call to wisdom. The triumph of the Bible in this regard is the union of heart and mind.

And yet I am speaking of joy as the capstone, as the heart of the matter. We come to a high point in the narrative when Jesus says, so simply and straightforwardly, "I have come that your joy might be complete." We read this as people who long to be happy; we were created for joy and

---

[2]I am grateful to David Baer, Isaiah scholar and former colleague, who made this observation in a Bible study I heard him give a number of years ago.

Christ has come that our joy would be complete.

What does this mean in a world wracked by conflict, difficulty and suffering? We get further clarification of Jesus' agenda in the next chapter, specifically in John 16:16-33. In these verses Jesus speaks in an interesting way, and on first reading his intent or meaning is not obvious—the perplexity of the first disciples is actually mentioned in the text as they seek to make sense of what Jesus is saying.

Jesus advises his disciples that their sorrow will be turned to joy. He speaks of sorrow as the condition of being in this world: in this world you will have trouble, he stresses (Jn 16:33). But because he has overcome the world (also affirmed in verse 33), the disciples can be confident that their sorrow is temporary, that it is only for a season; in the end they will know a joy.

He also speaks of a "little while," or of what seems to be a brief period of time: "A little while, and you will no longer see me, and again a little while, and you will see me" (Jn 16:16). And the disciples, we note, wonder about this among themselves. We read that they keep asking, what does he mean by the "little while"? The church has been asking this ever since. What did Jesus mean by the "little while"? The meaning is not immediately apparent.

Some commentators with good reason speak of this "little while" as the few days between the cross and the resurrection. And indeed, this was but a few hours. The disciples were in sorrow, of course, with the cross, but Jesus was assuring them that their sorrow would be turned to joy with the resurrection. This would be the act by which Christ would overcome the world (Jn 16:33).

Others suggest that, to the contrary, the "little while" is the period between Jesus' departure as he returns to the Father and his return at the consummation of the kingdom. From this perspective, Jesus' disciples will have sorrow in this world, but a time will come when they will have joy, and it will be a joy that will not be taken away (Jn 16:22).

So which is it? Is "the little while" the period between the death and resurrection of Jesus, so that the disciples are filled with joy post-resurrection? Or is the "little while" the period between the ascension and the return of Christ so that in this life the disciples have sorrow, but joy will come with the return of Christ?

Or is there a possible third reading? Lesslie Newbigin in his reflections on the Gospel of John suggests that there is a double meaning in Christ's words here.[3] And both meanings are crucial to our understanding of the interplay between sorrow and joy in this life. Yes, joy comes with the resurrection. Christians can and in a sense must live in joy; it is a primary means by which they witness to the gospel wonder that Christ is risen. And yet the Christian still lives in a broken and fragmented world. The complete measure of our joy that will never be taken away will not come until Christ Jesus makes all things well. In the meantime—and this is the critical matter at hand—our joy now in the midst of this deep fragmentation is a foretaste of what is yet to come; we live in a broken world, but our emotional focus is determined not by the fragmented world but by the reality that is yet to come.

Jesus speaks of our sorrow—our grief—and our joy. Our sorrow is only for a time; it is a reminder that all is not as yet well. In other words, our sorrow is appropriate and real; it is not a violation of our Christian identity but the very means by which we know that all is not yet well. It is a reminder that we anticipate the day when all will be healed and restored, that justice and peace will embrace.

But sorrow does not define us. It is not the central emotional space in which we live. What defines the church and the Christian, intellectually and therefore emotionally, is the deep awareness that all will be well. This means we will get angry; we will feel fear and we will get discouraged. And we will mourn the deep losses of life. And yet sorrow is not our true home. We were designed to live in joy; because of both creation and the redemption of creation through the cross and the assurance of this redemption in the resurrection, joy is our "default mode."

We are angry, but we do not live in a house of anger; we do not let the sun go down on our anger. We are afraid but we do not live there; we do not "camp there." Rather, we cast our cares on him who cares for us and receive the peace that even in this life transcends understanding (Phil 4:7). We are discouraged but we refuse to live in our discouragement. To live in discouragement is to allow cynicism to take seed in our lives—in our hearts.

---

[3]Lesslie Newbigin, *The Light Has Come: An Exposition of the Fourth Gospel* (Grand Rapids, MI: Eerdmans, 1982), pp. 218-19.

We will experience both sorrow and joy; that is the given. To not get angry means that we are not truly present to our world; it would be to live in nonreality. This is a world of deep wrongs. But the question remains: where is our emotional center? Where will we live emotionally? How will we begin each day and go to bed at night? What will be our emotional center? Will the emotional contours of our lives be shaped by the fragmentation of the world, or will the fundamental reality of the universe and of our hearts be that Christ is on the throne of the universe—the risen and ascended Christ—and that Christ will one day make all things well?

This is why the ascension is so critical to our Christian identity and worship. The liturgy of the church is about a real-time encounter with the risen and ascended Lord. And it is why we must speak of the ordering of the affections, which we will come to below. But first we need to stress the following: holy people are happy people. They know how to dance. And if they cannot dance with their feet due to the habits of their religious subculture, it should at least be evident that they know how to dance with their eyes.

They are not happy all the time, of course. It is important to stress that holy people feel keenly the fragmentation of the world. They sorrow with those who sorrow; they know how to be angry without sinning. They know what it is to be profoundly discouraged without allowing their discouragement to go to seed so that they are nothing but cynics. They know the pain and sorrow of mourning; they have experienced loss and they have walked with others who have experienced loss. And yet what defines them is an emotional center, an emotional resilience, an emotional maturity that is perhaps most evident in a deep and abiding joy.

Many have recognized in this the extraordinary wisdom of Julian of Norwich and the witness of her "revelations" that led her to the conviction that despite all the suffering and pain in the world, the Christian believer rests in a deep trust, a confidence, that God is there, that God is good and that in the end, as Dame Julian puts it, "All shall be well, and all shall be well, and all manner of things shall be well."[4]

---

[4]Julian of Norwich, *Showings*, trans. James Walsh (New York: Paulist, 1978). This line comes up many times in Julian's writings, including p. 225 of this translation.

These words are a reminder of the heart of the matter: the basis of joy is faith. It is the fruit of a life lived in confidence that God is good and that he has all in hand. We rest in this extraordinary reality and confidence.

THE ORDERING OF THE AFFECTIONS

In the little book I referenced earlier by Arthur Holmes, *Shaping Character: Moral Education and the Christian College*, in the chapter titled "Developing Character"—essentially the definitive chapter of the book—Holmes makes this observation: "Righteousness is not just a matter of right conduct but a matter of the heart."[5] He then notes that post-Enlightenment ethics tends to emphasize reasoning and decision-making, thought and deed. Holmes counters that it is crucial that the Christian community recover an appreciation of how all true moral education must address what he terms the "habits of the heart."

Holmes wrote this in 1991, and it was a prescient observation: the following two decades have produced a vibrant conversation about how indeed character development is first and foremost a matter of what is happening to us in the innermost recesses of our being—for which we typically use the language of "heart." While many of us grew up in religious communities that bifurcated heart and mind, we see an emerging insistence that true spiritual formation arises from the orientation of the heart, indeed the ordering of desire.

A key voice in this discussion has been that of Alasdair MacIntyre, whose work has stressed that in moral formation, morality is derivative of desire and that therefore if we care about character formation, the heart of the matter is not morality but desire.[6]

For the ancients in the spiritual heritage of the church—whether it is St. Athanasius on the Psalms or sixteenth- and seventeenth-century greats such as Ignatius Loyola or Frances de Sales—to speak of formation and thus of character development is to speak of the ordering of the affections. This was central to both John Wesley's and Jonathan Ed-

---

[5]Arthur F. Holmes, *Shaping Character: Moral Education in the Christian College* (Grand Rapids, MI: Eerdmans, 1991), p. 58.
[6]See particularly Alasdair MacIntyre, *After Virtue: A Study in Moral Theory*, 2nd ed. (South Bend, IN: University of Notre Dame Press, 1984).

wards's understanding of sanctification. This vision rests on an assumption that sin is not so much wrong actions—thought, word and deed—as it is misguided affections or misguided desire. And thus the goal of spiritual formation is not morality, however good and important and essential this is, but rather the ordering the affections in Christ. I should add that the essence of this argument is not so much that humanity's problem is unruly emotions that need to be tempered by reason. This would be to make "reason" and thus doctrine and right thinking the primary leverage point for spiritual formation. Rather, the focus would be the ordering of the affections.

Randy L. Maddox makes a fascinating observation when he notes that the major divergence of North American Methodism from its roots in Wesley's thought and practice was precisely at this point: the priority of the ordering of the affections for human life and Christian spirituality. This, Maddox notes, led to a debate on the possibility of instantaneous sanctification and a downplaying of the vital place of "the means of grace in empowering and shaping our affections." Yes, Wesley affirmed the call of the Scriptures to perfection and yes, he affirmed that it was possible to know the perfecting of our intentions. But Maddox reminds all heirs to Wesley that this was always with the assumption that there was continued formation—the ordering of the affections. Wesley called for the "tempering of the affections"—the passions—through disciplined practice.[7]

Yes, the affections are unruly! So how are they ordered? Certainly reason matters and theology and wisdom play a part, but the issue is not to control or suppress emotion with reason but rather to cultivate our desires—most notably, in the desire for the good. The affections, the deep loves, the desires and thus joys of our lives are "ordered."

This is ably captured by the recurring triad of faith, hope and love that emerges again and again in the apostle Paul's letters, including, for example, in the opening greeting to the Thessalonian believers, where he writes, "We always give thanks to God for all of you and mention you in our prayers, constantly remembering before our God and Father your

---

[7]Randy L. Maddox, "Holiness of Heart and Life: Lessons from North American Methodism," *Asbury Theological Journal* 50, no. 2 (1995): 151-72; and "Sanctification in the Benedictine and Methodist Traditions," *Asbury Theological Journal* 51, no. 1 (1996): 164.

work of faith and labor of love and steadfastness of hope in our Lord Jesus Christ" (1 Thess 1:2-3).

Having spoken at length about love in the previous chapter, I will focus here on faith and hope as the air that we breathe and the basis for our joy. Faith speaks of trust, of course, in the risen and ascended Christ and hope suggests confidence in the capacity of the ascended Christ to fulfill God's promises.

Faith and hope—a confidence in the presence, goodness and purposes of God—are the heart of the matter. And thus the necessary focus of spiritual formation is the cultivation of faith and hope. Joy is the pinnacle and the outcome, yes, but we come to this by cultivating faith and hope.

Faith is evident in freedom from fear, anxiety and worry; we take simply and seriously the call of Christ "Do not worry about your life" (Mt 6:25). We have learned that we will not live in anxiety but in the peace that transcends even our understanding (Phil 4), and we have learned to cast our cares upon God, knowing that God cares for us (1 Pet 5).

Just as faith is the antidote to fear, even so hope cancels our despair and any propensity we might have to cynicism. Hope is crucial in a world marked by profound suffering and disappointment. To live in hope is to believe and act in the conviction that though evil is strong, it does not have the last word. And thus Christian hopefulness is not irrational or escapist or merely another form of wishful thinking. The genius of our Christian hope is that it comes in the midst of a deep awareness of the reality in which we live and work. It is not mere optimism; we are not naive to the powers of darkness.

Hope is faith expressed in the passages of our lives in space and time; it frees us to live faithfully in time. Glenn Tinder thus suggests that hope is patient and stresses that we are responsible *in* history but not *for* history. History is in God's hands and in hope we allow him to do his work in his time and choose to live with patience, not with continual frustration or impatience with God or other people. Thus Tinder speaks of sin as an evasion of time, either a nostalgia about the past or an impatience regarding the future. Our call is to hopeful living in time.[8]

---

[8]Glenn Tinder, *The Fabric of Hope: An Essay* (Grand Rapids, MI: Eerdmans, 1999), p. 220.

To order the affections, quite simply, is to cultivate within our hearts—at the point of desire and longing, where we attend to what it is that matters to us most—our deep loves and our greatest aspirations. There, at that point, we cultivate the capacity to delight in the good, the noble, the excellent and the worthy of praise (Phil 4:8).

This cultivation requires that we attend to what is happening to us emotionally—where we are angry or in fear, where discouragement or mourning has entered our hearts. These negative movements of the heart are not evil or wrong; they may well be an apt response to the injustices, wrongs and losses we have experienced. But then also we nurture a delight, a deep joy, in that which reflects the goodness and providential care of God—in both creation and in his redemptive purposes in the world.

But this obviously requires that we believe something fundamental about the goodness of God: that indeed evil is but for a season, that evil will not have the last word, that the good will triumph. And this becomes the crucial question: do we believe this? And will we rest in this conviction? Will we act in a way that reflects a confidence that this is so?

In other words, will we have faith? Will we trust in that which is unseen? As we have already stressed, this trust is not in some impersonal and unknown force, but a confidence in Christ Jesus, our high priest and king. This faith is the basis for hope, for living in a deeply fragmented world where there is much that is wrong. In the language of Hebrews, this hope is an anchor for our souls (Heb 6:18-19).

And the evidence—the critical sign that we are women and men of faith—is surely joy. Joy is the sign that despite all that is wrong, despite the immediate evidence of the power of evil, we know Christ is the high priest and that as king he will one day make all things well.

It is typical in Christian teaching to distinguish between happiness and joy and to speak of happiness as resting on positive things, nice things, good things that happen, but joy in contrast is an orientation not dependent on daily disappointments and setbacks. However, this misses the point: joy rests on good things that have happened and that will happen—from the resurrection through the ascension the consummation of the reign of Christ.

So the readers of Hebrews, we read, had joy even as their property was plundered. They were not happy about the plundering, of course. But their joy—the emotional contours of their hearts—rested finally, as the author of Hebrews puts it, on a possession that was better and more lasting (Heb 10:34). This possession is described exquisitely by Peter:

> So that the genuineness of your faith—being more precious than gold that, though perishable, is tested by fire—may be found to result in praise and glory and honor when Jesus Christ is revealed. Although you have not seen him, you love him; and even though you do not see him now, you believe in him and rejoice with an indescribable and glorious joy. (1 Pet 1:7-8)

Yes, there will be loss and injustice; we will mourn these losses and respond appropriately to injustice. But we will not camp there; it is not our true emotional home.

Second, we need to ask, if faith and hope are so fundamental, how are these cultivated and sustained? Or another way to put it: how do we live in faith and hope? How do we live so that the emotional contours of our lives are shaped and informed—ordered—by the reality that Christ is the ascended Lord? Or, to use the fascinating phrase from the book of Hebrews, what does it mean "for the heart to be strengthened by grace" (Heb 13:9)? Let me suggest three basic elements to our lives that are both the expression of our joy and the means by which our hearts and lives are shaped, ordered and expanded. These are liturgy and worship, friendship and sabbath observance.

Regarding worship. Worship is both the supreme expression of our joy and at one and the same time the means by which our joy, our deep joy, is nurtured and cultivated. As soon as we make the ordering of the affections integral to holiness and spiritual maturity, we inevitably turn to worship—specifically to liturgy, that is, the order of our worship. But worship functions as the expression of joy and the means by which we foster the ordering of the affections only if certain elements, dispositions and orientations are in place.

First, and most crucial, worship requires a radical orientation toward the risen and ascended Christ—a real-time encounter with Christ wherein worship is not merely speaking or singing *about* Christ but a dynamic communion *with Christ*.

Furthermore, worship requires a deep emotional honesty. We must eschew the propensity to sing the "happy clappy" songs that provide no capacity for acknowledging and processing the pain and fragmentation of our world and of our lives. The ordering of the affections must include the capacity to sing, "When sorrows like sea billows roll."

It is imperative that we be alert to the great danger of contemporary worship practices to foster nothing more than self-indulgent moralistic therapeutic deism. We know the ordering of the affections only when our worship is grounded and saturated in the Scriptures and when it draws us into the presence of Christ. This suggests that while what is happening to us emotionally is critical in worship, the focus and goal is not to make worshipers "feel happy." While this is the derivative outcome of true worship, if our worship is oriented toward good feelings and a sense of personal satisfaction, the result is nothing more than narcissism.

Here is where the Old Testament Psalms are so valuable to our worship. It comes as no surprise that all ancient liturgies of the church draw heavily on the aptly called "prayer book of the Bible." The Psalms are the guide to true worship and the ordering of the affections. They are about the blessed life—specifically, they are a liturgical guide to what it means to be happy, the abiding theme of Book One of the Psalms, Psalms 1–41.

The Psalms open with "Happy are those who . . . delight in the law of the Lord" (Ps 1:1-2). We do not then polarize between the law and the Word, our freedom and our joy. Rather, our joy, our freedom, is found in deference to and delight in the truth that is revealed through the Word.

Psalm 2:12 speaks of the happiness of those who refuge in God. An echo of trust is found in Psalm 42:5, and Psalm 32 speaks of the joy of being forgiven. Psalms 41:2 and 106:3 describe the joy that comes to those who care for the poor and those who observe justice. Psalm 146:5 speaks of the happiness of those whose hope is in God.

The abiding sense is that joy comes to those who live by the law of God and in radical dependence on God—specifically the God who is revealed through the Word (the Torah). This is the essence of joy. And thus the essential way in which the Psalms order the affections is by fostering this radical trust in the Creator and redeemer of all things.

Thus we speak not only of the crucial place of worship, but specifically of the need for worship dominated by the Psalms. We urgently require this kind of worship in a society that longs for happiness and pursues it relentlessly.

Regarding friendship. Second only to worship and prayer, friendship is an act of freedom and joyous participation in the fulfillment of the reign of Christ. Friendship is the only kind of relationship that is, so to speak, eternal. It transcends time and space, though it is of course lived out in time and space. It transcends it in this sense: the relationship between parent and child, employer and employee, teacher and student, pastor and parishioner, even wife and husband is only for a season—inherently temporary. But in friendship we live with a foretaste of the kingdom that is yet to come.

And thus it is in friendship that we enter another sphere of life, one that is deeply congruent with ultimate reality. It is a means of participation in the joy of God. More than this, it is a mark of a person who lives in joy—a person who is mature in Christ will assuredly be marked by rich and life-giving friendships.

And these friends will likely, as a rule, be few in number—perhaps only two or three or four over the course of a lifetime. I say this to reiterate a point made by C. S. Lewis in his helpful distinction between friendship and companionship. Companionship along the way, in work and play and conversation, is surely a wonderful gift. And Lewis insists that he is not disparaging this gift. But friendship goes beyond this to an ineffable link between two human souls—fellow pilgrims with a shared vision, intuition and inner connection. Companionship is the necessary precursor to friendship; it is through companionship that friendship arises. And yet, friendship is much more than mere companionship.[9]

Lewis makes the helpful observation that lovers essentially face each other in mutual affection and service. Agape love, in turn, is outward-focused in generosity and service toward others. But friends together

---

[9]C. S. Lewis, *The Four Loves* (London: Collins, 1960), pp. 61-62.

look outward while they stand side by side.[10] They see and feel the world with deep and similar sensibilities that are mutually reinforcing. And it is then and there that our deep loneliness is overcome. Our deep craving for the presence of another in our lives—for a soul friend—is fulfilled.

We no longer live by pretense; we no longer fear rejection. We no longer live under the cloud of being judged or critiqued or assessed based on our looks, our talent, our opinions or judgments, our way of being, or our way of seeing the world. There is another person present to us who is of a remarkably similar bent but who also accepts us as we are. This is freedom—a freedom similar in kind to the freedom we know in worship. And in this freedom is joy. When we are in friendship we are no longer strange to ourselves, for there is another who is of the same "ilk" as we are.

Lewis also observes that friendship is not exclusive. Marriage is necessarily an exclusive relationship; lovers cannot incorporate another into their love without compromising it. But friends can bring in another who shares their rich camaraderie and perspective. In friendship there is no jealousy. Just as in worship others join in my worship, even so when my friend is a friend to another, nothing is lost. We don't own our friends or possess them, so we can free our friend to enjoy the company of others.

Many people confuse friendship with having acquaintances. In these cases a "friend" is a business contact, a person they know or see often, a connection for political advancement. These connections are defined by the usefulness. And when we confuse friends with companions and acquaintances, we end up wondering why we are lonely when we are no longer in a position of power or influence.

Friendship must be cultivated. And it takes time. We will have companions along the way, people with whom we work, worship and play. And as we journey we are alert and attentive to those who resonate more deeply, those with whom we experience less fear or, ideally, no fear. We look for times when we sense shared joy and the potential for a deeper camaraderie; we seek those with whom we sense a resonance of spirit.

---

[10]Ibid., p. 63.

We then venture, in the company of the other, to test and see if there is a friendship that goes deeper than companionship. We find opportunities for meals together, for walks and hikes, for mutual exploration, for time spent simply enjoying the company of the other. The word *enjoy* is crucial here. The meeting with the other is not utilitarian. We enjoy the company and presence of the other for its own sake, not for how it benefits us. The irony, perhaps, is that we do not ask the other to meet an ego need; we do not ask the other to affirm us or make us feel good. There are no demands. And thus, as in worship, being present to the other brings about the fulfillment of our deepest need for freedom and joy. We come by this fulfillment not directly but indirectly.

Friendship is also formative. We choose our friends carefully, for friendship is, as Lewis observes, a "school of virtue." It either makes us better or worse—or, as he puts it, "It makes good men better and bad men worse."[11] For indeed, in friendship our guard is down—again, in much the same way it is in worship. With a friend we have cultivated within us the good, the noble and the excellent, as suggested by the words of Philippians 4:8.

I suspect that for the apostle Paul there may have been only one person who was a friend in this way—we see hints of it here and there. I am thinking of the Gospel writer Luke. And yet another person also comes to mind who captures something of what I am seeking to express here. During a certain event in the apostle's life, worship and friendship seem specifically to come together. It happens when Paul is imprisoned in a jail in Philippi with his colleague and companion Silas (Acts 16:22-29). We read that at midnight the two were praying and singing hymns! I chuckle at the thought that at that moment these two men needed nothing: they were content to express their faith in joy-filled worship as pilgrims and friends along the way. Nothing else, in a sense, mattered.

Both worship and friendship are acts of defiance against the deep wrongs and the fragmentation of our world. They are acts of defiance wherein we insist that despite all that is so wrong, we live in hope and deep confidence that all is well and will be well. Christ Jesus is the as-

---

[11]Ibid., p. 75.

cended Lord. And in worship and friendship we learn to live this reality.

The pursuit of holiness is expressed, in part, in the resolve to nurture friendship. Many people grow older having been consumed with work or career, and as they move into their senior years they discover how alone they are. It is difficult to suddenly get into the practice of being a friend if one's whole life has involved seeing people as means to moving an agenda forward—a career or ministry or work-related agenda. In our senior years, both worship and friendship—finding joy in Christ and in the friends with whom we have journeyed along the way—become increasingly crucial in our lives.

Before I proceed to my next point, let me mention something that is linked with friendship. We need to speak of humor. Harry Blamires in his classic *The Christian Mind* makes the observation that a "sense of humor is fundamental to our sense of proportion and therefore to our very rationality . . . a bulwark against despair and insanity."[12] This suggests that we could speak of humor as essential to Christian wisdom, but here I want to stress that humor—insofar as it arises from the good, the noble, the excellent and the worthy of praise (Phil 4:8)—is a sign of faith. How can we laugh unless we know that evil is but for a time? Faith means we can delight in the moment, in the company of friends, in the ironies of life. And we can laugh.

It is for this reason that some suggest that in the dramatic arts, comedy is actually deeper and more profound than tragedy. The lightness of the comedy assumes the deep order of creation; we can laugh knowing that all is well and will be well. And yet it must be stressed that humor at its best, true humor, never degrades another person or another people. Also, something is very sad when we assume that a comic can be funny only if sexuality is part of the routine. We urgently need a humor that is God-honoring—perhaps even a humor that makes God laugh with us.

Regarding sabbath. I mentioned sabbath earlier in speaking of vocational holiness, and it comes up again here when we speak of joy and the ordering of our affections. Sabbath too is an act of defiance. How can we observe sabbath in such a needy world, when there is so much that "has"

---

[12]Harry Blamires, *The Christian Mind: How Should a Christian Think?* (New York: Seabury, 1963), p. 9.

to be done and when there is so much suffering all around us?

The practice of Sabbath is based on the fundamental rhythms of creation. We sabbath because are created beings, and built into the order of creation is the rhythm of work and sabbath. But we can go further. We sabbath because sabbath speaks of our hope, our deep confidence that one day all will be well. Sabbath is an act of defiance against evil and a deep act of trust in God to do what he will most assuredly do.

Indeed, through sabbath we signal that the future well-being of our world rests ultimately not on the strength of our arms, or our capacities, or our intelligence, but on God's gracious purposes and his power to fulfill those purposes. Sabbath means we trust God; it is an act of faith. Sabbath is about being present in this time and place with contentment and gratitude. Sabbath joy is always local; we are content in the intersection of space and time where we are situated.

To be happy, we need to live with a deep contentment; we are embodied souls and we will consistently be unhappy if we are fraught with itchy feet, always assuming that there is something better (greener?) just around the corner. We will be unhappy until we learn to settle, to rest—that is, to take part in sabbath rest—and be content here and now, in this place and at this time. This takes gratitude.

But it is also a matter of choice. We can decide to be present and grateful—in this geography (rather than constantly wishing one lived on a Greek island), in this topography (enjoying these magnificent prairies rather than harping after the mountains or the ocean), in this village or town or city (not comparing it to more exotic or glamorous locales), in this time (engaging in the present rather than harking back to the good old days or longing for a better time to come). To be content is to be present and to delight in this time and space. This too is sabbath.

In sabbath, we learn the power of play—whether it is a round of golf, a boat on the water with a fishing line, or the quiet intensity of a chess match and the thrill of a brilliant move. We also learn the power of the feast—of meals where there is that profound sense that time stands still, when with food and drink and the company of friends we live in the deep delight of the goodness and providential care of God.

In this interstice in time, we live in the reality that Christ is indeed on the throne of the universe. We listen to musicians, enjoy a standup comic and go to a baseball game, perhaps. In each case time stands still. And we give thanks for the entertainers in our midst: for musicians who give us a reason to dance, for comedians who give us reason to laugh and for athletes who give us a reason to cheer.

But sabbath has meaning only if we let go. We let go of our work, setting it aside because it belongs to God. We let go of our need to worry and carry our anxieties around in our bodies. We let go of our need to consume and buy more. And we rest.

Actually, sabbath is a means of grace for all four dimensions of the holiness of God, the holiness of being in Christ. Regarding wisdom, there is an ancient Jewish understanding of sabbath stating that we need leisure—that is, sabbath—to grow in wisdom. We need the sabbath to create the space to hear and receive the Word, to slow down and have heart-minds that are receptive. Without sabbath we live at a frenetic and superficial pace, mentally distracted and busy so that we cannot be fully present to the Word preached. Sabbath moderates the pace of our lives— we slow down so that that the Word of Christ can dwell richly within us.

Sabbath is integral to vocational holiness—in sabbath we rest from our work, and our rest actually gives integrity to our work so that we fulfill our calling out of the rest of God. Also, sabbath is essential for true community. And here I am suggesting that sabbath is a crucial means by which we open our hearts to the joy of God.

Worship. Friendship. Sabbath. Each of these is an act of defiance against the evil of our world, and each is an act that expands our capacity for joy. Each reflects deep wisdom—a living in the truth, in the wisdom that God is God. Worship, friendship and sabbath are means by which we live in the truth. Through worship, friendship and sabbath, our hearts are ordered, our capacity for joy expands and a heart that is oriented toward joy becomes part of our very DNA. Each is a means by which we can open up our hearts to the gift of joy. That is, our hearts are strengthened by grace (Heb 13:9).

Then joy comes on us like a bandit, as we read in Isaiah 35. Joy comes as a gift, not as something fabricated or manipulated, not the fruit of hype or some kind of escape to a fantasy land. Joy comes not because we have taken a thrill ride or a bungee jump, but because our hearts are open to receive the deep joy of God. This joy touches not the surface of our lives—it is not the "fun" of a "day off" before we return to the humdrum of daily life—but rather penetrates into the very fabric of our bones. It comes slowly but surely as through worship, friendship and sabbath our hearts grow in their capacity to receive this gift from God. Through worship, friendship and sabbath we turn from worry, cynicism, anger and bitterness.

And the joy that comes as a gift gives orientation to the whole of our lives. It is not that we are somehow happy on Sunday and then sad all week. Rather, the deep joy of worship, friendship and sabbath in turn permeates our entire existence, strengthens us and keeps us sane in the midst of the deep sorrows—the suffering and very real pain of life in a fragmented world.

I stress again: it is not that we are dishonest about the pain of this world. True worship is not escapist, and true friendship is not just speaking about nice pleasantries. Rather, the genius of this deep joy is precisely that we come by it honestly. Meaning—and this is crucial—we are honest about what is happening to us emotionally. We acknowledge sorrow. The lack of sorrow is a lack of engagement—of seeing and taking seriously the pain of this world. The call to rejoice is not an act of denial of the pain of the world.

If we are truly in the world—in but not of, nevertheless in the world—we will feel its pain. We will get angry when there is injustice; we will fear the loss of that which in Christ we treasure—especially the lives of those we love. And we will get discouraged if our work matters and if our passion for truth and justice and peace matter. There will be setbacks. Women and men of deep joy are not those who refuse to sorrow or grieve; rather they are those who sorrow but who have learned that this is not where they choose to live. They come back to the center.

In other words, they come by their joy honestly. My protest against the worship in my own tradition is, in part, our propensity to sing only the songs we hope will make people happy. The result is at best an escape, a fleeting but not lasting joy. In contrast, the Psalms foster joy through profound emotional honesty running the gamut of human emotion.

Thus worship acknowledges our pain but does not leave us there; it brings into the presence of the ascended Christ. And a true friend is one with whom we can share our deep sorrow—anger, fear, discouragement. If we have no place to share our pain, we have no space for growth in grace. Many pastors live in an unreal world because they live by pretense, not being honest with themselves or anyone else about what is happening to them emotionally. A true friend will hear our sorrow but not allow us to stay there.

INTERLUDE: THE QUESTION OF DEPRESSION

Before I continue, I need to say a few things regarding depression—not the blues, not the down-time midafternoon slump when our circadian rhythms have us feeling a bit low, not the disappointment we sense when things are not going well—but depression, the darkness that can lodge ever so deeply in the human mind. This is not the "dark night of the senses" or the "dark night of the soul," using language attributed to John of the Cross. Rather, this is a state of emotional dislocation. And I raise it here—in speaking of joy and religious experience—because there are those reading who feel that they are incapable of this kind of joy. Joy is elusive and depression is their constant companion.

What do we say to a person with an anxiety disorder, for example? Be happy? Not a chance! Such words are almost an act of cruelty. Trust God and know his healing touch? Not much better, actually. For even here, mental and emotional processes can come up against a huge wall, an obstacle that no amount of sincere faith and trust will overcome.

First, in response we must affirm the huge gift that is offered by the professional counselor—the gift of assessment of what is happening and guidance in a way forward. This person can help us understand, as best as we can, the source of the depression and begin to move toward resolution and constructive engagement. We can also give particular thanks to medical doctors and clinical psychologists who can provide an accurate diagnosis.

Second, we must also acknowledge that depression is the result of an interplay of diverse factors—while there may well be a spiritual or religious aspect to depression, it often cannot be assessed or treated without attention to the interaction of biological, psychological and relational factors. For example, a wise counselor will help a person think about depression in light of family dynamics that may be a significant factor in their lives.

Third, we must stress the vital place of community, the company of others who are present to us. For those we know to be suffering with depression, nothing is more crucial than community—the acceptance, compassion and support of a network of friends. These fellow travelers need patience, understanding and hope.

In speaking here of joy—and the deep joy of worship, friendship and sabbath—nothing I am offering by way of observation discounts the huge pain of those who live with depression. And yet my point remains: we are created to live in joy and in Christ even in a fallen, broken and fragmented world; this joy is God's gift to us. And so we are called to do all we can to expand our capacity for joy and to walk compassionately alongside those for whom this capacity seems so very elusive.

THE FUNDAMENTAL PLACE OF GRATITUDE

The call to joy is a call to worship, to friendship and to sabbath rest. And as such it is a choice we are invited to make. This means that we begin with the choice that is very much a part of biblical spirituality: we rejoice. Joy in the Bible is a way of being, a way of acting and responding. We choose to rejoice as an act of faith and an act of defiance against the fragmentation of our world. In so doing we refuse the self-absorption of self-pity; we refuse to mope and to live in despair.

We choose to be a joyful people. We resolve as we grow older that we will grow in our capacity for joy. We will not become bitter old people who are cynical about life, about the government, about our children or about God. We will choose to grow in our capacity for joy by cultivating, day in and day out, our faith in the risen and ascended Christ.

And for this, nothing is so crucial—nothing—as thanksgiving.

We can state it very simply: holy people are grateful people. Nothing so expands our capacity to know the joy of God as the insistence that we will give thanks. And while most assuredly this means we give thanks for the big things, the broad strokes of our lives, as a rule those with the capacity for thanksgiving are those who offer it daily and often. We begin the day with thanks for this day and for what is before us—the gifts of life and work and relationships that are offered on this day.

It is too easy—and, frankly, takes little intelligence and creativity—to complain, to be aware of all that is missing and all that is wrong. It is easy to complain about the rain or, if it is sunny, that it is too hot. It is easy to complain about the potholes and then complain that the road work crews who are repairing the potholes are delaying our commute to work. For some, it seems there is no other way to live. And these are unhappy people. What impresses me is that those who seem to complain the most often have much. And those who are grateful often seem to be lacking much but have chosen to give thanks for what they do have.

Facing Our Mortality

To be a saint requires that we have a grace-filled approach not only to how we live but also to how we die. To die well is a mark of living well, and it is thus a critical sign, ironically, of our capacity to live out our Christian vocation.

Thomas Ryan makes the apt point that we truly learn to live in joy only as we learn to face our mortality and then allow that awareness to speak to us about the preciousness of life, of this day and of this moment. We can savor life by allowing this awareness to transform each moment, each day, into an opportunity to live fully.[13]

Death will come. There is an inevitability to this that needs to shape our lives; we do not live in truth until we live in a way consistent with the fact that our days are numbered, as we read in Psalm 90:12. To live in wisdom means to engage our days with an awareness of the limits and fragility of human life. This awareness leads not to morbidity but to living in the truth. It means we are not surprised or blindsided by the process of aging, the limits of our bodies (and our minds); it means that we transition into our senior years with graciousness.

We do not grow old prematurely; we do not use aging as an excuse for inactivity. We keep active, engaged and generous with our time

---

[13]Thomas Ryan, *Remember to Live! Embracing the Second Half of Life* (Mahwah, NJ: Paulist, 2011).

and energy. So no fatalism or ageism here. But we will grow older, and wisdom calls us to transition into our senior years with grace and winsomeness.

Furthermore, though we accept the reality of death, we live insisting that death is an aberration. And thus there is an irony here. We accept that we are growing older and thus that we will die. And yet we accept this with grace, because we know that death is not the end. In other words, we face death knowing that it is a profound violation of the glory and beauty of God's creation. We feel the force of this, and we recognize that in death there is loss. Death is not a happy time. As Christians we will mourn in the fact of death. Along the way in the journey of faith, we learn to grieve the losses great and small that will inevitably intersect our lives.

And yet our mourning is qualified. It is not final; it does not ultimately define our lives. We are not first and foremost mourners. Why? Because of the resurrection. As Paul puts it, we do not suffer as those who do not have hope (Rom 8:18-21). There is no doubt that this is most difficult with a premature death, or a "tragic" death. The loss of a child to a strange disease, a father of young children caught in an auto accident, an artist at the prime of her creative life succumbing to cancer. And yet the principle remains the same: we do not suffer as those who have no hope.

Death will come. And we can face it with courage even though we know it is wrong, for we know that it is not the last word or final act. And so in the midst of the losses along the way, we will mourn. This is good and right. These losses are real. But as we mourn, we will find that our mourning is turned to joy.

And then also, we will face our own death with equanimity, knowing it will come and yet knowing it is not the end. In the meantime, we can and must revel in the life that is given to us: to delight in this day as a gift of life given to us now and with the knowledge that one day the ascended Christ will be revealed and will make all things well.

Thus the prospect of death does not diminish our joy. Indeed, to the contrary, it broadens our capacity for joy. And this joy is not merely the capstone of a Christian theology of holiness and spiritual maturity;

rather it infuses the whole of our lives and gives fundamental meaning and orientation to our relationships and our work. Joy fuels our capacity for wisdom and understanding, fostering deep learning and moral leadership. We do our work not only for the joy that is set before us—our deep desire and longing—but our work is an act of joy in the world. In mutual love and Christian fellowship, we share joy—indeed, love in many respects *is* shared joy.

Union with Christ: Reprise

And now we come full circle. We need to speak once more of the central dynamic of the Christian life—namely, union with Christ.

I have sought to stress all along the way that joy is not pursued in and of itself. This is the great lie, one might say, of our culture: that since we want to be happy we therefore should pursue whatever it is that makes us happy. Be happy, we hear, and do what makes you happy. The result, no surprise, is a narcissistic pursuit of pleasure.

But I have sought to highlight that joy is a gift and derivative of something else—therefore it is vital that we learn how to enhance our capacity for joy through worship, friendship, sabbath rest and, of course, giving thanks. And yet more than anything else our capacity for joy is directly linked to our capacity for God—specifically, for living in union with Christ.

Yes, Jesus affirms that he came so that our joy might be made complete (Jn 15:11). But he sets this up by inviting us to abide in him even as he abides in us (Jn 15:4). This is our joy: the mutual in-biding in Christ.

The gifts God gives us will come and they will go. We may love to run, but we will not always be able to run. We may love being with our friends, but we cannot cling to them or ask them to be what only God can be to us. We may love our garden, but we will not always have the pleasure of our trees, shrubs and flowers.

What Christians have known and affirmed for two millennia is that maturing Christians find their deepest and greatest joy in God himself. This is perhaps most apparent to us when God takes away the things that bring us joy: perhaps a friend or loved one, perhaps a job we love that in the providence of God is no longer ours. Perhaps it is a home we lived in, a space we deeply loved and enjoyed.

Along the way we learn that joy is not ultimately linked to money, honor, recognition or power. Rather, our deep joy is to be found in him. It is not a trust in social position, in economic structures, in political alliances or the strength of our arms. Indeed, Jacques Ellul is right in saying that until we repudiate each of these other false sources of supposed security, we will not know the liberation, the freedom that comes in finding the only true security, which is a security of being "in Christ."[14]

This joy comes when we stop seeking to sustain ourselves in our own power or justify or vindicate ourselves to others or to God. We rest in Christ, and joy is the natural byproduct of this rest. We find in Jesus the living bread and the living water that quenches the yearning of our souls. Only when we learn this and walk down this road are we truly freed to mature in joy. To receive God's gifts but not cling to them. To face our sorrows knowing that nothing—literally, nothing—can alter the great wonder that Jesus is our life, our strength, our joy.

I wonder if any hymnwriter has captured this more brilliantly and eloquently than Bernard of Clairvaux, the twelfth-century theologian and mystic. There are two hymns attributed to him that surely should be part of the worship repertoire of each Christian community—even if through translation. First, here are the magisterial words of "Jesus, the Very Thought of Thee":[15]

Jesus the very thought of Thee
With sweetness fills my breast;
But sweeter far Thy face to see,
And in Thy presence rest.

O hope of every contrite heart,
O joy of all the meek,
to those who fall, how kind Thou art!
And good to those who seek!

But what to those who find? Ah this

---

[14]Jacques Ellul, *The Ethics of Freedom*, trans. and ed. Geoffrey W. Bromiley (Grand Rapids, MI: Eerdmans, 1976), p. 97.
[15]Translation by Edward Caswall, 1814-1878; it sings very well to the tune of St. Agnes C.M.

Nor tongue nor pen can show;
The love of Jesus, what it is
None but his loved one's know.

Jesus our only joy be Thou,
As Thou our prize will be;
Jesus, be Thou our glory now,
And through eternity.

Equally significant is Bernard's contribution of the hymn translated into English as "Jesus, Thou Joy of Loving Hearts,"[16] which perhaps more than any captures what I am stressing here—that our joy is found in Christ himself. Consider these lyrics:

Jesus, Thou Joy of loving hearts,
Thou Fount of life, Thou Light of [all],
From the best bliss that earth imparts
We turn unfilled to Thee again.

Thy truth unchanged hath ever stood;
Thou savest those that on Thee call;
To them that seek Thee Thou art good,
To them that find Thee all in all.

We taste Thee, O Thou living Bread,
And long to feast upon Thee still;
We drink of Thee, the Fountain-head
and thirst our souls from Thee to fill.

Our restless spirits yearn for Thee,
Wher-e'er our changeful lot is cast;
Glad when They gracious smile we see,
Blest when our faith can hold Thee fast.

O Jesus, ever with us stay,
Make all our moments calm and bright;
Chase the dark night of sin away,
Shed o'er the world Thy holy light.

There is much that could be highlighted from these magnificent

---

[16]Translation by Ray Palmer, 1808-1887; it sings well to the tune of Hesperus (Quebec) L.M.

hymns to Christ; I will choose but two things pertinent to the call to joy in Christ.

First, both of these hymns capture something central to the Christian heritage: that our deepest joy is found when we learn to dwell in the love of Christ, to know how high and long and wide and deep is the love of God for us in Christ Jesus (Eph 3:18-19). And thus nothing in our spiritual practice is so fundamental as cultivating our capacity to live in the love of God.

Second, do not miss the exquisite reference to the Lord's Supper in the third verse of "Jesus, Thou Joy." The Lord's Supper brings it all together. Specifically it brings together Christ Jesus as the ascended Lord—our hope is in him—and Christ Jesus as the fulfillment of the deepest yearnings of the human soul. Alexander Schmemann speaks of how the Eucharist is "an entrance of the Church into the joy of the Lord . . . and to enter into that joy so as to be a witness to it in the world."[17]

The Lord's Supper is the supreme encounter between the risen and ascended Christ and his people. It is the event in which Christ in real time receives us in a joyous feast of celebration and anticipation. In this meal we declare that evil does not have the last word and that one day Jesus will make all things well. Christ hosts this meal, and each time we meet him at the table, we choose again to rejoice in him, to bring our sorrows again before the throne of grace, to once more delight in his good gifts and to receive afresh the deep hope without which we cannot live.

And then Christ feeds us—he gives us his very self, through the gracious power of the Holy Spirit, to go in peace, in joy and with courage into a fallen and broken world. Thus the benediction of Jude is fitting as we move from worship back into the world, as we move from our prayers into our work for the day. We face honestly our anger, disappointment and fear and choose on this day to live again in the joy of God:

> Now to him who is able to keep you from falling, and to make you stand without blemish in the presence of his glory with rejoicing, to the only God our Savior, through Jesus Christ our Lord, be glory, majesty, power, and authority, before all time and now and forever. Amen. (Jude 24-25)

---

[17]Alexander Schmemann, *For the Life of the World* (Crestwood, NY: St. Vladimir's Seminary Press, 1998), p. 26.

Congregations and Transformation

The Church and the Call to Spiritual Maturity

O LORD, who may abide in your tent?
Who may dwell on your holy hill?

Those who walk blamelessly, and do what is right,
and speak the truth from their heart.

PSALM 15:1-2

THERE ARE TWO AGENCIES THAT more than any other have the potential to be a conduit for this vision of the Christian life: the local congregation and the Christian college.

Speaking of the church, if we take seriously the clear biblical expectation and call to spiritual maturity, it will have a profound effect on how we envision congregational life and engage pastoral leadership. What would it look like for a congregation to be a venue for transformation, where the underlying assumption of congregational life is that through conversion one is initiated into a life of fellowship with the people of

God and that together they are on a journey of formation, indeed trans-formation, into the image of Christ? Of course, everything depends on what we mean by "church."

And what would it look like if pastoral ministry were oriented around this commitment?

This is Paul's vision for the church and thus for each congregation— evident throughout his writings, but particularly in Ephesians 4. It is clear: the expectation is that each congregation will be a maturing com-munity. This is the work of the ascended Christ, who gives gifts to the church to this end:

> The gifts he gave were that some would be apostles, some prophets, some evangelists, some pastors and teachers, to equip the saints for the work of ministry, for building up the body of Christ, until all of us come to the unity of the faith and of the knowledge of the Son of God, to maturity, to the measure of the full stature of Christ. (Eph 4:11-13)

Noteworthy, of course, is that religious leadership—identified in verse 11 as apostles, prophets, evangelists and pastor-teachers—is given to the church specifically to equip it to this end: that we would be mature in Christ.

This reference to Ephesians 4 is intended to highlight that everything depends—and this is not an overstatement—on those God has given as gifts to the church to equip the faith community and foster maturity in Christ. Everything depends on the evangelists and pastor-teachers, on the apostles and prophets. If those who are called into religious leadership do not preach and design their ministry around this passion and goal, it will simply not happen. Everything depends on evangelists and pastor-teachers rethinking their vocation: why have they been called and to what end?

Both the evangelists and the pastor-teachers have been given for this purpose: that the church would be mature in Christ. This was the deep passion of apostle Paul. He could not have articulated this commitment more clearly and poignantly than he does in Colossians 1, where he is speaking autobiographically about his own vocation. He writes:

> It is [Christ] whom we proclaim, warning everyone and teaching every-one in all wisdom, so that we may present everyone mature in Christ. For

this I toil and struggle with all the energy that he powerfully inspires within me. (Col 1:28-29)

Will pastors get a similar vision for their work and for congregational life? And will search committees and others who are part of the process of identifying pastoral candidates embrace this agenda? Will this be the defining priority that guides them toward those who serve in pastoral leadership in their congregations?

So, though I have written this book for all Christians who want to embrace the call to spiritual maturity, pivotal to this vision is that pastors in particular, along with lay and congregational leaders, embrace this as the defining commitment of congregational life.

Can we reconfigure our understanding of the nature of congregational life and the character of the pastoral calling? Can we see the church as having as its defining vision be the maturation of God's people, growing collectively and individually in faith? And what would it look like if this were the foundational vision for congregational life?

For starters, of course, we need to recognize not only the calling of the church but the fact that individual members need the church. James Davison Hunter makes the cogent observation that "character outside of lived community, the entanglements of complex social relationships, and their shared story, is impossible."[1] It is as simple as that. Character—spiritual maturity—is formed only if it is formed in community, which means that character is formed only when it is formed for community. Ephesians 4 puts it this way:

> But speaking the truth in love, we must grow up in every way into him who is the head, into Christ, from whom the whole body, joined and knit together by every ligament with which it is equipped, as each part is working properly, promotes the body's growth in building itself up in love. (Eph 4:15-16)

The text highlights that we will not know the transforming grace of Christ except as we are in fellowship with the body of Christ, the church. Yes, we are each responsible for our own lives; we need to take individual

---

[1]James Davison Hunter, *The Death of Character: Moral Education in an Age Without Good or Evil* (New York: Basic, 2000), p. 227.

responsibility for our journey in faith, hope and love. But we need the company of God's people. In his classic reflections on the theme of holiness, Stephen Neil has a fine segment that is somewhat autobiographical but that makes a critical point: in this journey of faith and in seeking to embrace the call to spiritual maturity, we do not walk this road alone. Indeed, we cannot do it alone. We need the company of others; we need the support and encouragement of the community of faith. He writes:

> If I am called to be a saint, if I am really expected to be so much like Jesus Christ that others will know at once and unmistakably that I am a Christian, then . . . I shall need all the help that I can possibly get. I know that I cannot climb this hill by myself; I shall need at every point the help, the encouragement, the understanding of those who have valiantly set themselves to climb it too. Holy Communion will not be one extra certificate of respectability for particularly pious persons; it will be the *Esca Viatorum*, the food of wayfaring men, without which I cannot cross the wilderness. I shall need the admonition from others when I fail, encouragement when I am weary, sympathy when the going is bad. And before I have gone more than a few yards on the way, I shall find that I am far more concerned bout others than about myself, and that a great part of my Christian life consists of trying to find ways in which I can be of service to them.[2]

While there are no doubt diverse descriptions of spiritual maturity, I am working with the understanding that, first and foremost, spiritual maturity is defined as union with Christ and, in and through him, it is a dynamic participation in the life of the triune God. Second, spiritual maturity has four particular expressions, each distinct but interdependent on the others:

- Wisdom: a mature Christian has a heart and mind informed by the truth, largely through the witness of the Scriptures.

- Good work: a mature Christian has clarity about his or her calling— with the courage and humility and capacity to fulfill this vocation.

- Ability to love others: a mature Christian knows how to love others in Christ as Christ has loved us.

---

[2]Stephen Neill, *Christian Holiness* (New York: Harper and Row, 1960), p. 114-15.

- Joy: a mature Christian lives with a deep and resilient joy, even in the midst of a fragmented world.

What would it look like if congregational life were oriented around this vision of spiritual maturity in Christ? Consider the implications for three dimensions of congregational life: worship, teaching-learning and mission.

- The church is a liturgical community—called to worship.

- The church is a teaching-learning community—called to the renewal of the mind.

- The church is a missional community—witnessing in word and deed to the reign of Christ.

Our formation in faith, hope and love is found through the dynamic and iterative engagement of all three. And all three are demarcated and infused with the resolve and commitment to love one another and grow in our capacity for joy. We can then say to an individual Christian, "To mature in your faith, you need the company of God's people." But specifically and to the point, it is not merely the gathering of Christians that a believer needs or even just fellow Christians in the vicinity: the Christian needs the church to be the church.

To those who provide pastoral and religious leadership for congregations, I offer the following: if your deep commitment is the spiritual formation and maturity of the members of your parish, as a pastor these are your three distinct leverage points where you can invest time and energy—three dimensions of congregational life that are the means of God's grace for faith formation. Well, three, plus a fourth of a different kind: I will also be speaking of the vital place of personal formation and spiritual direction. But first, the three dimensions of congregational life: worship, teaching-learning and mission.

Worship and the Formative Power of the Liturgy

First and foundationally, a commitment to spiritual maturity in Christ will mean that we take worship seriously; nothing is so formative in the life of the church and thus for each Christian as the liturgy. This is why

I always find it a little ironic when congregations say they have, for example, an associate pastor for worship and another for spiritual formation and discipleship. The irony is that whoever is associate for worship surely has a primary if not *the* primary leverage point in formation. Furthermore, if those called to provide liturgical leadership in the congregation do not appreciate their critical role in faith formation, then they do not truly understand the nature of worship and thus the role of worship in the life of the church.

Indeed, what I am suggesting here is that the entire pastoral staff have a shared vision for faith formation; all are "associates for spiritual formation and discipleship." Some may have responsibility for one aspect of congregational life over another, but every dimension of congregational life is to this end: that we might grow up in Christ.

What makes worship a defining and formative event in the life of God's people is precisely that it is an "encounter," and the encounter is formative. It is a real-time communion with the risen and ascended Christ.

The wisdom we seek is not that of an idea or concept but a wisdom found and known in the person of Christ. The calling of the church and our individual vocations in the world all arise from worship and are animated by the blessing or benediction of God through worship. Our love for one another is the fruit of our sensible awareness of God's love for us in Christ. And, of course, this is our deep joy—to know in real time the risen Christ present to us. Nothing so satisfies the longing of the human soul as Christ Jesus himself.

Thus every dimension of Christian holiness and spiritual maturity comes to its head and is given meaning through worship. Therefore, congregations that take the call to spiritual maturity seriously will take worship seriously. Or, better put, they will appreciate that when it comes to spiritual formation, nothing is so formative as worship, and worship leaders—or liturgists—will recognize that through worship they are "making disciples"; they have an eye for transformation.

What does it mean for worship to be transformative? Before we delve into this question, it is imperative that we affirm something quickly: the formative impact of worship is subtle and incremental. Its impact is cumulative—the fruit of repetition, ritual and consistency. Novelty distracts. Yes, we affirm creativity, and yes, there will be diversity in our worship. But the evidence of formative worship comes about over years of consistency and the power of repetition.

But then we have a huge challenge, especially those of us who worship in evangelical congregations. Increasingly over more than a generation we have fostered an approach to worship that is intentionally minimalistic when it comes to theological depth and breadth and banal when it comes to the cultivation of desire. I have often wondered if this is a kind of infantilization of the church, but a recent publication, *The Juvenilization of American Christianity*,[3] provides a better descriptor. That's it! The word *juvenilization* captures our dilemma precisely.

The impression one has in Sunday or weekend worship is that the youth group has taken over: worship is led by the twentysomethings, not by the mature and the wise, those experienced in leading worship. The tunes are catchy and light, catering to teenage sensibilities—a kind of cola thrill to the liturgical taste bud: nice feelings, hip-hop beats, accessible lyrics that focus on immediate felt needs. And it all assumes casual dress with a laid-back approach to teaching—sermons are tossed out as no longer hip, so they are replaced by a "talk." We no longer call for serious engagement with the text of Scripture but look for speakers who are first of all entertainers and whose charisma can draw a crowd.

The so-called worship war missed the point entirely; it was characterized as a battle between old and new, ancient and contemporary. The real issue is whether our worship caters to adolescent sensibilities or fosters a deeper orientation that nurtures genuine adult maturity in Christ. Let me stress something here: I am not protesting the involvement of youth in leading worship—not for a moment. It is rather that every dimension of congregational life—including teaching, governance and mission—call for wisdom and maturity. Those who are young necessarily learn from those who are older, who in turn pass on the wisdom from previous generations. Nowhere is this more crucial than in the most formative dimension of congregational life, worship and liturgy.

---

[3] Thomas E. Berger, *The Juvenilization of American Christianity* (Grand Rapids, MI: Eerdmans, 2012).

Our challenge is that mature worship is an acquired taste; when we have been drinking the equivalent of soda in our worship, with its immediate zing to the taste buds, it will take persistent and solid teaching to foster our desire and capacity for worship that is both biblical and formative.

What will this look like? Well, without any hesitation I insist that we will learn from those who have gone before us. Worship will be contemporary but it will draw on ancient motifs, perspectives and practices. We will learn from the masters, the spiritual masters from previous generations. We will not try to reinvent this or make it up or try to figure it out on our own.

In learning from ancient perspectives on the church, we find five features of liturgy or formative worship. First, it is consciously and intentionally trinitarian and christocentric. It is anchored by the great creedal heritage of the church and oh-so-intentionally an adoration of the Father through Christ in the grace and power of the Holy Spirit.

It is unabashedly about Christ and his reign in the world and in the cosmos. We will be drawn into a real-time encounter with the risen and ascended Christ. It is not about us; it is not about me. Yes, we might well, in the great evangelical tradition, celebrate the grace of Jesus, his love for us and his gracious provision for us—"amazing grace that saved a wretch like me." But the bottom line is our encounter with Christ.

Second, formative worship is penitential. There is a sense of continual realignment or, perhaps better, reorientation. In worship we are drawn afresh into an experiential awareness of the reign of Christ. We grow in understanding through the hymns, readings and proclaimed Word as the reign of Christ is announced, but we also grow in the ordering of the affections as we feel the force, the wonder, of Christ on the throne of the universe. And so in heart and mind we are ever so incrementally but just as surely aligned more and more to the reign of Christ.

Also, there is the simple act of confession where through repentance we recognize our need for mercy and even more for growth in faith hope and love. Through confession we seek not merely forgiveness but also renewed strength for the road. The act of confession is our plea for mercy; it is also our expression of desire for spiritual maturity.

Third, formative worship is by definition participatory. We are not merely observers; we are not merely singing along. We are not here for the ride. We the congregation are the choir; we are, in the company of our sisters and brothers, entering into the holy place. When worship leaders use either instruments or sound systems that drown out the voices of the congregation, they have moved, in effect, into entertainment mode. The genius of great worship leadership is that it prompts, it facilitates, it encourages and fosters the worship of the people of God.

Fourth, we need to also consider the interplay between space and liturgy. Space matters. We are embodied souls, and our spaces and places of worship are themselves formative. And here's the key in this regard: do our spaces and places of worship reflect our theological convictions about worship and the character of the church? Is there a congruency between the space and the witness to the reign of Christ?

Fifth, I need to again speak of the Psalms. As noted in the chapter on joy, Christian worship is at its best when infused with the Old Testament Psalms. This is the prayer book of Jesus, and as we worship Christ and pray with him, it makes sense for us to draw heavily on it. As Bonhoeffer puts it so well, when our worship is infused with the Psalms, we learn to pray according to the Scriptures, we learn what and how we should worship, and we learn what it means to worship together.[4] With the Psalms, our worship is a worship with Christ and with one another.

But now, sixth, I must speak of the form of formative worship, which is the ancient modality of Word and sacrament. This duality of Word in sacrament is foundational to the life of the church and the mission of God in Christ. It is evident, for example, in the words of Jesus when he commissions his followers in Matthew 28, enjoining them to make disciples by baptizing them and teaching them to obey. Sacrament and Word; Word and sacrament.

Take for example the description of congregational life found in Acts 2:42, which reads, "They devoted themselves to the apostles' teaching

---

[4]Dietrich Bonhoeffer, *Life Together and Prayerbook of the Bible*, Dietrich Bonhoeffer Works vol. 5, trans. Daniel W. Bloesh and James H. Burtness (Minneapolis: Fortress Press, 1996), pp. 55-61.

and fellowship, to the breaking of bread and the prayers." This is the baseline: a congregation committed to spiritual transformation in a manner consistent with the witness of the Scriptures and the practice of the early church will, very simply, have a twofold commitment in its worship: one, to the apostles' teaching and fellowship and, two, to the breaking of bread and the prayers.

As a beginner preacher I used to preach this as a great four-point sermon—that is, until I began to see that the grammar of the text did not indicate four distinct commitments, and the supposed "four" items listed in the text were not of a kind. I was mixing apples and oranges. There really are only two fundamental actions to which the early church devoted itself.

The early church community is described as having a commitment to the apostles' teaching—within and as part of their shared life in the fellowship of the Spirit. Indeed, transformative worship will be evident in this: the words preached will not be clever insights and engaging stories from a person who gives a "talk" but rather a gracious making plain of the teachings (the writings) of the prophets and the apostles—that is, the Old and New Testaments. More on this below.

And then we see the reference to the breaking of bread and the prayers. "The prayers" is in the plural, suggesting the shared worship of the people of God, and the "breaking of bread" is short-hand for the Lord's Supper or Eucharist. The evidence of the practice of the early church suggests that they celebrated the Lord's Supper each time they gathered for worship. Not once a month on the first Sunday of the month—for which there is surely little if any theological justification—but weekly, each time they met for worship.

I perhaps need to clarify and expand a little on this last point. I made the observation in chapter 2 that the theology and practice of holiness depends on a full-orbed christology: a truncated gospel is not the foundation on which we can build this house. We need a theology of Christ's work that fosters not merely the idea of a transaction that has been done for us but a participation in his ascended life.

But we could also add this: the theology and practice of holiness requires a particular *ecclesiology*. So much depends on how we understand the character, witness and purpose of the church. Consider, then, what we might call an economy of holiness.

Our understanding of holiness and spiritual maturity needs to be trinitarian. We speak of the calling of the Father, a calling to union with Christ that is the fruit of the Spirit's work in our lives. To be truly trinitarian, we must speak of the work of the Spirit.

And yet we must still ask, how does the Spirit do the work of transformation? And for this we must speak of the church and of the means of grace. To put it simply and directly, the vision for spiritual maturity and holiness in the New Testament is distinctly *ecclesial*: the transformation of God is effected in our lives through the grace and witness of the church.

The church is not merely a gathering of assorted individuals who meet regularly for religious activities. For the church to be a means of God's transforming grace, we need to then consider what makes the church the church and what actions by the church constitute the means by which the Spirit does the Spirit's work. The answer is straightforward: Word and sacrament.

- Jesus commissions his followers to make disciples by baptizing and teaching (Mt 28:19).

- Jesus reveals himself to them through the exposition of the whole counsel of God and in the breaking of the bread (Lk 24:13-35).

- The believers devoted themselves to the apostles' doctrine and the fellowship, and to the breaking of bread and the prayers (Acts 2:42).

Thus, our vision for holiness and maturity in Christ is trinitarian but also, thoroughly churchly or ecclesial. The church is the means by which the triune God, through the Spirit, is at work in the world and in our lives. And thus we speak of the church as the fellowship of the Spirit—and, specifically, as the fellowship of the Spirit, the venue for Word and sacrament.

If just any one piece is missing—if it is not fully trinitarian or does not elevate both Word and sacrament within the life of the church—our theology and practice of holiness will be left wanting. And it will not be biblical or consistent with the ancient witness of the church.

The evangelical church has sought to respond to the call to make disciples and develop maturity in Christ with an emphasis on Bible teaching but with a diminished role for the sacraments: downplaying baptism as a means of grace and celebrating the Lord's Supper only occasionally. But the power of the Word is found precisely in counterpoint with the celebration of the holy meal. It is not that we have one of the two means of grace (one is better than none and, if we have to choose, best to go with Scripture). Rather, they function in tandem as mutually reinforcing. This is so in part because we are not merely people of the book: what defines us is not the text of Scripture, per se, but the risen and ascended Christ.

And it is important to consider the interplay between the text and the risen Lord. Paul at one and the same time speaks of preaching the Scriptures, making them plain and preaching Christ (and him crucified). We truly preach the Scriptures only when we preach Christ Jesus. Thus there is a powerful and clear christological hermeneutic to the Scriptures: we read the Scriptures and interpret their meaning in light of the incarnation, life, death, resurrection and, of course, ascension of Christ Jesus, high priest and king.

This means on one level that we preach each text in light of the Christ event; we read the Scriptures with the Gospels as the canonical center from which we read and preach everything from Genesis to Revelation. This is good and important, but not the heart of the matter.

While the Scriptures are vital to the purposes of God in the church and in the world, and while there is no formation in wisdom without the teaching of the Scriptures, we are not ultimately people of the book but a people who look to Jesus. Our understanding of the wisdom of God is deeply christological; we see and understand all things in light of Christ. But more, by virtue of the ascension, Christ is now, in real time, the high priest and king. The one through whom all things were created (Heb 1:2) is now the one through whom all things are being redeemed.

And so we look to Jesus; we consider Jesus; we behold and indeed contemplate Jesus. I wonder if we can put it this way: the genius of spiritual formation and character development is a matter of dual attentiveness—we listen to the Scriptures with an eager and open heart and mind even as we look to Jesus, the pioneer and perfecter of our faith.

And the Scriptures, of course, are given to us and taught to us so that we might grow in our faith in Christ, in Christ himself.

And who is this Christ? He is the crucified one: our wisdom is the wisdom of the cross. And he is the ascended one: our wisdom, the wisdom we teach, is the wisdom of the reign of Christ, of the in-breaking of the kingdom of God. Indeed all of life is viewed through this twofold lens: the cross of Christ and the reign of Christ.

Surely this is the fundamental character of all effective preaching—all transformational preaching. It is not so much oratory, or brilliant exegesis, or charisma and gravitas, or compelling illustrations and anecdotes, as it is this: that the ancient text is faithfully opened up and made plain in the light of and in the presence of the crucified, risen and ascended Christ. We sustain this dynamic awareness of the presence of the ascended Christ by the profound consciousness of Christ that pervades our worship and, I am suggesting, by the essential counterpoint of Word and sacrament.

We have a deficient theology of the Spirit if we do not foster an appreciation of the relationship between the Spirit and the Word and between the Spirit and the sacramental actions of baptism and the Lord's Supper. The apostle Paul is unequivocal: we do not know and live in Christ except by the Spirit (see especially Rom 8:1-16). But he is equally insistent on the place of baptism and the Lord's Supper. In Romans 6 he stresses that baptism re-presents to us our vigorous and dynamic union with Christ in his death and resurrection, and the Lord's Supper speaks of our participation in the life of Christ—his body and blood—as he stresses in 1 Corinthians 10:16-17. We do not then choose between Word and Spirit or between the sacraments and the Spirit; Word and sacrament are the very means by which the Spirit draws us into union with Christ.

The main point here: it is time that we recover and embrace a biblical understanding of the character of God's transforming work in and through the church.

With worship structured around Word and sacrament, the church lives in dynamic union with the risen and ascended Christ. But these practices—indeed all spiritual practices—are significant and efficacious only insofar as we walk in them in the Spirit. Thus we must be much more explicit about our radical dependence on the Spirit. Christ is the center and focus; the ascended Christ stands in our midst as the one in whom we have our being and in whom we live and dwell. But we cannot live in him and worship in truth until and except as we are equipped, empowered and enabled by the Spirit. Regarding the central acts of Word and sacrament, this means we are more intentionally explicit in our approach to the Word and in how we participate in baptism and the Lord's Supper.

This will be evident in the public rubrics of our worship. All ancient liturgies include the appropriately named "prayer for illumination" as we come to the preaching of the Scriptures. So it makes full sense that this would be an intentional prayer for the Spirit to illumine our minds, rekindle our hearts and strengthen our wills through the Scriptures.

Baptism should then also necessarily include an explicit reference to the Spirit: our only hope to live out our baptismal identity—anchored in Christ, rooted and established in him, growing in our identity as those who are united with Christ in his death and resurrection—is through the Spirit. We make it clear that in the Spirit we live out our Christian faith. How do we signal this? For the ancient church, it was through the oil of anointing—a "chrismation" wherein the one baptized was also confirmed in the Spirit.

Also crucial is that our celebration of the Lord's Supper include the aptly named "epiclesis"—the prayer for the Spirit to come upon our gathering, fill us and draw us into the presence of Christ, and consecrate the elements so that they are truly the body and blood of Christ to us.

If in the Word or in baptism or the Lord's Supper we neglect to mention the work of the Spirit, we will consistently and perhaps unwittingly foster the idea that somehow we can do this on our own—we can become Christians and live out our Christian identity in our own capacities. But, of course, it is in the grace of the Spirit that we meet Christ Jesus, who is present to us in the Word and in the sacramental actions of the church. Both, then—and this is crucial—Word and sacrament are not ends in themselves. They are a means by which we meet Christ in real time. The Lord's Supper, for example, is not merely a remembrance of Christ and his work but an actual dynamic and real-time participation in the life of Christ (again, see 1 Cor 10:16-17).

The Gospel of John portrays this in a particularly powerful way. While affirming the priority of the Spirit as the means by which we live now in union with Christ—see John 14 and 16—John's Gospel also highlights two other vital means by which this union is fostered. First, regarding the Word, we are reminded that Christ himself is the divine Logos. We have reference to his words as vital to our following and communion as essential to the message of God. John 10 focuses on sheep who hear the voice of Jesus; John 15 stresses our abiding in him and his words abiding in us (Jn 15:7). Those who appreciate the sacramental character of our union with Christ highlight a parallel thread in John's Gospel, noting the direct link between John 1:14 ("And the Word became flesh") and John 15:4 ("Abide in me as I abide in you") and the remarkable exchange in John 6:56 where Jesus insists, "Those who eat my flesh and drink my blood abide in me, and I in them."

In other words, the mutual abiding in Christ is charismatic (Spirit), evangelical (Word) and sacramental (Lord's Supper). The church does not in the end need to choose between these: we can be charismatic, evangelical and sacramental. Indeed a full theology of holiness is all three.

The Christian lives in the world with spiritual practices—including personal prayer and the study of Scripture, of course—that foster the capacity to be in the world as one who is in union with Christ. But what grounds and gives an essential orientation to the individual life is precisely the work of the church—that is, the liturgy: a real-time encounter with Christ through Word and sacrament. And both are received as a dynamic dimension of the grace of the Spirit in our lives.

THE CHURCH AS A TEACHING-LEARNING COMMUNITY

The local church is not a school, but it very nearly is. It is a teaching-learning community. In contrast to a school, this is not its essence or fundamental character. And yet without it—without teaching and learning—it is not truly the church.

A congregation is first and foremost a worshiping community that in turn has been called into service in the world, into mission, as a sign of and embodiment of the kingdom of God. I say that the church is not a school because of the critical priority of worship and the ongoing commitment to mission. And yet the church cannot fulfill the call to worship and service unless the good work of worship and the engagement in mission are grounded in and animated by study—the genuine learning that leads to the renewal of the mind.

While the orientation to worship and mission is crucial—essential to our identity and purpose as the church—we are a teaching-learning community with no apology. As a congregation we are resolved to cultivate a Christian mind, recognizing that we are transformed by the renewal of our minds (Rom 12:2). We are resolved to be learners; we are, as the church, a community that recognizes the priority of teaching to our common life.

Pastoral leadership has a liturgical or priestly function, leading the people of God in worship. And, furthermore, pastoral leadership has a missional role, encouraging and equipping the faith community to witness to the reign of Christ in word and deed. But the pastoral office will be, perhaps first and foremost, a teaching responsibility. Pastors are teachers, and they equip the people of God for worship and mission through their teaching.[5]

The whole of the Christian Scriptures witness to the deep link between understanding—an informed appreciation of the truth—and spiritual maturity. This is the underlying assumption of the entire book of Hebrews: that readers need to see and understand something about Christ and that this understanding shapes and determines everything else. The whole of spiritual life is lived through the lens of a particular vision of the crucified and ascended Christ. All reality is considered from this vantage point, from this "world view," one might say. What is patently clear is that

---

[5]No doubt Anglican-Episcopalian readers will immediately insist that the first calling of the pastor is to lead in worship, and those within my own tradition, the Christian and Missionary Alliance, might well press instead that a pastor is first called to equip and empower the congregation for mission and service. But here I am inclined to think that the Presbyterians got it right in referring to the pastoral office as that of the "teaching elder." In the end, all three are fundamental to the work of religious leadership, but the New Testament witness to pastoral leadership seems to put the emphasis on the work of teaching. This is how disciples are made (with baptism, Mt 28:19), and this seems to be the primary emphasis of the pastoral epistles—in everything Timothy and Titus do, teaching is both central and fundamental to their ministries.

to be mature in Christ, quite simply, one requires this understanding. And this understanding is the result of good teaching.

Here is the crucial piece that must not be missed: moral intelligence and integrity are located within a broader vision of spiritual formation and character development. And this broader vision is a theological understanding of God's purposes in the world. Thus Ephesians 1–3 is the basis on which we come to the specific elements of character and moral maturity described in Ephesians 4–6. Ephesians 4 begins with the line "Lead a life worthy of the calling to which you have been called" (Eph 4:1), and this is based on the great vision articulated in chapters 1 through 3. Christians cannot expect to live out the Christian life without a theological vision and foundation for the life to which we are called. We cannot preach the content of chapters 4 through 6 without equally articulating the great theological vision of chapters 1 through 3.

In almost any cross section of the church we encounter, we hear about the need to "develop character." We are concerned with the level of spiritual immaturity in the church and we wonder how transformation will come. A very common response is that we need to pray more. We speak of the need for renewal and revival, and we love to quote the line in 2 Chronicles: "If my people, who are called by my name, will humble themselves and pray . . . " (2 Chron 7:14 NIV). We conclude that if we want major renewal to the church, we need to get down on our knees and ask God for it. We have "concerts of prayer," where through half-day or daylong seasons of intercessory prayer, we ask for God's renewing grace.

Well, prayer is indeed essential to the life and witness of the church. And prayer both speaks of and fosters our radical dependency on God and his grace to bring about the renewal of the church. And yet what must not be missed is this: when God wants to bring about the maturity of his people, to foster character development and moral intelligence, he sends teachers. We make disciples by teaching. Timothy is urged to preach and teach, in season and out of season. The renewal of the church, its formation in Christ, is through cultivation of the mind of Christ. This is how the church is edified, renewed and strengthened; this is how the church is equipped to be the sign of the kingdom in the world.

Prayer without teaching will lead only to frustration and futility. Prayer without teaching is, quite simply, a subtle form of disobedience. Jesus commissions us to make disciples by teaching them. There is no easy out. We must avoid the thought that if we just pray there will be some dramatic or, as we like to think, "miraculous" personal and social transformation of our people and our church through "revival." Yes, we must pray for revival, but it comes, slowly and incrementally, as we attend to the process of teaching and learning, of immersion in the wisdom of God. We long for the Spirit to make all things new but often neglect the fundamental means by which the Spirit makes all things new—the teaching ministry of the church.

The objective of this teaching-learning is that God's people would be equipped to think theologically about life and work and relationships. Indeed, a good point of departure is to have a solid theological orientation to what it means to be the church, specifically to be the church in worship and the church in mission. That is a good place to begin as a way to foster the cultivation of a Christian mind: to see our worship in its Godward orientation and to see our mission in its orientation to the reign of Christ. Otherwise, worship is nothing but sentimentalism and mission is nothing but pragmatism.

But when we have a theological vision, our worship and our engagement in the mission of God in turn provide the crucial orientation points for our study and learning. We study and learn as those who move into worship and come from worship; we study and learn as those who are called to be in the world in generous service, and we bring our experience of being in the world right back into the venues and spaces of teaching and learning. It is our worship and our engagement in mission that fosters an integration of heart and mind through our teaching and learning.

The Scriptures and religious education. So, then, what do we study together? I stressed above that the passion for teaching and learning in the church is to cultivate a theological vision for life, work and relationships. To this end, our primary resource is the Scriptures. We teach the Bible. Nothing is more fundamental, more crucial and thus more central than the study of the Old and New Testaments.

And yet, perhaps the line "We teach the Bible" is not quite accurate as a way of speaking about how wisdom is formed and how we cultivate the capacity to think theologically. It is too bald a statement, one that requires greater nuance. Affirming the vital place of the Scriptures is not enough; we must also speak to how they are read, how they are engaged and in what way they are to the church a source of wisdom and thus of transforming grace. What is it that makes the Scriptures formative?

While much is being said on the place of preaching on the one hand and *lectio divina* on the other, I will just suggest the following as a guide. First, we recognize the authority and unity of the Scriptures. The Scriptures are the testament to the wisdom of God, the story of God and the ways of God. Those who would be wise and the community that would grow in wisdom will foster the capacity to read the Scriptures, proclaim or preach the Scriptures, and live the Scriptures.

Second, we need to read the Scriptures in light of two crucial and essential interpretive grids: the story of God in the narrative—most helpfully expressed through the lens of creation, fall and redemption—and the trinitarian and creedal faith of the church. Little is gained if the Scriptures are treated as a moral code, textbook or encyclopedia of religious truths rather than as a means to be brought into the redemptive story of God's grace. Many people know their Bibles well, but the experience of knowing their Bibles, which they read regularly, has not transformed their thinking, their minds, their way of seeing.

Third, the reference to the creedal history of the church is a reminder that our reading of the Scriptures and indeed our growth in wisdom is intimately connected to the life of the church. The Bible is not our personal book; it is the sacred text of the church. And we do not come to wisdom on our own but in humility accept the wisdom of the church as the "rule of faith" by which the Scriptures are read. There is no wisdom without an acceptance of the authority of God, and the authority of God is revealed through the Scriptures and the church God called into being.

So we learn to read the Scriptures in community, listening with others and in mutual submission to others. We learn to read in historic continuity with the ancient witness of the church, recognizing the authority of the great tradition, most notably the creedal heritage of the church. We always read the light of some tradition; those who ostensibly reject "tradition" as a source or guide to their reading of Scriptures simply make themselves the authoritative tradition. True learning—in community and in humility—recognizes the intellectual, moral and spiritual authority of the church historic and the wisdom that is cultivated through what Stephen E. Fowl and L. Gregory Jones have called "socially embodied traditions."[6]

Fourth, and just as crucial as anything mentioned above, we read Scripture in its social, economic and religious context. The Scriptures and the creedal heritage of the church—and Christ himself, of course—provide a consistent voice and unity to the church catholic. But this does not diminish the deep particularity of the gospel and of the wisdom that emerges as the Scriptures are read in diverse cultural settings. And so we can speak of a Christian wisdom that emerges in Africa as Africans read the Bible or a wisdom that emerges in Finland on the same conviction.

And then also, we acknowledge that the contemporary church is in conversation with earlier generations in the history of the church—the church is always thinking and reading the Scriptures and conversing and thinking some more and considering what it means to be wise in this time and space, in this particularity. Thus, for example, Kwame Bediako can speak of the conversation between African Christians and other contemporary Christians but also of the conversation between African Christians and theologians of the second century.[7] Christian wisdom is always simultaneously catholic (universal) and local or particular.

I would also add that we read the Scriptures in conversation with the wisdom of our own religious and intellectual heritage. The Scriptures are always primary and uniquely authoritative, but why would an English person not read the Bible as one who is also familiar with Shakespeare, or a Filipino Christian not read the Old Testament Proverbs as one who is familiar with the traditional proverbs of her cultural heritage? In other words, wise people do not merely read the Bible. And yet

---

[6]Stephen E. Fowl and L. Gregory Jones, *Reading in Communion: Scripture and Ethics in Christian Life* (Eugene, OR: Wipf and Stock, 1998), p. 10.
[7]Kwame Bediako, *Theology and Identity: The Impact of Culture upon Christian Thought in the Second Century and in Modern Africa* (Oxford: Regnum, 1992).

we can hardly overstate the primacy of the Scriptures for our formation in wisdom.

As an aside, but an important aside, I would also note the following from Bediako. He stresses that part of the genius of the Christian Scriptures is that they remain "in every respect the Word of God" in the vernacular—that through the witness of the Holy Spirit and by virtue of what happened on the day of Pentecost, all Christians can grow in their understanding of Jesus Christ by the witness of the Spirit in their own language.[8]

Catechism and rites of initiation. This vision for a teaching-learning congregation will be fulfilled only when we foster, right from the beginning, that a person comes to faith in Christ through a process of teaching and learning—more specifically, through catechesis. Matthew 28 and the commissioning words of Jesus provide a very helpful guide to how we think about conversion, rites of initiation and the church as a teaching-learning community:

> And Jesus came and said to them, "All authority in heaven and on earth has been given to me. Go therefore and make disciples of all nations, baptizing them in the name of the Father and of the Son and of the Holy Spirit, and teaching them to obey everything that I have commanded you. And remember, I am with you always, to the end of the age." (Mt 28:18-20)

Consider what this might offer us as we think about conversion and rites of initiation. First, of course, our primary reference point for teaching and learning is the authority of Christ and the in-breaking of the reign of Christ over all things, in heaven and on earth (verse 18). The ascension—or, better, the ascended one, Christ Jesus—is central to our vision of wisdom and theological formation. This is the baseline that undergirds our entire approach to mission and the invitation we make to those who inquire after the gospel. To come into the household of faith and respond to the gospel is to come under the benevolent authority or reign of Christ.

Second, we represent this transition into faith in Christ and life under the reign of Christ through the sacramental act of baptism; we are, one

---

[8]Kwame Bediako, *Jesus and the Gospel in Africa* (New York: Orbis Books, 2004), p. 32.

might say, made disciples by baptism. Thus in Acts 2:37-38, when Peter and the others are asked after Peter's Pentecost sermon, "What should we do?" they answer, "Repent, and be baptized every one of you in the name of Jesus Christ so that your sins may be forgiven." Baptism then becomes a sign or symbol, a sacrament of our union with Christ and our appropriation of his forgiveness, of the gift of his Spirit that fills us and our identification with the faith community that now witnesses to and embodies what it means to live under the authority that has been given to Christ Jesus. (Noteworthy, of course: baptism is markedly *trinitarian*. More on this below.)

Third, disciples are made through teaching, specifically teaching unto obedience. There should be no surprise in this reference to obedience, of course, given the authority Christ mentions in Matthew 28:18. Teaching has a clear purpose: making disciples. Few texts of Scripture so challenge our contemporary propensity to separate evangelism and education as does this passage of Scripture. Indeed, one could easily get the impression from this text that evangelism *is* teaching; people come to faith in Christ through the teaching-learning process. But, of course, we already recognize that the church community itself is a teaching-learning community. So initiation into the faith will by definition mean "catechesis." One becomes a Christian through a catechetical process of teaching, learning, instruction in the faith, specifically the faith lived in obedience to Christ.

But then there is a question to consider, one that perhaps does not get enough air time. The trifold declaration that demarcates the character and contours of our baptism is often treated as little more than a kind of formula that somehow legitimizes one's baptism. And yet could it be that these words—"in the name of the Father and of the Son and of the Holy Spirit"—are not so much a formula as a theological vision that informs the very meaning of baptism? Furthermore, if "make disciples" is presented here as two acts—baptism and teaching for obedience— should we not ask about the relationship between these two, the relationship between baptism and catechesis?

In particular, this leads me to suggest the following. For Christian initiation, baptism and catechesis are both essential and each is the necessary counterpart of the other. Baptism without teaching is an empty sign. What gives baptism its meaning is precisely that it is accompanied by teaching. And the logic would follow: it could and perhaps should be teaching that is trinitarian in content if not also in form. In other words, the theological vision of baptism requires teaching that gives meaning to the sign or symbol of baptism. But the reverse is also true: that cate- chesis is grounded and expressed concretely, tangibly and thus sacra- mentally in baptism. We teach for obedience, and the supreme sign of that obedience is baptism. But more, baptism is the act of whole-person, embodied appropriation of that which the initiate has learned and is learning through catechesis.

In trinitarian teaching we are reminded that we are deeply dependent on the ancient creeds to provide the contours or, one might say, the grammar, the architecture for our catechesis and thus for our growth in wisdom. But then the creeds are not an end in themselves; rather they speak of a vision for life that leads to transformation. We long for trans- formational teaching, teaching that leads to wisdom and thus spiritual maturity, but even more, teaching that fosters union with Christ. We have no interest in knowledge as an end in itself, but only teaching for obedience, for transformation, for wisdom and the grace to abide in Christ as Christ abides in us (Jn 15:4). Could it not be that baptism grants this to us, that the sacramental life of the church is precisely what keeps our teaching from being one-dimensional, cerebral and not holistic?

The faith community is a teaching-learning community; we are on a journey together to grow in wisdom. I am suggesting that Christian ini- tiation—the evangelistic ministry of the church, that ministry by which people are incorporated into the life of Christ that is embodied in a faith community—should itself be a teaching-learning process that is for the new Christian the beginning of this journey toward wisdom.

In this regard we give new Christians many tools, of course. But perhaps one of the most crucial capacities is that we introduce them to the Scriptures and teach them, as basic Christianity 101, how to read the Bible for themselves. This is fundamental; it should be part of the evan- gelistic process of all churches so that new Christians can begin to read and pray the Bible in their personal prayers and are equipped to participate in the preaching and teaching ministry of the church.

We also need to add the following: the books of Job and Ecclesiastes remind us that in the process of evangelism and witness to the reign of Christ we must reject facile answers to the evil of this world and indeed sustain an awareness that the problems of this world are complex and not easily answered or resolved. To have a credible witness we do not have pretend "wisdom" in the face of evil; rather, we witness to the wisdom of the cross.

THE CONGREGATION IN MISSION

The church is first and foremost a liturgical community; nothing so defines the identity of the people of God as that they worship God in spirit and truth. Furthermore, the church is a teaching-learning community called to make disciples by teaching them to obey all that Christ has commanded. But also, we can and must speak of the church as a missional community. And in the vision for spiritually mature believers this will be evident in at least two ways.

First, the church collectively is a witness to the reign of Christ in the world and in the cosmos: our shared identity in community is evident in part by our collaborative participation together in the mission of God. Together we are part of congregations that locally and globally witness to the reign of Christ in deeds of compassion, seeking justice and through our words calling women and men to the worship of Christ. Spiritual maturity requires a keen awareness of the kingdom purposes of God in the world, and in the church community we are invited to participate in this mission.

Members of the church are not observers but participants. It is not that we hear mission reports from those we view as missioners of the church but that we are active with our sisters and brothers in this very mission. This does not mean that we do not have missioners who are sent to other regions and peoples for purposes of Christian mission. And it does not mean that we should not receive reports of the work of God in and through them. It is rather that the church is missionary in its very character, meaning not so much that we "send" missionaries as that the community is collectively, in word and deed, attentive to and participating in the kingdom work of God. This will mean a dual commitment to what God is doing locally and what God is doing globally; it will mean an equal resolve to be present to a local community and to witness in word and deed.

As a side note here, I should stress that we often think of mission as global and international—"to the regions beyond," as they say. But just as mission by definition is witness in word and deed, each mutually authenticating, similarly mission is both local and global, and the global has credibility in part because of the local commitment. We can ask of a congregation, what is your local witness and commitment in word and deed? What is your global witness and commitment—again, in word and deed?

But the main point here is that participation in the mission of the church is formative: mission participation is not merely the fruit of growth in faith, hope and love. It is rather a very means by which we mature in our faith. Through shared participation in mission, in generous service together in word and deed, we are drawn into the vision of God's purposes in the world.

For several years I served as the executive director of a mission agency, and one of the abiding impressions of those years was the work of the board of directors to which I reported. I was consistently amazed how that shared work on the board was for most if not for all a means of grace. Through active and generous service with others, in work to which we had together been called, we saw and learned and grew in our understanding and our faith, developing a resilient hope. And this emerged even as we recognized that we were only participants in what was clearly first and foremost the work of God. While I would like to think we did good work as a board and as an administrative team, I often think that the main benefit of our work was the spiritual renewal and growth that came for each of us, and for our group as a whole, through our participation in this shared ministry. We grew together in faith, hope and love.

Service is formative. For the church in mission it is noteworthy that what is formative—what fosters faith, hope and love—is shared participation in the mission purposes of God in the world. It follows then that as the church we are not only in mission and not only encouraging church members to affirm and support what the church is doing, but we are providing as many ways as possible for each person, old and young, new Christian and more mature, to be involved.

First, then, the church in mission draws its members into shared participation in the mission of God. But second, and just as important, the church in mission empowers its members individually to fulfill their own God-given vocations. The individual personal vocation is always the counterpoint to this calling of the church community. The church's vocation does not co-opt our individual vocations. Jesus called some to religious ministry but not all (witness Zacchaeus), and Paul did not encourage his converts to leave their occupations and devote themselves to the work of the church. In other words, the individual Christian has a calling, and this has weight, substance and integrity in its own right. We are participants in congregational life and in the mission of the church, but this is not the whole of our vocational identity or commitment.

And so the other vision of the church is to empower and equip each member to complete or fulfill his or her vocational identity. I will speak to this more in my next point, but here consider that part of how this is fulfilled is through the preaching and teaching ministry of the church.

The in-breaking of the kingdom of God comes not Sunday morning in the gathering of the people for worship; it is rather on Monday morning when those empowered by Word and sacrament, through fellowship and mutual encouragement, are heading into every sphere and sector of society: into schools, businesses, doctors' offices, construction jobs, art studios and the daily routines of raising families and making homes.

For many Christians this creates tension. Which comes first, they often ask: Is it my calling into the world in business, the arts, education or the raising of my children? Or does my local church have priority on my life and my time? Which takes priority: God's calling on my personal life, my vocation? Or the work and ministry of the church community of which I am a part?

Or might this be a false question? Yes, we are of course members of and participants in the work of the church in the world. But our identity as Christian believers is not reduced to our churchly identities; we are not merely members of the church. Our being in the world will necessarily be informed by our lives as participants in the church—the people of God. Our church identity is not incidental to our lives. To the contrary, the church defines our way of being. It is an organic and essential dimension of our lives and to our capacity to be in but not of the world. But the church does not consume us or our time, and the mission and collective call of the church does not co-opt the individual and personal vocation to which we are each called.

God is calling women and men into every sphere and sector of society. The in-breaking of the reign of Christ happens not so much Sunday morning as it does on Monday as the members of the church fan out to fulfill their God-given vocations in the world. Most pastors, unfortunately, equate kingdom growth with the growth of their churches. They are inclined to think they are successful if ever more people come to their church and are active in it.

But could it be that the most effective congregations are defined not so much by how large they are and how quickly they are growing, but whether or not their members are equipped and empowered to be the people of God in the world? Indeed, what would it look like and feel like to be part of a church where the driving concern of the pastors and the board was not attendance and budgets and buildings but equipped and empowered people who are able to discern their vocations and then fulfill those vocations with courage, wisdom and generosity? What would pastoral ministry look like if the pastor said to a member, "You are not here for me—to support my ministry and give your offerings and work diligently to help with the ministries of this church," but rather, "I am here for you—to equip, encourage and empower you for the work to which you are called: in business, in hospitals, at home and in schools. If you are an artist, then the mission and purpose of this church, as an integral part of our commitment to each member, is to think with you about your calling to the arts and provide a theological foundation and orientation for your work, then to encourage you again and again when the going is difficult, and then to celebrate your work as vital to the kingdom purposes of God in the world."

This needs to be evident in our preaching and teaching and prayers:

we live, as a congregation, deeply conscious of how our members are in the world. And it means we do not judge or value them solely for what they give to the church in time and financial support.

Can larger mega-congregations do this? Perhaps. But it is likely the smaller congregation of two or three hundred that is better positioned to truly be an agent of transformation in a society, if for no other reason than that it has a far better read on the vocations of its individual members. Either way, we need to learn to judge a church not by the number of Sunday morning attendees but rather by a more subtle and significant criterion: are these people being drawn into the mission of God and equipped for service for Christ through their vocations in the world?

This means we speak this vocation as often as we can. "If you are in business, we believe in you—that is, we believe in business as good work, not merely a means to support the work of the church."

"If you are a teacher in the local high school, we believe in you, not merely as a witness for Jesus, but because the work of teaching history in the local high school is good work."

When I say we equip women and men to fulfill their vocations, this includes, at the very least, the following: first, that we provide a theological foundation and orientation for good work, demonstrating in our sermons, our prayers and the teaching of the church that God calls people into every sphere of society and that therefore business, the arts, education and homemaking are all good work—indeed, the work of God. It means we stop using the phrase "God's work" or "the Lord's work" to refer to church-related activities. When Christians are called into banks, dentists' offices, schools and the design of gardens, they are being called to do "God's work." What they urgently need is the theological vision to see this, feel this and then act in and through their work in a way that is congruent with the kingdom purposes of God in the world.

Second, it means we will be a discerning community, providing each member with the capacity to discern his own calling in the light of his own potential, as well as the economic and social context (and limits) that inevitably are part of vocational discernment.

And third, it will mean a regular and constant commitment to encouragement. Everyone lives and works in a fragmented world. We all need encouragement. Athletes know that however much their coaches and trainers are teachers and mentors and facilitators of their prowess, they are first and foremost resident encouragers.

And so I say to a pastor of a church: do you have a young person who senses a call into the arts, or business, or education? Then work with her as teacher and friend to help her see how her vocation is integral to the purposes of God in the world. Help her discern if this is truly her calling; avoid any inclination to press her into "religious work" as though that work, your work, were somehow more spiritual or sacred. And then, in sermons and prayers and hymns sung in worship, as well as through the personal encounters that are integral to pastoral ministry, find every way you can to encourage your parishioners in the work to which they have been called.

And then preach not only for moral reform but for participation in the reign of Christ. We preach to draw God's people into the wonder of the risen and ascended Christ. Preaching at its best is the faithful proclamation of the Scriptures wherein Christ is preached and the assembly of God's people is drawn into his reality. We preach the kingdom, and through preaching we empower God's people to see and feel the power of the gospel, to know the weight of the glory of the risen and ascended Christ, and to, in the words of the letter to the Colossians, "set our minds on things above" so that we live in the world with this vision, acting and reacting as those who know that Christ reigns over all things.

Preaching is never just public therapy or advice giving—the inevitable talk on Father's Day on "how to be a good dad," for example. Rather, good preaching draws out the big picture of the purposes of God in our world, locating our lives in the God-story, the in-breaking of the reign of Christ. Against the backdrop of the big picture of the reign of Christ, we can consider how each member of our congregation is being called to be God's person in the world as a co-creator and co-redeemer in Christ. This our passion: that each would know the power and grace of God for the work to which they are called.

This process of empowering and equipping God's people for their

vocations in the world should begin early in the faith journey. As with
the teaching-learning process and formation in wisdom, it could
begin as soon as someone starts to participate in the life of the church.
Early on, all newcomers to the faith community should hear the
gospel of the mission of God in the world being preached. And they
should be caught up in the realization that each person has a calling
and that this congregation believes in that work and seeks to support
them in that vocation.

As a newcomer is initiated into the life of the church and to the faith,
the mission of God should be front and center. There should be a clear
sense in which a new convert is invited to consider his own sense of call
and how that call is an expression of the purposes of God in his life and
in the world. He should begin to see and feel how worship is not escapist,
a denial of the world, but rather an ordering of the affections for those
who are called to be in the world.

Baptism should clearly signal this: at the baptism we signal and declare that this individual, baptized in Christ, united with Christ in his
death and resurrection, will now live out his baptismal identity as one
called to witness to the reign of Christ in the world. Again, it needs to be
clear and explicit. This person, through his baptism, is not merely forgiven; this individual is also filled with and anointed by the Spirit to
fulfill a God-given vocation in the world.

If this vocation is known and recognized, why not make it specific? If
he is called to be an artist, medical officer, carpenter or stay-at-home
dad, why not speak to this at his baptism? If his vocation is just emerging
or not yet unknown, we can speak of his work in the world as that to
which his baptism will take him.

SPIRITUAL DIRECTION AND PERSONAL PASTORAL CARE

The church is a liturgical community, a teaching-learning community
and a missional community. Each of these is a vital part of the formative
work of the church in the life of each member, and the interplay between
them is interdependent and iterative. But one more thing must be added:
we must speak of the personal and pastoral work of spiritual direction,
spiritual guidance or spiritual companionship—the catalytic element

that provides the crucial integration of the three dimensions of congregational life.

Can a person come to maturity in Christ without personal, one-to-one pastoral care and nurture? It is, of course, theoretically possible. And yet it is likely the exception. Normally maturity in Christ requires the labor-intensive work of personal spiritual formation. Many things happen in groups: worship, teaching and shared participation in mission. And much of our formation in the faith takes place in the company of others. The historic witness of the church unequivocally affirms the value of shared experiences of formation. But there is also an abiding witness to the indispensable and formative influence of one person providing personal formation in the life of another.

The ancient language for this ministry has been that of *spiritual direction*. Whether this language is used or not is neither here nor there; the crucial piece is this: that if we are going to mature in our faith and grow up in Christ, most of us need a personal connection with someone who is pastor, spiritual friend and counselor.

Most ancient models of pastoral ministry recognized that the public work of preaching and presiding needed to be complemented by the more intimate and personal work of visitation: the requisite investment of time and energy, one-on-one, in the life of each parishioner. As churches grow numerically, it is simply not possible or reasonable for the pastor to bear this full responsibility. But this is not inherently a problem: anyone in the church who is older, wiser and more mature should recognize that inherent in the Christian calling and identity is a responsibility to invest time, personally and generously, in the lives of others. Jesus was never so busy that he could not take time for a Nicodemus. Paul's ministry can be appreciated only when we also see his substantive and personal investment in others, such as Timothy. This form of ministry is integral to the life of a church that is truly committed to discipleship and spiritual maturity. In time, it is woven into the very fabric of congregational life.

This work is done quietly; it does not appear on a job résumé. It is the work of blessing and encouragement. It is the work of listening first and offering counsel only after we have listened well. It is the ministry of teaching, admonition and good counsel. It is the work of the father or mother to a spiritual son or daughter—the transmission of a maturing faith from one generation to another. It is the work of commending wisdom: "Hear, my child, your father's instruction, and do not reject your mother's teaching" (Prov 1:8). It is offered with patience and compassion, not judgment.

The genius of this ministry is that it is particular: to this person at this time and at this point in the journey of faith. Often, though not always, this personal, pastoral and focused ministry will be in times of crisis or during rites of passage—birth, transitions into adult faith, baptism, marriage and, of course, death. Each transition is an opportunity for reflection and the appropriation of the grace for this hour and this time of life.

This suggests that a vital dimension of the ministry of the church is fostering these kinds of connections and providing time and space for them to be integral to the life of the church. And it means that women and men mature in their faith are both encouraged and equipped to provide this kind of personal investment in the life of others. They come over time to recognize that as they move into their senior years, they have a calling to invest in the life of another. And young people come to know that their only hope for navigating life and work and relationships in a messy, complicated and confusing world is the company of those who will come alongside and patiently listen, encourage and provide good counsel.

Thus the four dimensions of congregational life. If we have a commitment to spiritual maturity for the church and its members, we will invest energy in the following: worship; teaching and learning, specifically of the Scriptures; mission and vocation; and, also integral, personal spiritual formation. All four of these are, of course, demarcated by a resolve and commitment to love another—the fellowship—and to journey together in joy.

There is no community without love. Thus spiritual formation and character development will and must include the cultivation of our capacity to love the other. It begins in our homes; it finds definitive expression in the life of the church—as a community demarcated by love.

And then it marks every dimension of our engagement with the world: with colleagues, with those in our communities, with those near and far, and with our enemies. The church is a school of love where we learn what it means to love within each dimension of our lives.

And it is a community of joy: joy in worship, joy in our teaching-learning, joy in our shared participation in the mission of God, and joy in our capacity, encouraged by the church, to do good work. This suggests something of prime importance: effective congregational life is not about doing more and more and more—I am thinking here of such mantras as "pray more, give more, serve more." Instead we need to do less, most likely, but do the right things; nothing is gained by making church life so busy that church activities are all-consuming. We must preserve time for play, for meals together, for sabbath rest.

CONCLUSION

Finally, regarding the church, I will offer some comments and observations about the character of theological education. I noted earlier that Paul's self-identity, passion and commitment as a leader of the church was to "present everyone mature in Christ" (Col 1:28). It would follow, then, that the formation of pastors for religious leadership would have as its defining vision not the management of church systems, not so much the establishing of new congregations, not the techniques for fostering church growth, but rather to "present everyone mature in Christ."

I am not suggesting that church systems and new congregations and church growth do not matter—not for a moment. It is merely that perhaps the most crucial and defining capacity of a graduate of a theological seminary should be the capacity to foster maturity in Christ in and through the church.

This would suggest the following fundamental and requisite capacities, corresponding to the four dimensions of congregational life identified in this chapter. First, it is necessary to have a nuanced understanding of the character of congregational worship—to know the history of worship, its ancient sources among the people of Israel and what it means now to worship in Christ in the new covenant. Of course, this involves the capacity to preside at worship—which means knowing more than a standard chord sequence for the guitar.

Second is the capacity to preach and teach, for indeed the church is a teaching-learning community, and specifically this requires the capacity to preach and teach the Scriptures. A pastor is a minister of the Word. Third, a pastor is an equipper, fostering the capacity of the congregation to be "in mission" and to help each individual Christian recognize and respond to his or her own vocation. And, fourth, it means a seminary graduate is trained for the good and vital work of personal pastoral care and spiritual formation.

Is there more to pastoral ministry? Must there be other elements to a complete program of theological education? Certainly. My point is only this: if a seminary is committed to spiritual maturity and radical discipleship, its graduates will have these four capacities.

CHRISTIAN HIGHER EDUCATION

A Passion for Wisdom and
Spiritual Transformation

How can young people keep their way pure?
By guarding it according to your word.
With my whole heart I seek you;
do not let me stray from your commandments.

PSALM 119:9-10

WHEN WE CONSIDER THE CALL to spiritual maturity, we need to speak of the potential impact of educators, specifically the faculty and administration of institutions of higher learning, notably Christian universities, colleges and theological seminaries. Few agencies and institutions have as much influence and potential leverage as Christian colleges and universities—undergraduate and graduate programs in the liberal arts, sciences, business administration, fine arts and ministerial formation. Indeed, Dallas Willard suggests that the "greatest issue facing the church today is whether or not Christian schools will say loudly and clearly that they have essential knowledge that non-Christian schools do not have."[1]

While I am inclined to think that the greatest issue we face is the nature and character of the church and of congregational life, I am sobered by Willard's observation. He writes from the vantage point of the public or secular university, encouraging those who lead and teach within Christian institutions of higher learning. He obviously recognizes the formative influence of Christian universities and colleges; he recognizes both—the potential impact of a university on a society and culture and then, of course, the potential impact of a Christian institution of higher learning on the church, on the cultural context in which it is located and beyond into the public square.

Perhaps there are indeed two crucial leverage points for the church today: the congregation and higher education. For the congregation, of course, much depends on the institutions where pastors are formed—theological schools and seminaries. So our approach to teaching and learning in higher education is pivotal to this entire vision—to anyone who takes seriously the call to maturity in Christ.

WHY CHRISTIAN HIGHER EDUCATION?

Christian higher education is at a crossroads. We are asking the question, particularly in evangelical and Protestant circles: to what end and with what purpose do we do education and, specifically, higher education? Why do we establish and sustain postsecondary academic institutions? Is there a place for the Christian university or college and, if so, what makes such an institution distinctly Christian? What is the "essential knowledge" of which Willard speaks? And what is the place of Christian higher education in the mission of God and thus in the mission of the church?[2]

---

[1]Dallas Willard, "The Failure of Evangelical Political Involvement," in *God and Governing: Reflections on Ethics, Virtue, and Statesmanship*, ed. Roger N. Overton (Eugene, OR: Pickwick, 2009), p. 90.

[2]The current conversation on this score is rich and diverse in both Roman Catholic and evangelical-Protestant circles. Particularly noteworthy for evangelical schools is the contribution of Stanley Hauerwas, *The State of the University: Academic Knowledges and the Knowledge of God* (Oxford, UK: Blackwell, 2007), note especially pp. 92-107, and James K. A. Smith, *Desiring the Kingdom: Worship, Worldview, and Cultural Formation* (Grand Rapids, MI: Baker Academic, 2009).

I offer these comments as one whose primary experience over the past thirty years has been with theological seminaries—as an administrator, consultant and faculty member. And what impresses me in the exchanges between those doing theological education and those engaged in liberal arts education is that educators in both spheres are facing remarkably similar challenges. The issues at stake are on the whole the same. Both Christian universities and theological schools are asking what it is that makes education Christian and what in the end provides some kind of unity, defining principle or purpose for what we are doing.

Whether in theological education or in the arts and sciences, when it comes to asking the question "why?"—why engage in higher education or formal theological study or why higher education at all?—the answer tends to be one of two possibilities. Either (a) for understanding and knowledge, or (b) for vocational preparation and credentialing.

Regarding knowledge, it is argued that if you go to a university, you will study and you will know stuff. If it is a Christian university, it will be knowledge that is "Christian"—with a Christian worldview, perhaps, or a Christian perspective on the discipline or topic. The second typical answer to the "why" question is to assure the prospective student that she or he will be trained and qualified for a particular occupation—with theological schools, of course, one will be prepared for and competent in religious leadership.

There is typically a recognition of the need to cultivate the spiritual life. But the basic assumption is that professors are responsible for their specialized knowledge of an academic discipline; they are called to pass on knowledge to their students. Within the training model, instructors are expected to deliver capacity and competency. Both typically look to another group that complements the academic process in caring for the spiritual formation component of the academic community. Teachers teach and train; those in student life and chaplains, perhaps, are responsible for matters of spirituality and character development.

The assumption remains that the essence of Christian higher education is either a Christian perspective on academic disciplines or credentialing for a particular responsibility (or both). You will get a

Christianized view of biology or a Christian perspective on doing business.

When there is a critique of higher education, the focus tends to be at one of these two points. Most typical of theological seminaries, for example, is a criticism that graduates do not have the requisite capacities for what is "needed" by the church. This has led some larger churches to start their own seminaries—in the basement, perhaps—so they can do their own skills cultivation. Often they critique the seminary for being all about knowledge and not about practice.

But the same occurs in the undergraduate liberal arts school. Students come to a Christian university or college with the hope of getting two things: a Christianized version of what they would otherwise have received at the public or secular university and, if all goes well, a well-paying job when they complete their studies. They hope that this institution will integrate faith and learning. They are looking for a university or college where Christian faith is taken seriously and thus not threatened by critical reflection and reason. It is common for Christian universities to tout how they integrate faith and reason.

Students who come to these institutions further hope that they can move into either the church or the marketplace and get a good job with the capacities to succeed in that job. And Christian universities love to celebrate their alumni who end up in high-profile political, church, business and professional positions. Education in this scenario is reduced to either knowledge (albeit hopefully a Christian knowledge) or capacity and credentialing.[3]

And yet is this the "essential knowledge" Willard claims Christian institutions have at their disposal? Is this really what makes them Christian and thus defines their mission? Is this all they have to offer?

Both of these things matter. We do need to cultivate a Christian vision of reality, a Christian worldview. One of the compelling features of Christian institutions of higher learning is that they foster this way of seeing, understanding and believing. Faith and reason are indeed integrated. And yes, it is important to foster the capacity for gainful em-

---

[3] I particularly appreciate the way that Jens Zimmermann expresses this in "The Passionate Intellect," *Direction: A Mennonite Brethren Forum* 37, no. 1 (2008): 19-37.

ployment. Pastors need to be competent in their ministry, business-people in the management of their shops and teachers and musicians in their craft. And it is surely vital that they do this work in a manner that is deeply congruent with a biblical understanding of ministry, business, the arts or whatever their occupation.

But neither of these is compelling enough to justify the existence of these institutions. Neither of these is the "value-added" of an institution of higher learning that claims to be Christian. It is not their greatest potential legacy.

HIGHER EDUCATION AS TRANSFORMATIVE LEARNING

Instead, surely the crux of the matter, the heart of the issue, is that Christian institutions—colleges and universities of higher learning—have the potential to offer *transformative* learning. Surely these institutions are spheres for personal and corporate transformation; the Christian academy at its best views education as a means by which the Spirit fulfills the Spirit's agenda in our lives. It needs to be stressed right up front: this is not, as is often thought, achieved by downplaying the academic side of higher education. Rather the academic process can and must be viewed as the means by which God brings about his transformation in the lives of individuals and the transformation of communities of learning.

In other words, this vision assumes a stress on the value of and commitment to academic excellence, the academic process and the classic academic disciplines. But with this commitment, the bottom line is ultimately and finally not academics but transformation.

Christian universities and colleges, in other words, pursue academic excellence not because they want to have a positive reputation with the Ivy League schools of the world but because it is good for the soul. If it is not good for the soul and for soul formation, then let it go—it is the world's agenda and why should a Christian institution of higher learning play that game? But perhaps the vision of academic excellence is actually something that is deeply Christian. And, furthermore, perhaps a case could be made that the commitment to excellence in research and teaching that is the mantra of the secular or public university is actually something that was planted there in the original vision for these universities—a vision that was unapologetically Christian.

The most significant gift the Christian university or college can give the church and the world is women and men who have experienced, through the process of quality teaching-learning, the transforming power of the gospel. The greatest value that higher education offers the world—whether for the marketplace or the church—is wise men and women of mature character who are capable of providing vibrant moral leadership. And this means we do not judge the academic community from a shortsighted pragmatic point of view. Rather, we recognize the crucial place of the arts and the humanities in the work of academic formation. To cut out art departments because they do not bring a financial return is to fail to appreciate their transformative potential.

And so we ask the obvious question: what would this look like? What is the content, the character of this experience of grace in the educational process? And what is the particular way in which an institution of higher learning can contribute to this objective?

IN CHRIST

First and without equivocation we can speak of the entire academic agenda as having a single unqualified focus: to know, love and serve Christ Jesus. And more, through the process of study, learning, research, writing—along with the cocurricular agenda of worship, community, sports and the arts—we are responding to the call of the Father and the working of the Spirit that draws us into dynamic union with the risen and ascended Christ.

The grace we seek is to understand the world through the lens of Christ Jesus, the one in whom all things exist and have their being. We see all things through the wonder of Christ as the one through whom all things are created and are being redeemed—meaning not only that there is a christological hermeneutic in our reading of Scripture but that we have a christological hermeneutic to our reading of all things. Every discipline, from law to business, from biology to religious studies, is pursued with this passionate desire to see and understand all things in Christ. In the words of 2 Corinthians 10:5, we "take every thought captive to obey Christ."[4]

But we go further: we do not merely talk about Christ; we study that we might live in obedience to Christ. We study with a vision and passion for service, for lives lived under the authority of the ascended one. Even more, our commitment is not merely to an idea of Christ but to Christ himself. Thus the energy that animates our studies, our teaching-research, our life in as an academic community is Christ—not the idea or principle or concept of Christ but the person of the risen Lord. Our prayer each day is that the Spirit of Christ would infuse our relationships, our academic processes, our way of being, animating our lives and our work everywhere from the library to the classroom to the academic offices to the soccer field.

FOUR ELEMENTS OF OUR LIFE IN CHRIST

With this identity, in Christ, as the given—not as one feature of our identity as a university but as the defining reason for our lives and our work—we can speak of each of the elements of a theology of the Christian life. I have suggested that a helpful way to think of the theology of transformation in Christ is in terms of four essential elements or dimensions. A person who is mature in their faith will have these qualities or characteristics:

- Wisdom—recognizing this as the vision of maturity in Christ, informed by the wisdom literature of the Old Testament and given Christian expression by the apostle Paul in Colossians 1.

- Vocational holiness—the capacity for good work in response to God's call and equipping.

- Love—the capacity to love as one has been loved.

---

[4]This phrase from 2 Corinthians 10:5 has inspired a number of books and articles, including D. W. Gill, *The Opening of the Christian Mind: Taking Every Thought Captive to Christ* (Downers Grove, IL: InterVarsity Press, 1989); K. W. Hermann, *Every Thought Captive to Christ: A Guide to Resources for Developing a Christian Perspective in the Major Academic Disciplines* (Kent, OH: Radix Christian Studies Program, 1985); D. W. King, *Taking Every Thought Captive: Forty Years of Christian Scholar's Review* (Abilene, TX: Abilene Christian University Press, 2011); R. L. Pratt, *Every Thought Captive: A Study Manual for the Defense of Christian Truth* (Phillipsburg, NJ: Presbyterian and Reformed, 1979).

- Joy—the capstone, a joy in Christ in the midst of a fragmented world, a joy that is the crucial evidence of faith in the risen and ascended Christ.

I propose that we can say to a prospective student, this is what we hope for you and long for you and offer to you. This is what we are about. This is what it means to be part of this academic community, this university, this seminary.

- You will grow in wisdom and in your capacity for wisdom.

- You will mature in your vocational identity and calling, and you will receive the inner tools and resources for a lifetime of vocational discernment.

- We will grow together in love and in our capacity for love, even as we are loved.

- You will become a happier person: you will know the joy of God, but more, you will grow in your capacity for joy.

Can a Christian university deliver on this agenda? Well, why not? Why not make this our vision and mission, our commitment and our institutional orientation? On the one hand, what have we to lose? But more importantly, can we seek anything less?

If this is our agenda it makes all the difference, of course, in the recruitment of faculty. It means that competency in their discipline—biblical studies, music, philosophy or history—is important. Crucial, actually. But that competence is only a means to an end. The end is not capability in the discipline but transformation in Christ. And yet each discipline is crucial and competence in the discipline is crucial, because each discipline is an essential means to that end.

We need gifted philosophers and sociologists and musicians and historians. But the genius of a Christian university or seminary is a passion for transformation, and so we would recruit and welcome faculty who have this as their passion and commitment along with strong capacity. They are master-teachers who through the academic process know what it means to foster transformation and the capacity for transformation. They know the art of classroom instruction; they know that grading and assessment are all part of an investment in the formation of students.

They affirm at each point of the academic process that they are committed to transformation. This is vital. It is not that they make it a point to say nice things about Jesus or are sure to offer a prayer before the lecture or bring in a few Bible verses here and there, or even that they are sincerely and truly kind, generous and compassionate (though we certainly hope they are!). Rather, what we are after is scholar-teachers who know how to teach their specific discipline with a vision for transformation and who can see and feel in their gut the power of the teaching-learning process to foster and encourage transformation in Christ.

So, then, what do we seek—through each discipline, through each element or dimension of the academic process, curricular and cocurricular, within the academic community? First, wisdom—briefly here, since I will expand on this more below. We seek intellectual maturity, a maturity infused with wisdom, the orientation of those who in reverence for Christ seek the renewal of the mind and thus the capacity to know the truth and live in this truth.

This includes the basic elements of moral intelligence: integrity in our finances, in sexuality and in speech (the three recurring marks in the wisdom literature of the Old Testament, the Sermon on the Mount and the New Testament Epistles). Character development is anchored in wisdom and growth in wisdom. All higher education needs to be committed without apology to character development. But we must not confuse moral formation with spiritual formation. Moral and character development are derivative of union with Christ. Furthermore, true intellectual development is fundamentally formation in wisdom, which in turn includes and informs Christian moral commitments.

Second, we must also speak of vocational holiness—the capacity to discern what God is doing in the world and participate in this kingdom work in a way that is deeply congruent with one's own sense of calling. While I have suggested that it is not adequate to speak of the university as having a mission to "credential," this does not mean we are not passionate about good work and even good work that is a means of gainful employment.

But we do not reduce the curriculum to helping someone get a job or be successful at that job. Rather, the whole of the curriculum is about highlighting what God is doing in the world as Creator and redeemer. It is the constant question for Christians in higher education: not merely "What is truth" but also "What is God doing in our world and how are we potential participants in this work?" This vision for the work of God as Creator and redeemer, maker and healer, then frees us to grow in self-knowledge, to be freed in the university or the seminary from pretense and even from competition and to seek the wisdom that includes mature self-understanding—the essential starting point in vocational discernment.

Furthermore, vocational holiness includes the capacity for hopeful realism. Whether in sociology or in business, in pastoral ministry or medicine, we can develop the capacity to make a diagnosis—to read the situation, to understand one's times and one's circumstances and to see these circumstances with grace and deep hopefulness. For a pastor, this means both the resolve and capacity to get an accurate understanding of a congregation and the community in which it is located. The crucial piece is that we see the congregation and the situation as it actually is rather than as we wish it were. This perspective, this capacity, is always hope-filled. The abiding and underlying ethos of Christian education is always and persistently hopeful, even in the face of tragedy, darkness and setback.

From here and in this context, then, we foster the capacity for vocational discernment. To a prospective seminary student, we do not say we will make you a competent and skilled pastor. To a potential student in our school of business or education we do not say we will make you a gifted and capable business person or teacher. Well, okay, we do. But this is almost secondary—more like a case study in good work and the craft of a particular occupation. What should be clear is that our passion in a Christian institution of higher learning is to foster your capacity for a lifetime of vocational transitions and thus vocational discernment at each of these transitions. Vocational holiness means we appreciate the work of God in the world, know how to read and see ourselves in the light of this work and know how to read our times, our circumstances—and then, of course, to respond with courage and creativity.

Many of our students will have no idea what they will be doing ten or twenty years from now. Even if they are business majors or philosophy majors now, that does not mean that ten years hence they will be businesspeople or teaching philosophy in the community college. Knowing this means we give them the intellectual and emotional tools for a lifetime of good work and a lifetime of vocational discernment.

And this is deeply practical—lest we think of it as disengaged from the actual marketplace. Employers in many different sectors of society are looking for staff and leaders who can think critically with creativity and with a capacity for innovation and who are capable of working collaboratively with others. They are looking for leaders who can be aligned with a knowledge base and complex economy who have the capacity for continuous learning. Christian universities, colleges and theological seminaries can deliver on this. And they will anchor this capacity for critical thinking, creativity, innovation and collaboration in the gospel.

Institutions of Christian learning will approach vocation in terms of a lifetime of skills for good work, with a vision for students that know how to debate, how to make a compelling case for a cause with confidence, how to function in a pluralistic, multifaith context with humility but with moral authority. Formation will mean fostering students' capacity to face an ever-changing world with courage and discernment. And, furthermore, students who in the workplace will know how to exercise power with compassion and skill—with a commitment to the common good, using power for the sake of others. Central to this capacity for good work is prudence—wisdom that is timely and fitting, apt actions and apt words for this time and this place. Prudence is the interface of wisdom and good work.

The third part of the Christian institution's vision is to create people who love as they are loved. I wonder how a typical high school graduate would respond to the university advertisement that read, "Enroll at [distinguished Ivy League want-to-be] Christian university, and you will learn how to love." Since one of young people's great longings is to love and be loved, you would think that would solve all numerical goals of the recruitment department!

But it sounds too soft, too sentimental, too disconnected from serious academic processes. And yet why not? Why not highlight and insist on this: the great energy that sustains the world is the love of God, and therefore growth in wisdom, understanding and excellence in our work through our studies will include, as something that infuses the whole curriculum and our way of being, the deep conviction that to be human is to be loved, and to be all we are called to be means we learn how to love.

If we fail on this point, we create only noisy gongs (see 1 Cor 13:1). If we are not minimally effective on this point, everything else we do is suspect. So why not be up front about it? Why not state this as one of the points of commitment and passion, something that without apology demarcates our common life and thus our vision for the academic enterprise?

This is desperately needed in a society terribly confused about the meaning of love. And surely, if we grow in wisdom and our capacity to fulfill God's call on our lives, then we have to learn along the way what it means to love a spouse, a child, a friend, what it means to love a colleague or a competitor, what it means to love an enemy—both the enemy closer at hand and the enemy with whom our country is at war—what it means to love with a deep passion for truth, justice and freedom. How does the call to love affect how we function on the public stage and vote for political parties and advocate for specific agendas?

This love is learned in the classroom as we think practically and substantively about love and reject sentimentalized or eroticized versions of "love." But this learning to love and be loved is not merely talked about; it is also embodied in the life of the community, in professors who actually love their students, in faculty who live in mutual love for one another, in students who learn with faculty how to process conflict, wrongs and difficulties—these become the actual grist for learning how to love.

We learn what it means to offer and receive hospitality—whether it is the hospitality of a shared meal or, so very crucial, being gracious and hospitable toward another whose ideas, opinions and manner may strike us as wrong or problematic. We learn that to love is to serve, and this call—a generous sacrificial passion to be Christ to the church and to the world—infuses the whole curriculum. What drives us, motivates us, through the academic process is not professional success, prestige or advancement, but generous service. What catches our attention through the process of learning is not so much Wall Street as the far side of the tracks—not those in power, but those who are at the margins. We foster in the entire curriculum a capacity to see the world as the Old Testament prophets saw the world.

In all of this we link love with wisdom; to grow in love is to grow in discernment. We foster an increasing capacity to love well, with prudence and wisdom. As I will be stressing below, this wisdom is central to the curriculum of the Christian university.

And, fourth, joy. The palpable longing of the human soul is to be happy. And Jesus assures us that he has come that our joy would be complete. Well, then, can we not say to a potential student, you want to be happy and Jesus wants to make you happy. We want to deliver on this agenda, this mission, this divine intent for your life.

Dare we say it more bluntly? You will be happy and know what it means to be a happy person! We engage in Christian higher education, we function as a Christian university or seminary, so that we can be happy and so that you can know a joy that permeates into the very core of your being. Our agenda is that you would know joy during your studies—and this means learning to delight in the good, the noble, the excellent and the worthy of praise. You will learn in the course of your studies that what you thought you needed to be happy—property, prestige and power—are all vacuous in the end. Your deepest joy is finally found only in God and in a life anchored in his wisdom and his call on your life. When you find this, you will be "blessed" (see Ps 1).

Our school of business will be as intentional as our school of theology in insisting that we are not about the accumulation of property, prestige and power. But more, we can say to them, your university and seminary studies will not only be a delight, they will enhance your capacity for joy. The entire curriculum will be infused with a passion for the truth that sets us free, the vision for generous service that aligns us with the kingdom purposes of God in the world. A vision for Christ and the beauty of Christ can—yes, it really can—satisfy the deepest longings of the human soul.

This means that we will face the pain and sorrow of this world with honesty and compassion; we will not be naive to the massive injustice that demarcates life in this fragmented world; we will not be immune to each other's pain. We will face the wrongs squarely, but we will do so through the lens of the crucified, risen and ascended Christ. We will learn how to be angry without sin, how to mourn loss but allow our mourning to be turned to joy, how to be discouraged without becoming cynics and how to be afraid but not live consumed with anxiety. What is happening to us emotionally will not be incidental to our academic agenda; we are committed equally to both intellectual and emotional maturity—marks, when taken together, of a genuine wisdom.

And as an aside here, it merits reminder that there is no learning without joy—no deep learning, no transforming learning, without delight in the very learning process. True intellectual development is about the ordering of desire or, as the ancients stated it, the ordering of the affections. It is about fostering the capacity to delight in the good—to find in the good our deepest satisfaction.

Wisdom, good work, love and joy. Each is a dimension of being in Christ. And for each, one's university or seminary studies are but a point of departure. There will be growth and development during one's studies, of course. But the genius of higher education is in fostering the potential for growth. University studies are about learning how to learn, how to live and how to grow in one's capacity for wisdom, good work, love and joy.

WISDOM AS A UNIFYING COMMITMENT

In this articulation of the character of mature Christian spirituality, particular attention needs to be given to the place of wisdom in the mission and educational purpose of the Christian university or seminary. A church is first and foremost a liturgical community. The church has a passion for teaching and learning and a deep commitment to mission and to fostering the vocational capacity of its members. But it is fundamentally a liturgical community. In contrast to a church or congregation, an academic institution is not first a liturgical or missional community but a teaching-learning community. And for institutions of higher learning, wisdom is the primary leverage point for spiritual and moral formation and character development.

One of the urgent needs in higher education is to find a unifying theme or focus that will bring together the deep disciplinary fragmentation that has history and science teachers doing their work in silos rather than out of a commitment to a shared vision and mission for the university and seminary. First and fundamentally, Christian institutions of higher education sustain an overarching affirmation of the glory of Christ in the world. But how? Specifically, the glory of Christ is affirmed through the academic process of teaching-learning, and thus wisdom presents a compelling possibility as a unifying and integrating reference point for the work of faculty, student life directors and administrators.

- Wisdom as the fruit of teaching and learning.

- Wisdom as the ballast for good work and the capacity for good work.

- Wisdom as the necessary counterpart to love—informing and animating the call to love one another.

- Wisdom as the foundation for joy.

The university as we know it is essentially a medieval creation. And the vision of the early universities was simple and clear: the pursuit of understanding, formation for life through the cultivation of virtues and habits and equipping for service for the common good.[5] This vision for the university was a Christian vision; every university in the West was an institution of the church. The church had a vision for higher education and it established centers of learning as a vital part of its understanding of the church's mission in the world.

The genius of the medieval university was the interplay between scholastic theology and mystical theology: critical intellectual study, learning and reflection on the one hand, and the learning that is informed by prayer and contemplation on the other. Both were viewed as integral to each other in the defining vision of the university: the love of God.

---

[5]David F. Ford, *Christian Wisdom: Desiring God and Learning in Love* (Cambridge, UK: Cambridge University Press, 2007), p. 308.

Implicitly if not explicitly the university was about formation in wisdom, and wisdom was found specifically at this point of integration between critical scholarship (scholastic theology) and the intentional fostering of spiritual vitality with reflection on the nature of the spiritual life (mystical theology). Each informed the other; the counterpoint between them fostered growth in wisdom.

This integration of learning and the spiritual life was fostered in particular in the monastic movement. This is profiled in the classic *The Love of Learning and the Desire for God* by John Leclercq.[6] This examination of monastic culture may well be more relevant than ever, partly because the monastic movement is providing a counterbalance to the pragmatism of contemporary Western (and evangelical) approaches to higher education. Furthermore, in a post-Christian secular society, the monastic movement suggests practices that may well have continuing relevance for the church as a whole and thus for Christian universities, colleges and seminaries in the twenty-first century.

Leclercq reminds us that the genius of the monastic movement was an unqualified affirmation that the purpose of study and learning— indeed of all spiritual practice—is union with God in Christ. And that thus even if we speak of wisdom as the immediate goal of study and learning, the ultimate goal without with the immediate goal makes no sense. And this means that study, learning and scholarship must be infused with prayer and worship. It is by prayer and worship that our study is located within the broader purposes of God in our lives. Prayer and worship give focus, clarity and purpose to study, to the academic endeavor. Constant prayer is then the air that is breathed as we pursue our studies and scholarship.

Bernard of Clairvaux insisted that we are not wise until we live in the fear of God and are drawn up into the love of God. And thus monastic theology is the essential completion of scholastic theology.[7] What impresses me from Leclercq's study of monasticism is that for all his celebration of the monastic approach to learning, he does not pit monas-

---

[6]John Leclercq, *The Love of Learning and the Desire for God: A Study of Monastic Culture*, trans. Catharine Misrahi (New York: Fordham, 1961).
[7]Ibid., p. 223.

ticism against scholasticism. To the contrary, he affirms that scholasticism is almost a necessary counterpart to monastic culture, with its diligent focus on the grammar of Scripture and the recognition of the need to draw on non-Christian sources for our learning, including philosophy.

Leclercq also notes that monastic theology needs scholastic theology in order to engage the culture—the social and intellectual context in which theology is to be lived and expressed. And Leclercq has an oh-so-brief appendix in which the theological work of St. Anselm is celebrated precisely because he was both a scholastic—a first-class scholar on the public stage—and also deeply monastic, a lover of God and a man of prayer.

This all seems alien to the contemporary university. And in many respects it is. The original vision for learning and study toward wisdom seems a far cry from the experience of a typical university student in the twenty-first century. And yet the split between prayerful piety and critical scholarship actually has a long history. Indeed, Mark A. McIntosh observes that by the sixteenth century, a split was already beginning to emerge—between scholastic theology and mystical theology, between learning through critical scholarship and the life of *devotio*.

Mystical writers, he notes, were increasingly speaking of the interior life in terms of their own experience, with less and less appeal to the Scriptures or ancient authorities.[8] Conversely, scholasticism became increasingly suspicious of mystical theology, the experience of faith and the study of the interior life. Erasmus and others were scathing in their critique of scholasticism for its failure to integrate heart and mind and to prepare one for life and service. For Erasmus, scholastic theology was disconnected from life, from spirituality and thus from service and ministry.

Yet there were always those who insisted on holding them together. A noteworthy example is the Society of Jesus. David J. Hassel, a member of the Society of Jesus, in his book *City of Wisdom: A Christian Vision of the American University* contends that Jesuit higher education sought from the beginning to avoid this split between scholarship and devotion

---

[8]Mark A. McIntosh, *Mystical Theology: The Integrity of Spirituality and Theology* (Malden, MA: Blackwell, 1998), p. 68.

and insisted on sustaining the original medieval vision of higher education as the pursuit of understanding, formation for life and equipping for service.

The early Jesuit vision for higher education was initially described in the Jesuit Constitutions and then more fully articulated in the *Ratio Studiorum* of 1599 (the "plan of studies"). This early Jesuit ideal has continuing relevance for any Christian institution resolved to hold together three defining values and commitments: a commitment to radical apostolic service in the world, prayer and depth of piety, and critical scholarship. The Jesuits were and continue to be perhaps the greatest missionary order in the history of the church. The Spiritual Exercises of Ignatius of Loyola were their classic guide to the interior life of prayer and discernment. And they insisted on the vital place of scholarship in the purposes of God in the world.

The Ratio Studiorum starts with and insists on the primacy of the Scriptures but then calls for a full and all encompassing curriculum that explores every dimension of human learning. Then, alongside the process of critical learning, we see two parallel and embedded commitments: all learning is oriented toward a life of service for the church and for the world, and all learning is to foster the interior life along with virtue and formation of character.[9]

This, Hassel suggests, is wisdom, and wisdom is the integrating point of the curriculum as well as that which provides operational unity to the university, illuminating administrative decisions.[10] Wisdom fosters a panoramic Christian vision integrating knowledge, skill and art. And this vision encourages the academic community to draw on wisdom from wherever it comes, in that all truth is God's truth. It is, in other words, world-embracing and world-affirming: celebrating culture, art and philosophy. But, and this is crucial, this vision fosters discernment and prudence as well. Thus a Christian philosophy and a biblical theology are the essential anchors to the curriculum.

---

[9]John W. O'Malley, "The Jesuit Educational Enterprise in Historical Perspective," *Jesuit Higher Education: Essays on an American Tradition of Excellence*, ed. Rolando E. Bonachea (Pittsburgh: Duquesne University Press, 1989), pp. 16-20.

[10]David J. Hassel, *City of Wisdom: A Christian Vision of the American University* (Chicago: Loyola University Press, 1983), p. 353.

I mention this particular example from the history of the church for a reason: to indicate that this understanding or vision of higher education is not new, but also, just as critically, to highlight that first-class scholarship and an orientation to transformation and formation for service are not a threat to one another. The Jesuits have perhaps not always sustained this ideal. But their commitment to scholarship is unmatched; they have demonstrated that this comprehensive vision for higher education does not threaten high-quality scholarship. To the contrary, the two are mutually reinforcing and mutually dependent. Good scholarship fosters depth of piety; piety, in turn, animates scholarship.

It is encouraging, then, to see this theme of wisdom and higher education emerging in significant publications in this century. I will reference two in particular: Daniel J. Treier's *Virtue and the Voice of God: Toward Theology as Wisdom* and David F. Ford's *Christian Wisdom: Desiring God and Learning in Love.*[11] Treier writes from the conviction that theology is essential to the mission and ministry of the church and, more, that this task is the work of wisdom, a wisdom marked by an authentic engagement with our contemporary context, for the truth proclaimed by the church is "public" truth. The substantive contribution of this book is the way in which he provides the reader with this comprehensive analysis of the place of wisdom in biblical revelation. He is explicit that his agenda is to understand theological formation as formation in wisdom, and so he establishes his argument by a thorough outline of the place of wisdom in the Scriptures, with special attention given to Proverbs 3:13-18. And he demonstrates that wisdom can provide the church with the unifying element needed for theological education.

But then, as Treier notes, it is one thing to say that the end of theological education is wisdom; we then need to ask, what is the "material

---

[11]Daniel J. Treier, *Virtue and the Voice of God: Toward Theology as Wisdom* (Grand Rapids: Eerdmans, 2006); Ford, *Christian Wisdom.* I am not suggesting these are the only voices; there are many others, including Charles Wood, *Vision and Discernment: An Orientation in Theological Study* (Decatur, GA: Scholars Press, 1985, perhaps the strongest critique of clericalism); Max L. Stackhouse, *Apologia: Contextualization, Globalization and Mission in Theological Education* (Grand Rapids: Eerdmans, 1988); and Ellen Charry, *By The Renewing of Your Minds: The Pastoral Function of Christian Doctrine* (New York: Oxford University Press, 1997).

content" of this wisdom?[12] For Treier, that content, arising from his extended theological interpretation of wisdom, is the knowledge of God by the Spirit in and by the Scriptures. This naturally leads him to probe what it means to read the Scripture as Scripture as he argues for the unity of the Scriptures, a postcritical understanding of rationality, the idea that theory and practice must inform each other and, finally, that we can and must speak of a theological interpretation of the Bible.

While Treier's publication makes the case that theological education is formation in wisdom—something that should perhaps be self-evident—David Ford harkens back to the original medieval vision of the university as a venue for formation in wisdom. He also bemoans the loss of the powerful interplay between wisdom and the university, and his description—his critique—of the contemporary university is telling. He sees a trend toward the university serving the economy, with students being consumers of a product that will hopefully foster their career aspirations.

Ford does not discount the need for attention to pragmatics and agrees that there are legitimate economic goals to higher education. But what he grieves is the loss of the pursuit of understanding for its own sake, the lack of a commitment to well-rounded formation through education as students are formed for the common good and that, indeed, "the inattention to all-round formation underlines what is perhaps the most glaring weakness of contemporary higher education."[13] He notes that in his own university, Cambridge, the aim of forming wise people for the common good may be implicit in some forms of the university but wonders why it cannot "be made an explicit issue in discussion, negotiation and deliberation relating to universities."[14] Why can we not, Ford asks, sustain such a comprehensive ideal, one that would integrate knowledge and practice?

Ford has the challenge of articulating a distinctively Christian vision for the public university within a multifaith and secular context. For the Christian university—be it Catholic or evangelical—there is no reason

---

[12]Treier, *Virtue*, p. 24.
[13]Ford, *Christian Wisdom*, p. 322.
[14]Ibid., p. 323.

at all for this vision to be anything but explicit and for us to actively seek this very integration of knowledge and practice.

WISDOM AND PRACTICE

But then, of course, we need to speak of practice. When we use the language of "wisdom" we are making a notable distinction between knowledge and wisdom. There is no wisdom without knowledge, but knowledge alone is not wisdom. Wisdom is knowledge in practice, knowledge that is lived. And so to speak of wisdom we must speak of practice. And one of the vibrant conversations of the late twentieth and early twenty-first centuries has been shared reflections around practice.

The key contributions to this conversation have been those of Craig Dykstra, Miroslav Volf, Greg Jones and Dorothy Bass.[15] They note how theology is formed within us only if it is practiced and that, therefore, practice is the essential counterpart to theological and spiritual formation. It is through practice that virtue is cultivated. They speak of spiritual practice as that which Christians do together by way of formative routines and actions—repeated, routinized, signifying faith and cultivating faith. It is not merely a good deed done or a ritual observed but the routine observance that marks Christian identity and fosters that identity.

A primary catalyst for this conversation was the work of Alasdair MacIntyre and the publication of his book *After Virtue*.[16] MacIntyre speaks of social practices that foster a particular set of dispositions and thus a way of being and way of behavior. What these Christian theologians have done is to take MacIntyre's understanding of the place of practice in forming virtue and see it through a distinctly Christian and theological lens. They have done so on the conviction that we must not separate thought from action. They insist that word and deed, thought

---

[15]The defining publications for this conversation include Craig Dykstra, *Growing in the Life of Faith: Education and Christian Practices* (Louisville: Geneva Press, 1997), and then the revised edition (Louisville: Westminster John Knox, 2005); Dorothy Bass and Craig Dykstra, eds., *Practicing Our Faith: A Guide for Conversation, Learning and Growth* (San Francisco, Jossey Bass, 1997); and Miroslav Volf and Dorothy C. Bass, eds., *Practicing Theology: Beliefs and Practices in Christian Life* (Grand Rapids, MI: Eerdmans, 2002).

[16]Alasdair MacIntyre, *After Virtue* (South Bend, IN: Notre Dame University Press, 1984).

and action form and reform each other and that certain defined and intentional practices foster this interface between word and deed, between confession and behavior.

From understanding to practice: there are two sides to this. First, we need to be intentional in the practicing of our faith. In the move from confession to action, it is practices that give us tracks on which to act in a manner consistent with our confession. Thus, for example, the practice of triune worship reflects and expresses our conviction that God is triune. And the practice of hospitality reflects a conviction that we are to show hospitality. If you say something matters, it should and will be evident in practice. If prayer matters, then you will pray.

What matters most to us in life will be evident in the practices that track those things into the contours, routines and rhythms of daily life, the cycle of the year and, indeed, the seasons of life. And we do these whether we feel like or not. We do not act spontaneously but deeply rely on routines and practices to form our deepest convictions—our values— into virtues within us. If we believe God is good; we will give thanks.

But second, this whole discussion affirms that even as understanding informs practice, so practice informs understanding. Thus, for example, we do not really know that God is triune until and unless we worship God as triune; it is through the practice itself that this knowledge is cultivated. It is through doing hospitality that we come to see and understand its character. And, furthermore, practices form our hearts and minds in their repetition. It is in routine and indeed ritual observance— in practice—that what we believe is embodied and thus known.

Thus, practice matters. And it is formative. If worship practices are narcissistic with superficial and escapist melodies, they will cultivate such perspectives or dispositions. Theologically weak or thin practices, particularly in the context of worship, do not form us in wisdom. Worse, they distort understanding and practice. If worship is not trinitarian, it will powerfully undermine any attempt in a lecture hall to speak of God as triune. Practice influences understanding.

Thus, if I were to say that I cannot pray because I have no faith, these authors would urge me to pray so that faith might grow in me. The effect between understanding and practice is iterative. If I believe God is good,

I will give thanks, but more, in giving thanks I enter slowly but surely into a deeper awareness of and appreciation of the goodness of God. And a fundamental means by which I come to an appreciation that God is triune is through baptism and the Lord's supper. Indeed, our practice should reflect our understanding of the nature of God. We do not really "get it"—the Trinity, that is—until we practice it, and specifically practice it in the actions, the embodiment, of baptism and the Lord's Supper. We don't get it until we do it.

These "patterned activities," to use the language of Dykstra and Bass, gradually and incrementally lead to transformation.[17] I must stress this point: the effect of a shared spiritual practice is gradual and incremental. Yes, practices foster a knowledge of God, of self, of the other and of the created order. And yes, they are a means by which we know the grace of God, the grace by which we are transformed and made new. But the fruit of these practices is known over time as slowly but surely the truth, wisdom, is formed within us. Critical to this discussion is the fact that these are not merely activities of an individual but of a community. In shared practices the community is formed together in a common faith.

This brings us back to where I began—the medieval and monastic vision for education. This call to practice is not a new suggestion; it is ancient—it is inherent in the medieval and monastic understanding of prayer and learning. This ancient vision offers the contemporary academic community some wisdom of lasting value.

The vital place of worship and prayer. First, this commitment to transformation and scholarship assumes the central place of prayer and worship. This is the defining practice. This suggests to us that for the individual there is no substitute for prayer, and for the learning community, whether a theological seminary or Christian university, the shared liturgy is a unifying and defining practice of our shared life and our commitment to learning and wisdom—our learning is anchored in our worship of the living and ascended embodiment of the wisdom of God, Christ Jesus. We come to recognize we do not study well until and unless we pray well. And thus, teaching our students to pray is funda-

---

[17]Bass, *Practicing Theology*, p. 26.

mental to our purposes as an academic community.

The study of the Scriptures. Second, the essential complement to worship as central to learning and thus to formation in wisdom is the Scriptures. The ancient monastics made engagement with the Scriptures foundational to all learning. And yet it was not biblicism, for their study of the Scripture was complemented by their engagement with the theology and wisdom of the church fathers. What anchored their learning was the primacy of the Scriptures, yes, but their engagement with the Scriptures was guided by the theological heritage and tradition of the church.

It is important to affirm, though, that their study of Scripture was never as an end in itself; one came to Scripture from prayer and the Scriptures in turn informed their practice of prayer. Thus the contemporary practice of *lectio divina* is really an ancient practice, fostered by the monastic movement and an essential spiritual practice for the church today as well as for every student in a theological school—the capacity to read the Scriptures in prayer with attention to grammar and exegesis but with ultimate attention to the one who is revealed through the ancient text.

Study and engagement with the world. Third, we must beware of succumbing to the common stereotype that monasticism was about disengagement and not about the call of the gospel and of the church to mission—specifically mission to the city and the urban poor. One did certainly step aside from the demands of the world for study, prayer, contemplation and the focused practices of a disciplined Christian community, especially in the Benedictine tradition. But this observation is simply not accurate for later monasticism. And even the Benedictines had an extraordinary commitment to hospitality.

I think of the Friars who left the cloister, whose houses of life and worship were located in the very heart of the cities and whose lives— think of the Franciscans and the Dominicans, for example—were marked by profound commitment to the urban poor in word and deed. And then we have the Society of Jesus, the first apostolic order. They did not establish monasteries but sustained the commitment to prayer and study with the resolve to be, as they put it, "contemplatives in action."

So can this vision for wisdom be the integrating point for Christian higher education? Does the ancient commitment to wisdom have relevance for the Christian university and theological seminary in the twenty-first century? Why not? Why can we not teach for wisdom—a wisdom that is lived and practiced in community through individual spiritual disciplines but with the continued caveat that central and pivotal is worship, the shared liturgy, as the defining practice of the faith community? Why can we not affirm a wisdom that recognizes the priority of the Scriptures in the shaping and informing of a Christian mind but also draws on the whole of God's revelation, a teaching for wisdom that fosters the capacity to live with courage, creativity, character and skill?

By implication, this vision suggests that the liberal arts are about learning to think and act holistically. But it also means that professional programs—education and music and business and church ministry—are not defined in purely pragmatic terms. They are not merely about learning the skills of good business or effective pulpit communication. Rather, the Christian university and the seminary are about the foundational vision of cultivating wisdom as a central means by which we foster the capacity to be in Christ and in service for Christ in the world.

And so, an invitation to faculty: yes, you are trained and you are an expert in a discipline—philosophy or science or business administration or New Testament exegesis. And yet each discipline is but a lens through which we celebrate that all truth is God's truth, and each discipline is a means by which we grow in our capacity for the wisdom found in Christ. And so we say to a faculty member, your job in the end is not to teach history or mathematics or music but to teach these disciplines as a means by which we seek the renewal of the mind, cultivate mature reasoning and thus moral intelligence, and equip men and women to provide moral and spiritual leadership for the church and the marketplace.

TEACHING FOR WISDOM

What does it mean to teach for wisdom—for sapiential holiness? First, a quick note on what it does not mean. Formation in wisdom is the antithesis of indoctrination. Formation in wisdom fosters an open mind and an open Spirit, an eagerness to test theories, to press against borders, to see new ways of framing the truth. There will be diversity of opinion and space for ambiguity.

But then, more to the point, what does it mean to teach for transformation? First, to teach for wisdom is to teach from a clearly defined intellectual tradition; without apology we affirm that our teaching arises from a distinctive theological or philosophical vantage point—a tradition. Lesslie Newbigin states this well in writing, "When reason and tradition are opposed as separate or rival criteria of truth, then the nature of reason is being misunderstood. . . . There are not 'truths of reason' except those that have been developed within a historical tradition."[18] All learning requires that we apprentice within a tradition and submit to the authority of that tradition, for as Newbigin insists, "Innovation can only be responsibly accepted from those who are already masters of the tradition, skilled practitioners of whom it can be said both that the tradition dwells fully in them and that they dwell fully in the tradition."[19]

For the Christian this means that we begin with faith—faith seeking understanding. But more, it is the faith of the church—the creedal and spiritual anchor that locates all understanding and thus all teaching-learning. We stand within a particular tradition. This location for critical reflection does not mean we are arrogant or incapable of new learning, including new learning that challenges that tradition. It is merely that wisdom is anchored; it is located. It is traditioned. This means that a faith-based institution of higher education can and should be unapologetic about its own theological and spiritual tradition, not as a kind of dogmatism or indoctrination and not from an assumed position of superiority, but merely because there is no other way to teach toward wisdom but to teach from within such a heritage—be it Reformed, Anabaptist, Benedictine or Wesleyan-Holiness. We of course teach with a generosity toward other traditions and with an eagerness to learn from others, but our

---

[18]Lesslie Newbigin, *The Gospel in a Pluralist Society* (Grand Rapids, MI: Eerdmans, 1989), p. 57.
[19]Ibid., p. 47.

teaching-learning is located and arises from a tradition as, at the very least, a point of departure.[20]

Second, to teach for transformation is to recognize the primacy of the Scriptures that provide the grand narrative that shapes our vision of the world. In some classes and courses this will be explicit; the biblical narrative will actually be the focus of study. The massive advantage of the Christian university is that this can be clearly incorporated into the curriculum: all students study the Scriptures as a core requirement and commitment. But then it is not that every course is a Bible course; it is rather that we are formed in wisdom as those for whom the Scriptures— the ancient text—are the very air that we breathe, the subtext of our critical reflections, the baseline from which we distill our learning and make sense of our world.

Third, wisdom by its very nature is passed on from one generation to the next; to teach for wisdom is to introduce students to a conversation that has been going on for many decades, centuries and perhaps millennia. As a theologian, this means that patristic theology inevitably is a crucial reference point in my classes; indeed for each of the main courses I teach—Conversion and Transformation, the Meaning of the Sacraments, Spiritual Discernment—we begin with the church fathers. For philosophy, it surely means we go back even further.

Fourth, to teach for wisdom is to foster the capacity for discernment— specifically, the discernment of our times, our culture, our social mores. Wise people are able to interpret their situation and make sense of their world—to read the newspaper, to observe the behavior of a family, to hear a popular song on the radio, to sit through a business meeting of a congregation or to observe the marketing campaign of a major corporation—and to observe and interpret with discrimination and good judgment. Quality learning fosters the capacity for hermeneutics—of our times, our culture, our society, our history. And so, whether it is a course in medieval history, modern American poetry or the ethnog-

---

[20]See especially in this regard Richard T. Hughes and William B. Adrian, *Models for Christian Higher Education: Strategies for Success in the Twenty-First Century* (Grand Rapids, MI: Eerdmans, 1997), with their compelling contrasts and comparisons between universities within Roman Catholic, Lutheran, Wesleyan, Reformed, Mennonite and other traditions.

raphy of Russian youth culture, we learn with a growing capacity for interpreting and making sense of our world and doing so with a discerning eye.

And finally, to learn for wisdom is to practice what we learn—to live our learning. This should not come too early, actually, but it must come. What I mean is that there is an advantage to learning that fosters waiting, processing and distilling what we have heard and seen. We do not act prematurely; we are to wait, see and consider. But not for too long. For wisdom to be the outcome of our learning, it will mean that our learning is in time embodied—actually lived out in our way of being, from understanding to practice and back to understanding. It is, to use the ancient phrase, a practical wisdom.

What must be stressed is that good teaching cannot be reduced to technique. When I think back to my greatest teachers, they were a diverse lot, but they were all wise. And they had a passion for their discipline and for truth and for life. Most had a keen sense of humor. Most did not rely on teaching "aids"—early equivalents to contemporary PowerPoint. Most came to their teaching with a profound respect for their student that was evident in their patience, compassion and attentiveness to their questions and interests. They had no patience with facile arguments, no toleration of pretense or posturing, little capacity to suffer fools. But mainly, I stress, they were a diverse group of people, each comfortable in their own skin.

For the Christian, of course, to teach for wisdom is to teach for this particular end: the genius, the "essential knowledge" of the Christian university is that it can be explicit—to know, love and serve Christ Jesus. We study to the glory and grandeur of Christ, we foster through our studies a passion for Christ (loving Christ with our whole minds) and with a passion to serve him in the church and in the world. And this is evident in part in a profound love of learning—a passion to know God and know more about the ways of God as creator and redeemer.

If this vision is going to shape our vision of theological education, we will have to learn from earlier generations of Christian theologians, educators and scholars. Particularly we will learn from those who did not see reason and spirituality as in tension but as necessary to each other.

SEEKING TRANSFORMATION IN THE SECULAR UNIVERSITY

While I am considering here the call or mission of the Christian university or the theological seminary, I must also reflect on the potential for transformation for those who enroll in a public or secular university. This was my world and thus my experience. I did an undergraduate degree, a joint interdisciplinary major in anthropology and history (I smile as I write this, realizing that this interdisciplinary option was a great gift to those of us who either did not know what major to choose or who wanted to major in everything).

The university at the time was dominated in the social sciences by faculty with a strong sympathy toward a Marxist-Leninist agenda. And the chair of the history department, Professor Zaggorin, led the honors senior seminar. I have a vivid memory of his eloquent articulation of a view of history where truth was in the eye of the beholder. I came to that course as one taken with the argument that there is "evidence that demands a verdict" and was speechless in response to his retort regarding the resurrection of Jesus that "it may be true for you, but that does not make it true for your neighbor."

I have since given much thought to what I wish I had said at the time, but my main point here is that I did my undergraduate studies not in a Christian university or college but in an institution that had a powerful inclination to discount not only the Christian faith but also what I viewed (at that time) as the basis for that faith.

In retrospect I am very glad that I chose this option for my undergraduate studies. And I am deeply grateful for the local chapter of Inter-Varsity Christian Fellowship, which was a key resource and support network through the duration of those studies. I have since come to value and appreciate other campus ministries, both evangelical and Roman Catholic, in their vision to be a means of grace within the public and secular university.

But also, I must confess, there was a noteworthy gap in my formation: the local church. In my initial two years of university studies I attended one of the churches that was walking distance from the university. And week after week the message was the same—the preacher routinely disparaged the university as a waste of time and money, dis-

counting the value of higher education in general but particularly that
from a secular university. He was only barely tolerant of the local Bible
college, which at least affirmed the study of the Scriptures. But the university had no redeeming value for him. And I vividly remember the
day that I walked out midway through the sermon and wondered if I
could ever embrace a Christian faith that did not take seriously the life
of the mind.

In the providential goodness of God, some time later I heard about
and headed to a place called L'Abri in the village of Huemoz, Swit-
zerland. I was welcomed into a community that was both very Christian
and very affirming of the life of the mind—including my involvement
as a student in the secular university. The L'Abri community was pivotal
in my eventual journey to a maturing faith in Christ. But I often think
back and wonder what could have been if the church down the street
from the university had had a greater vision for supporting, encouraging and equipping both students and faculty members whose calling
and vision was to be part of a teaching-learning community that was
avowedly secular.

Can we speak of formation and transformation in the critical university years for those who enroll at the public university? If the answer
is yes, it seems to me that there are two indispensable agencies essential
to the process of transformation. First is the student ministry and
second is the local church. The ideal, of course, is that they work in
tandem, with the church recognizing the need to support and encourage
campus ministries (they have expertise and time that few churches
have) and the campus ministry affirming that they are not the church
and that students need to be part of a faith community as an integral
dimension of their faith formation.

The campus ministry needs to engage a vision for a three-to-four-
year "curriculum" that complements the academic curriculum. They
need to avoid the inclination to think that they need to convert as many
students as possible to Christian faith as quickly as possible; they should
avoid any inclination to force to the matter or press prematurely for a
"decision" for Christ. Rather, campus ministries need to view this entire
three or four year season of life as a time of discovery, learning and thus

potential transformation. For those from a Christian upbringing, this is an opportunity with some distance from parents to come to an adult faith. For those from nonreligious backgrounds, this is an opportunity to—slowly and without anything being forced—consider the claims of Christ Jesus and the meaning of the gospel.

The college years are a formative time of life both for those who have made a Christian commitment and for those who may be inquirers. For all, why not have a curriculum that is geared not so much to get young people to make a faith commitment but rather to establish the foundation and practices for a lifetime of growth in faith, hope and love?

For growth in wisdom, consider a focused approach to fostering an understanding of the Scriptures so that the ancient text is increasingly the frame of reference by which we make sense of our world and thus of all of our studies. In my own experience, nothing was so crucial as this: that the campus ministry believed in and encouraged regular Bible study—and more, it provided students with the capacity to read and study the Bible as the counterpoint to the university curriculum. This parallel curriculum should also include an introduction to the ancient creeds as the baseline for reading the Scriptures and for fostering a trinitarian vision of life, work and relationships.

For growth in vocational holiness, campus ministry can be an ideal time to create spaces and places for students to reflect on and discuss the character of good work. With new distance from home and parents, university students have their first real opportunity for what developmental theorists call "differentiation"; social separation from parents can open up the possibility of real self-knowledge. Students typically come to the university years with massive expectations from parents regarding "successful" careers; now is a time for them to step back from the pressure points of families and immediate communities to—with time and space, new friends and acquaintances—learn, in the language of Romans 12:3, to take a "sober" look at themselves.

And in a world so very confused about the nature of love, the university years must be a time and space, a season of life, in which students learn what it means to grow in love: both the experience of love and what it means to love one's neighbor. The parallel curriculum of campus ministry should surely also address the character of joy—the ordering of the affections, the nurturing of desire.

All this is good, but can the campus ministry do it all? The ideal, and surely an achievable vision, is for campus ministries to establish intentional partnerships with local churches: to identify churches with a vision for the university student, who do not view students as a bother because they are not big givers and are around for just a few years. To have a vision for hospitality for the university student and who will seek, among other things, to demonstrate the love of Christ.

The local church should consider its potential impact on the life of a university student. Every two years or so, I teach a graduate-level theology course titled Conversion and Transformation. One of the requirements for the course is a theological interpretation of a conversion narrative, and students typically use their own narrative as the basis for this theological analysis of religious experience.

They begin with a description of their journey to an adult faith. And as I read these, I am amazed at how frequently there is reference to a church they attended during their university undergraduate years. It is not uncommon that a key element in their journey to faith in Christ will be a Baptist or Pentecostal or Anglican-Episcopalian or Presbyterian church, perhaps just down the street from the university, whose calling included a vision and passion for supporting, encouraging and equipping students. What left a lasting mark and legacy on their lives was simply this: radical hospitality, worship that drew them into the presence of the ascended Christ, fellowship with Christians from all walks of life and who were both older and younger (not too homogeneous!), and orientation in preaching and congregational life toward the mission of God in the world.

Some larger congregations may actually have a campus minister, but most will naturally partner with a local campus ministry. In my first pastorate, in Peterborough, Ontario, the main campus minister was with the Navigators, and we had him in our pulpit once a year and regularly gave him the opportunity to encourage our congregation with a vision for the university. We viewed him as an essential presence on the campus that we could not provide but we could support.

The church provides the campus ministry with a critical counterpoint: the sacraments of baptism and the Lord's Supper, the fellowship of a broader community of Christians, and the patterns of life in a faith community that they will hopefully incorporate into their lives and that will serve them well long after they are students in a university.

THE PLACE OF WORSHIP IN ACADEMIC COMMUNITIES

But now, back to the character of a Christian university or a theological seminary. I have proposed two things in particular. First, the goal or purpose of higher education is, without qualification, transformation. The immediate objective is not merely knowledge with a Christian worldview or a commitment to the integration of faith and reason. Neither can it be reduced to professional training or credentialing; it cannot be defined in purely pragmatic terms. Rather, the commitment of the Christian university and the seminary is spiritual maturity and character development in Christ. Second, I am also suggesting that the primary leverage point for this agenda is wisdom—that formation in wisdom can be the unifying point of integration for the curriculum of the university or the seminary.

But now we need to speak of worship. For wisdom to provide this leverage point as a means by which the Christian university or seminary fulfills the agenda of teaching and learning as transformation, worship—the shared liturgy—is crucial and pivotal. Earlier I indicated that the university is not a liturgical community. And yet what should be evident at each point of our reflections is that our studies, our teaching-learning, will be fundamentally secular with nothing but a religious veneer without worship.

If the crucified and ascended Christ is to be the defining center of the academic vision, if in our studies our passion is not merely knowledge but wisdom, if we are not merely seeking to train for a job but to know what it is to do good work in response to the call of Christ, and if throughout the entire program we are to grow in love and our capacity for love and joy, then worship is fundamental. The vision for wisdom affirms again and again that wisdom is the fruit of diligent study and intellectual rigor. But it is first and foremost a gift from God, and thus worship and prayer are the essential counterpoint to the work of the classroom and library.

It would make sense that the chapel—the venue for formal, liturgical worship—be architecturally placed at the very center of the campus, a visual reminder that all study, all research and teaching, every dimension of the academic life of this institution is oriented toward the greater glory of God: *ad majorem dei gloriam*, as Ignatius Loyola so aptly put it. I celebrate the new chapel on the campus of my own alma mater, the Ateneo de Manila University in the Philippines, with its exquisitely designed center of worship that can be seen from almost every corner of the campus. And then I also think of the chapel that is housed within the Loyola school of theology on the campus of the Ateneo: it is immediately adjacent to the library, signaling what I am speaking of here. We go to the library as those who are worshipers with the intent that our research be informed by our prayers, and we come to our worship as those who have been to the library, seeking a worship of God that is informed by study, learning and critical reflection.

With worship at the center, worship, study and learning are offered to God as a sacrifice of praise, and our affections are ordered according to the wisdom of God, that is, Christ Jesus himself. Worship slows us down so that there is a measured pace to our studies, and this pacing humbles us, fostering teachableness but also discernment. Worship has the capacity to infuse the whole academic program with an awareness of the ascended Christ who calls us to our study, our service and to our work in the world. It is an integrating event that keeps our study from being purely cerebral. And its place in the week reminds us that our study— our work as scholars, teachers, students and administrators—is not an end in itself but an act of worship offered back to Christ.

How often should worship take place? At least weekly, but in many institutions there is the option of daily worship. Perhaps there is a weekly gathering of the whole community along with the availability of daily morning worship in a smaller venue. The worship can be simple and concise: readings from Scripture, the sharing of a psalm, hymns that celebrate the God who in Christ has created and redeemed all things, prayers for the community and for the world, perhaps a brief meditation on the Scripture readings. And then a benediction wherein we return to our studies with Christ's blessing. In some contexts, the regular celebration of the Lord's Supper would be possible and appropriate.

This gathering is necessarily governed by the Scriptures read and preached. I think also of the deep commitment to the Psalms within the Benedictine monastic tradition and in the preachers' seminary overseen by Dietrich Bonhoeffer as he describes it in *Life Together*. They prayed the Psalms in recognition that nothing so integrates our lives and our prayers and teaches us to pray as immersion in the Psalms.

In our worship, our singing should reflect our keenest theology; the genius of the great hymns is that they translate theology into prayer (Luther: "When we sing we pray twice"). The depths of our theological reflection should be reflected in the depth of our singing. There is something deeply inconsistent when we engage in profound reflection on the nature of the Trinity in theology class but then sing superficial choruses in chapel. In like manner, there should be a deep congruency between the study of the sciences and the worship of the Creator in the chapel.

Surely the leadership for the chapel should be the same as the leadership for the classroom; while student involvement is important, it makes sense that the president, dean and faculty own the leadership of chapel—shaping its priorities, leading the prayers, ministering the Word. A vital means by which we teach is through example; we teach our students how to pray and how to worship and how to lead worship by our own participation and by the leadership we give to chapel.

We recognize that students learn how to pray in their personal prayers by following the example of our common or corporate worship and prayers. Thus, for example, if we neglect the Scriptures in our common worship, they will surely neglect the Scriptures in their personal prayers. If we include confession as integral to our weekly worship, it follows that our students will appreciate how crucial confession is to their personal and private daily prayers.

For students at a public or secular university, may there be a church in the vicinity that provides the weekly worship that is vital to our faith orientation—and perhaps even the option for noonday prayers and the celebration of the Lord's Supper. As a pastor of an interdenominational church in the Philippines, it was an easy call to continue the practice established by my predecessors: a brief noontime celebration of the Lord's Supper each Thursday for those in the neighboring offices and institutions of higher education who could slip in during their lunch break.

With these university years being so formative, it is essential that worship—corporate liturgical worship and personal, individual prayers—be part of the routine and rhythm of the life of a student and an academic. Thus Leclercq's study of monasticism comes down to a single defining observation: the last sentence of his magisterial book reads, "In the liturgy, love of learning and desire for God find perfect reconciliation."[21]

Conclusion

This is my prayer: that congregations and institutions of higher learning would embrace this vision and passion for their mission and their work, for the routines and rhythms that demarcate their shared lives—either as faith communities or as faith-based universities or seminaries. That vision being to seek with passion and diligence the spiritual maturity of those they have been called to serve. And specifically, it is my prayer that we not view this as either marginal to the identity of a congregation or to higher education but as integral to what it means to be the church and what it means to be a Christian university or theological seminary.

---

[21]Leclercq, Love of Learning, p. 251.

Name Index

Subject Index

Scripture Index